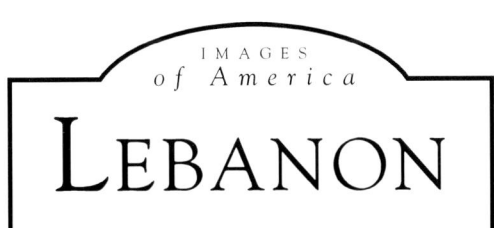

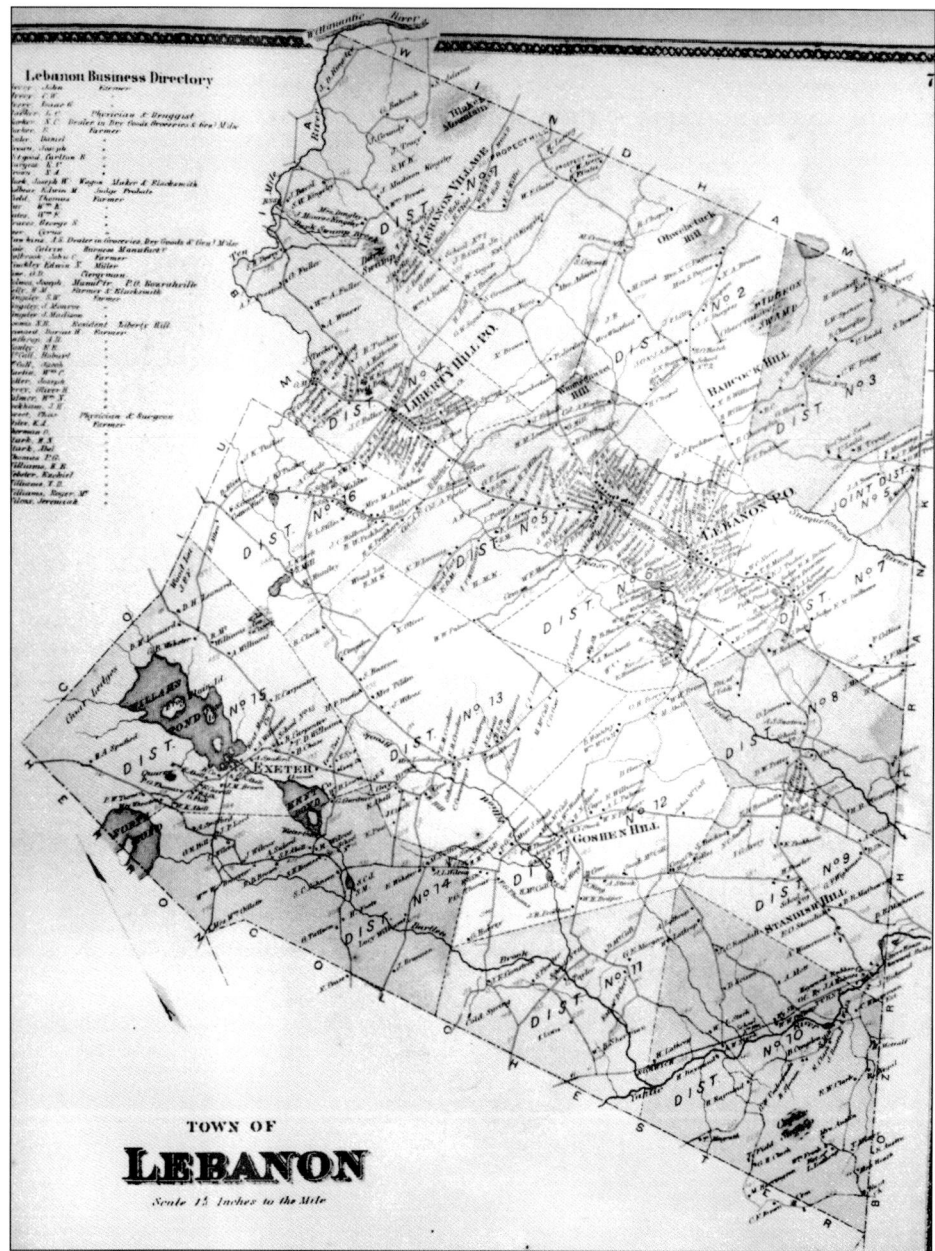

A MAP OF LEBANON, 1868. This map outlines the 16 school districts and includes a local business directory. It was published by F. W. Beers & Company of New York City.

On the cover: THE LEBANON CREAMERY. Once the largest creamery in the state, the Lebanon Creamery opened for business in 1885 in a converted building on Susquetonscut Brook, below the present elementary school on Route 207. Butter from the creamery was shipped by rail to city markets. When markets changed, business gradually fell off. The creamery assets were finally sold at auction in 1933. (Courtesy LHS.)

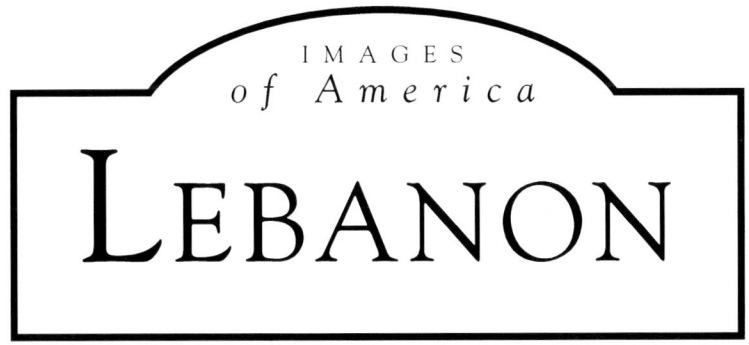

IMAGES of America

LEBANON

Alicia Wayland, Ed Tollmann, and Claire S. Krause
for the Lebanon Historical Society

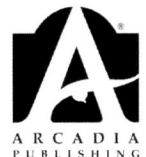

Copyright © 2004 by Alicia Wayland, Ed Tollmann, and Claire S. Krause
ISBN 978-0-7385-3573-9

Published by Arcadia Publishing,
Charleston, South Carolina

Printed in the United States of America

Library of Congress Catalog Card Number: 2004101194

For all general information, contact Arcadia Publishing:
Telephone 843-853-2070
Fax 843-853-0044
E-mail sales@arcadiapublishing.com
For customer service and orders:
Toll-free 1-888-313-2665

Visit us on the Internet at www.arcadiapublishing.com

To the men and women of Lebanon who served in the armed forces throughout our nation's history.

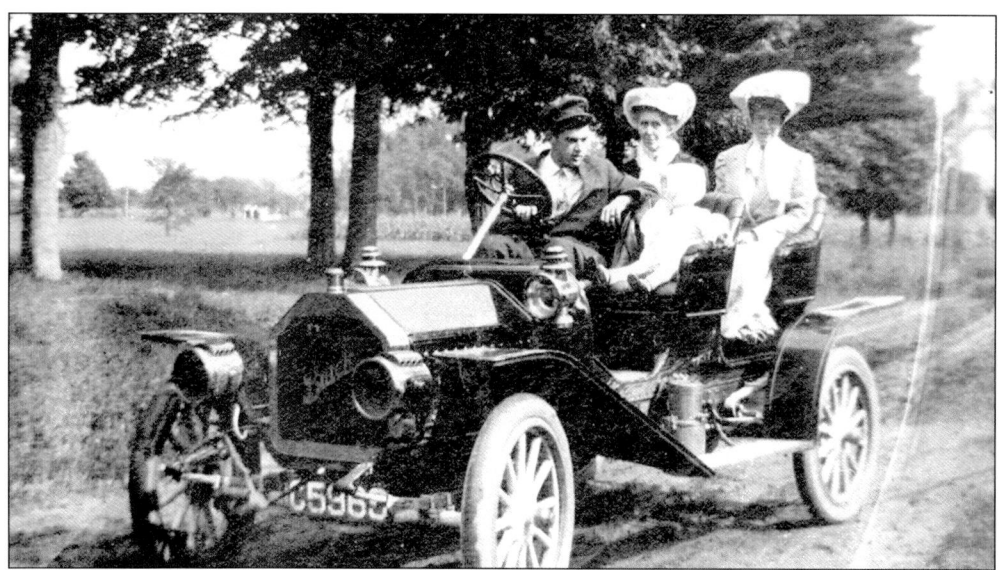

DRIVING 'ROUND THE GREEN. Mercy Tucker Gillette, who lived on West Town Street, owned one of the first automobiles in Lebanon and loved to drive around the town green to show off. In this early 1900s photograph, she appears on the far right; her sister Phebe Tucker Irish is in the center. The driver and the child are unidentified. Mercy was the wife of Isaac Gillette, judge of probate from 1885 to 1906. (Courtesy Arlene McCaw.)

Contents

Acknowledgments   6

Introduction   7

1. Notable People and Places   9
2. Houses of Worship   19
3. The Liberty Hill Neighborhood   31
4. The Farming Community   57
5. The Village Hill Neighborhood   69
6. School Bells   89
7. Lebanon in World War II   99
8. Lebanon Then and Now   109

Acknowledgments

This book would not have been possible without the support of the board of directors of the Lebanon Historical Society, who graciously agreed to make the historical society's archival material available to the authors for use in the book. Photographs, postcards, and maps from these collections are credited as LHS, whether the item was received through gift or purchase. As we examined these records, we realized the debt owed to the people who contributed material to the LHS archives over the years. We extend our thanks and appreciation for their contributions to the preservation of Lebanon's history. Photographs and postcards that are privately owned are credited by the name of the contributor. We are grateful for their permission to use these items.

Special thanks are due Grace Sayles, who scanned all the materials produced in this book with her customary professionalism and good advice. She was indispensable to our efforts.

The idea for the book arose from the desire of Ed Tollmann to share his extensive collection of Lebanon memorabilia with a larger audience. Alicia Wayland and Claire S. Krause share his passion for our town's history. All three authors joined forces to bring together some of the stories of Lebanon people and places for your enjoyment. Alicia Wayland compiled the introduction and chapters 1, 2, 4, 6, 7, and 8. Ed Tollmann compiled chapter 3. All images in that chapter are from his personal collection. Claire S. Krause compiled chapter 5.

—Alicia Wayland, Ed Tollmann, and Claire S. Krause

Introduction

Lebanon was called Poquechaneed by the Mohegan Indians, who hunted the hills and valleys before the arrival of the first English settlers in the 1690s. In 1692, four proprietors from Norwich and Stonington purchased the first land tract in Lebanon from Oweneco, sachem of the Mohegans. The tract was called the Five Mile Purchase and encompassed most of present-day Lebanon.

Settlement of the town began in 1695 on land granted by the proprietors to settlers from Connecticut and Massachusetts. Earlier land grants by the General Assembly and other purchases from the Mohegans adjacent to the Five Mile Purchase, including the Clarke and Dewey Purchase to the north, were also being settled.

On October 10, 1700, these tracts of land were incorporated by the General Assembly as the town of Lebanon, an area covering 80 square miles. Boundaries were established and permission to gather a church was given. The First Congregational Church was organized shortly thereafter. In 1804, the northern section of town, called the North Society or Lebanon Crank, was set off as the town of Columbia. Columbia shared equally in Lebanon's history until that date.

By 1725, Lebanon was a thriving agricultural town with sawmills, gristmills, tanneries, and other trades connected with farming. Much of the prosperity of the early years was based on stock raising. Cattle were driven to market in Boston and Norwich, and later the town was the center of the colony's meat-packing industry. The census of 1774 indicates Lebanon was one of the largest and most prosperous towns in the colony.

Lebanon is best known for its role in the American Revolution. Among its patriots were William Williams, signer of the Declaration of Independence, and the rebel Gov. Jonathan Trumbull, the only colonial governor to become the governor of a state when independence was declared. Trumbull directed Connecticut's great contributions to the patriot cause, primarily from his War Office across from the town green, giving Lebanon its nickname of "the Heartbeat of the American Revolution."

During the 19th century, Lebanon farmers concentrated on dairying, first in butter and cheese and then in the production of whole milk. The Yankee population dwindled as many residents left town for jobs in the cities or to take up new western lands. Many of the Irish, Jewish, Slavic, and German settlers from Ukraine who migrated to Lebanon during this period continued farming the land.

In the mid–20th century, improved roads made Lebanon attractive to city dwellers, spurring a growth in suburban development. Agriculture is still the major economic activity, preserving the rural landscape, but now 90 percent of the residents commute out of town to work.

Lebanon is the birthplace of five of the state's governors, more than any other town. They are, with terms of office, as follows: Jonathan Trumbull, 1769–1784; Jonathan Trumbull Jr., 1797–1809; Clark Bissell, 1847–1849; Joseph Trumbull, 1849–1850; and William A. Buckingham, 1858–1866. Lebanon is also the birthplace of Dr. William Beaumont, a U.S. Army surgeon who discovered the secret of human digestion.

The town's most distinctive feature is the mile-long town green, listed on the National Register of Historic Places. The northern section of the green is a vast, open meadow of 27 acres where neighboring farmers make hay. It is the only town green still in agricultural use. The southern end of the green is the site for many civic, cultural, and recreational activities that take place throughout the year. A favorite event is the Lebanon Historical Society's annual outdoor antiques show, held on the green on the last Saturday in September.

Museums and other historic sites around the town green tell the story of Connecticut's significant role in national history during the Revolutionary period, as well as Dr. Beaumont's unique place in medical history. The Lebanon Historical Society Museum and Visitor Center features local history exhibitions, a research and genealogy library, and visitor amenities.

Each generation has made its mark on the town throughout more than 300 years of town history. This pictorial history provides glimpses of some of the people, places, and events that make Lebanon a town to remember from past to present.

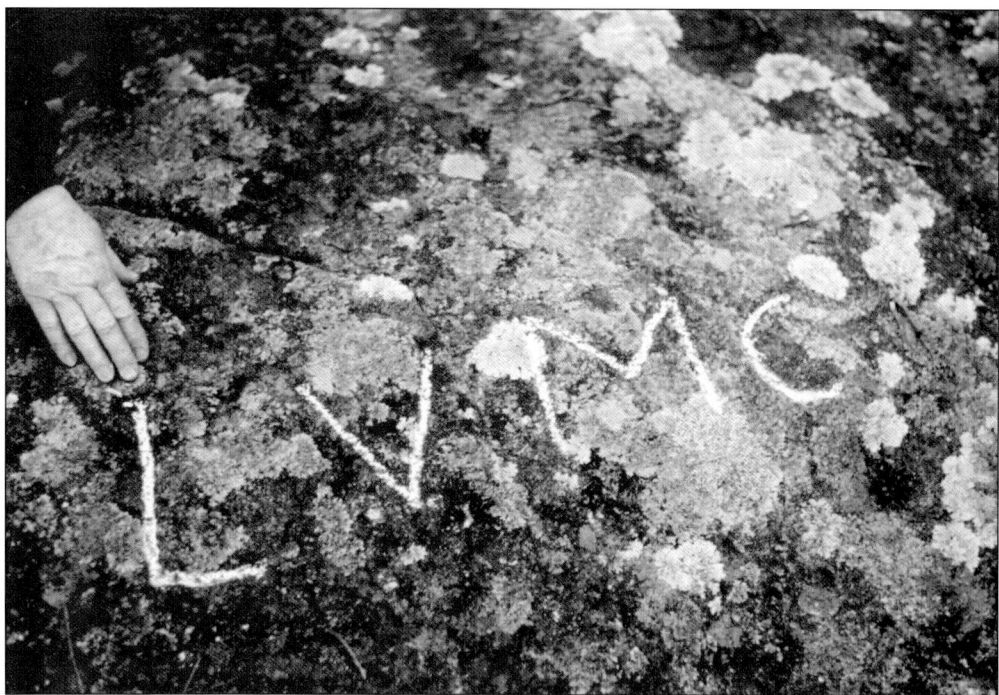

FIVE MILE ROCK. This rock marks the southwest corner of the Five Mile Purchase. The chiseled letters LVMC stand for "Lebanon Five Mile Corner." In 1705, the General Assembly finally confirmed Oweneco's 1692 sale to the four original proprietors and all subsequent land transfers, then ordered a survey of the tract with marked rocks to be set in all corners. This corner rock is located off Randall Road on private property. (Courtesy LHS.)

One

NOTABLE PEOPLE AND PLACES

During the early settlement period, land was cleared, crops sown, buildings erected, and primitive roads constructed. After the initial hardships of settlement, the town grew rapidly. The colony census of 1756 counted a population of 3,274, making Lebanon the sixth-largest town in terms of population, greater even than Hartford.

Much of the prosperity of the early years was due to Joseph Trumbull, who moved to Lebanon from Simsbury in 1704. He drove local cattle to city markets, where he exchanged the herds for manufactured goods to sell in his store. He was also involved in the West Indies trade, the largest outlet for colonial provisions.

Jonathan Trumbull (1710–1785), Joseph's son, greatly expanded the family business, carrying on an extensive overseas trade. He was increasingly influential in colony affairs as a member of the General Assembly, and he was elected lieutenant governor in 1767. In 1769, Jonathan Trumbull became governor, a post he would hold for nearly 15 years during one of the most tumultuous periods in the nation's history.

When news of the April 1775 Lexington-Concord alarm reached the area, Governor Trumbull turned his former store into his headquarters. During the American Revolution, more than 500 meetings of the Council of Safety were held in this building, known as the War Office.

Throughout the entire war, at least 677 Lebanon men served in the militia and the Continental Army at some time. This figure represents more than 50 percent of the adult male population.

William Williams was one of the most ardent supporters of independence. As a delegate to the Continental Congress in 1776, he was one of Connecticut's four signers of the Declaration of Independence. Williams was also married to the governor's daughter Mary Trumbull.

Governor Trumbull's office was the command post for Connecticut's outpouring of provisions to the war effort. He responded repeatedly to Gen. George Washington's urgent pleas for provisions for the Continental Army. The cattle drives from Connecticut saved the starving soldiers at Valley Forge and Morristown. Connecticut is called the Provisions State for these efforts.

Washington also called on the governor to supply the French army, led by the comte de Rochambeau. Two years after France entered into an alliance with the United States, transport ships landed 5,000 French soldiers at Newport, Rhode Island, in July 1780. In November of that same year, Rochambeau sent about 220 hussars from the duc de Lauzun's Legion, the cavalry unit of his army, to Lebanon, where forage for horses was more plentiful.

Washington stayed in Lebanon the night of March 4, 1781, on his way to Newport to meet with General Rochambeau. Here, he reviewed the French legionnaires before continuing his journey. Shortly after the visit, Jonathan Trumbull Jr. accepted Washington's invitation to become his military secretary. He remained by Washington's side until the army was disbanded in 1783.

After a seven-month encampment, Lauzun's Legion left Lebanon in June 1781, as the French army marched from Newport through Connecticut to meet Washington on the Hudson River. Four months later, the allied armies crushed Lord Cornwallis and the British at the Battle of Yorktown in Virginia. The surrender of Cornwallis on October 19, 1781, virtually ended military operations, although New York City remained occupied until 1783.

Throughout the war, the fidelity of Connecticut's patriots was upheld through military defeats, financial chaos, and wartime shortages by the leaders who organized the state's contributions to the patriot cause from their modest buildings around the town green.

The preservation of these historic buildings and the role of these leaders in securing the nation's independence led to the establishment of the Lebanon Green National Register District in 1979. The town green is still the heart of the community and continues to inspire visitors as they walk in the footsteps of patriots.

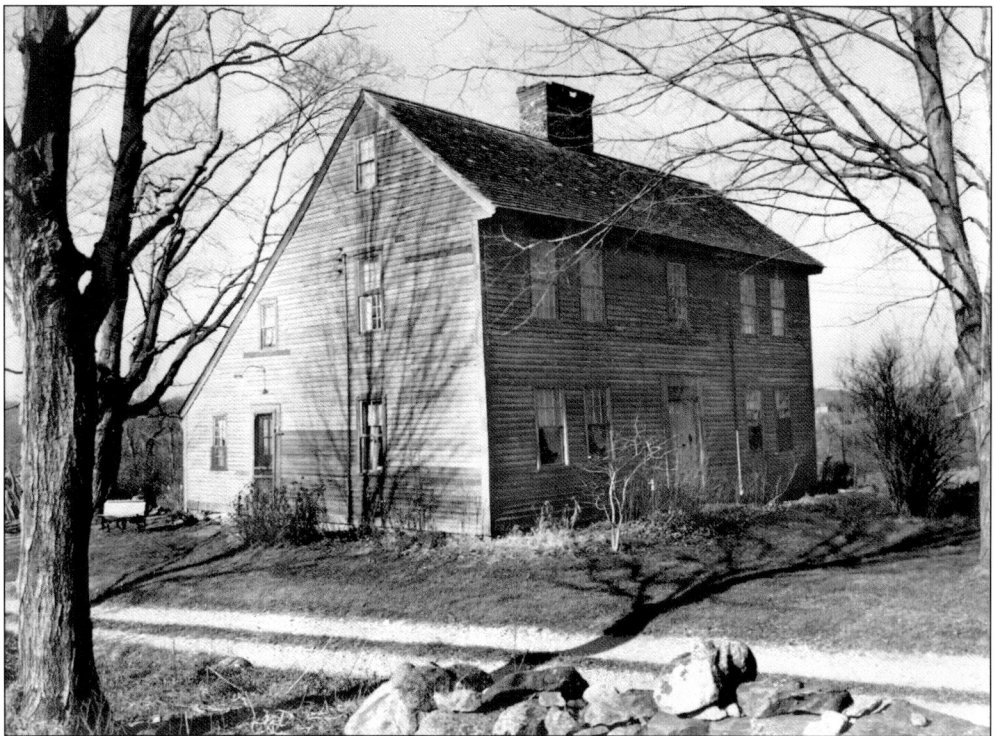

THE CLARK HOUSE, C. 1708. The oldest known surviving house in Lebanon was built by Moses Clark on Madley Road. It is the birthplace of Col. James Clark (1730–1826), who led the Lebanon militia to Cambridge in 1775, then fought at Bunker Hill. Clark also fought at the battles of Harlem Heights and White Plains. This early 1900s photograph shows the house before it was restored. (Courtesy LHS.)

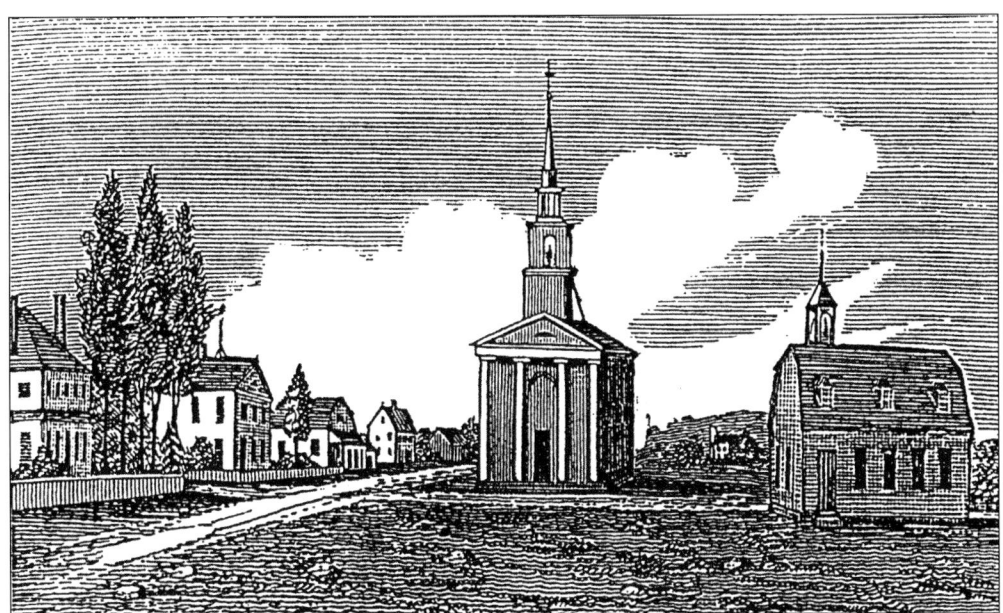

THE TISDALE SCHOOL. Jonathan Trumbull and several townspeople founded the Tisdale School as a subscription school in 1743. In 1762, the original frame structure was replaced by the two-story brick building shown on the right. The school was named after Nathan Tisdale (1732–1787), a brilliant teacher who drew students from as far away as the West Indies. The building was torn down sometime before 1844. (Courtesy John Warner Barber, *Connecticut Historical Collections*, 1836.)

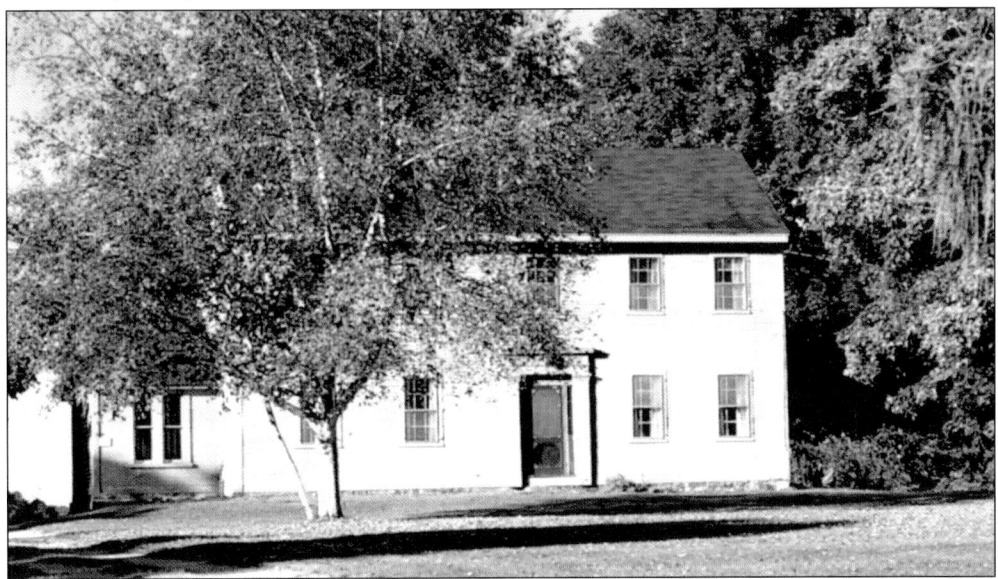

THE WELLES HOUSE, 1712. Solomon Williams, the third pastor of the First Congregational Church, purchased this house in 1722. His eight children, including William, signer of the Declaration of Independence, were born here. Solomon was a leader in the founding of the Philogrammatican Library in 1738 and kept the library books in this house. Only the third library in the colony, it was dissolved in 1792. (Photograph by Grant Huntington; courtesy town of Lebanon.)

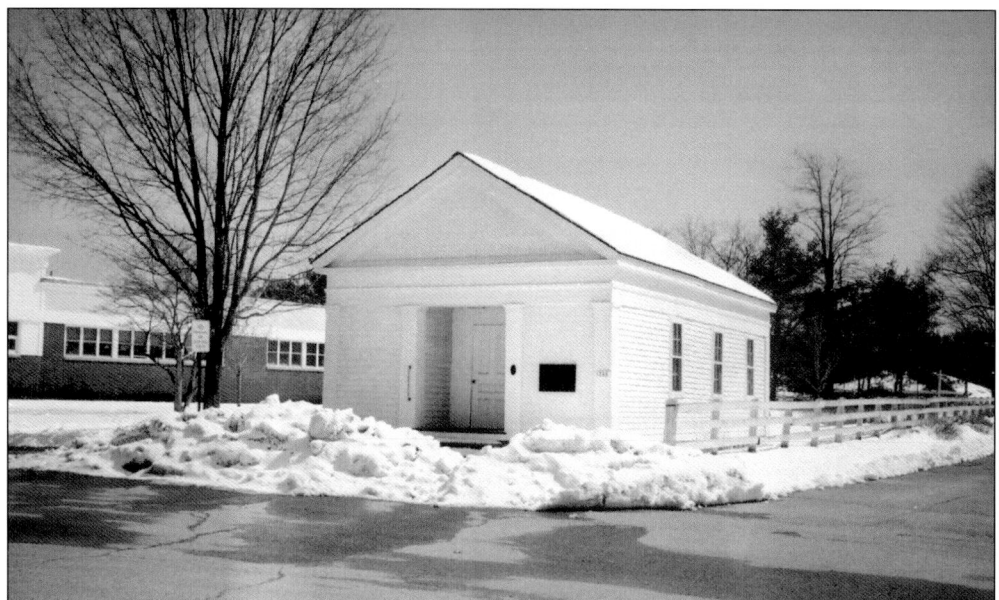

MOOR'S INDIAN CHARITY SCHOOL. In the North Society (now Columbia), Pastor Eleazar Wheelock opened a school for American Indian children in 1754, where he trained both whites and American Indians as missionaries. In 1769, Wheelock moved his school to Hanover, New Hampshire, and also founded a new college named after the Earl of Dartmouth. This school building, considered the forerunner of Dartmouth College, is a historic landmark in the center of Columbia. (Courtesy LHS.)

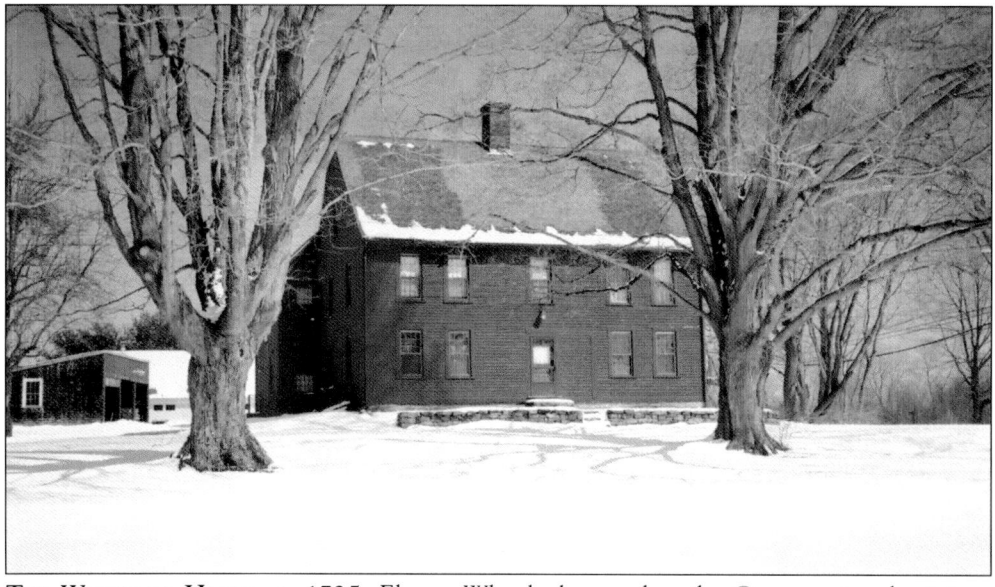

THE WHEELOCK HOUSE, C. 1735. Eleazar Wheelock served as the Congregational minister of the North Society from 1735 to 1769. During this time, he also conducted a school for college-bound boys in his home. His most famous pupil was Samson Occom, a Mohegan Indian who studied there from 1743 to 1748. Occom was the first Mohegan to become an ordained minister, and his success led Wheelock to open the school for American Indian children in 1754. (Courtesy LHS.)

THE REBEL GOVERNOR. Jonathan Trumbull was the only colonial governor to become governor of a state when independence was declared in 1776. He served from 1769 to 1784. During the Revolution, he mobilized the state to provide men and supplies for the patriot cause. His leadership was critical to the final victory. When Trumbull died, Gen. George Washington wrote that his service placed him "among the first of patriots." (Courtesy town of Lebanon, special collection.)

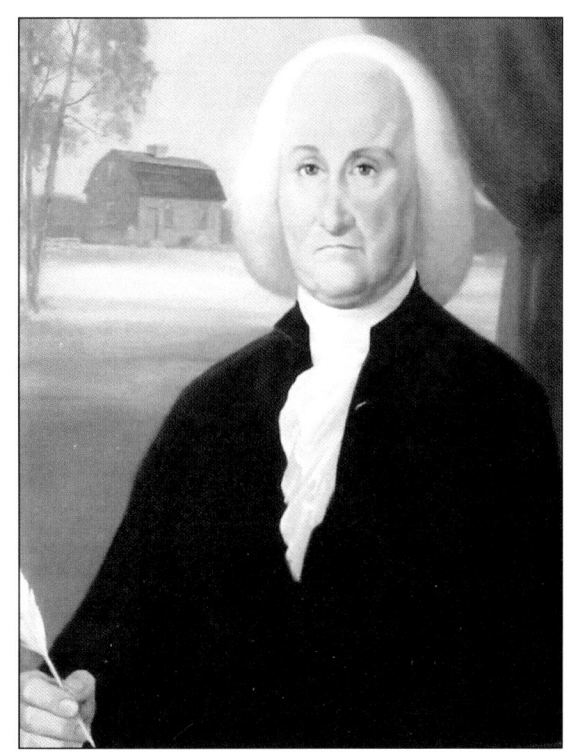

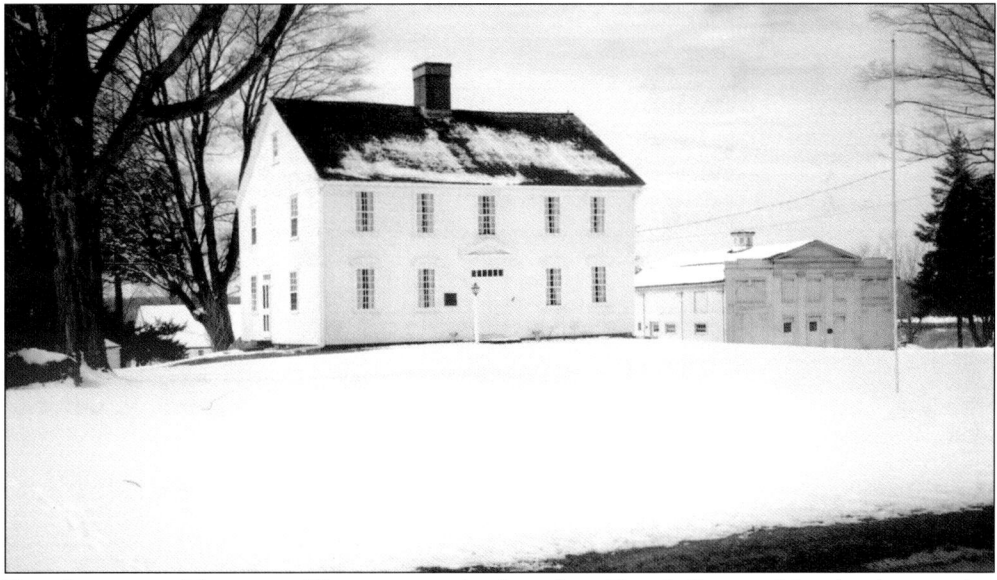

THE GOVERNOR TRUMBULL HOUSE, C. 1740. Jonathan Trumbull moved his family into this house when he inherited it from his father in 1755. His youngest child, John Trumbull, a patriot and artist of the Revolution, was born here in 1756. The Wadsworth Stable, originally located on the estate of Col. Jeremiah Wadsworth in Hartford, was moved here in 1954. Both buildings are now museums owned by the Connecticut Daughters of the American Revolution. (Courtesy LHS.)

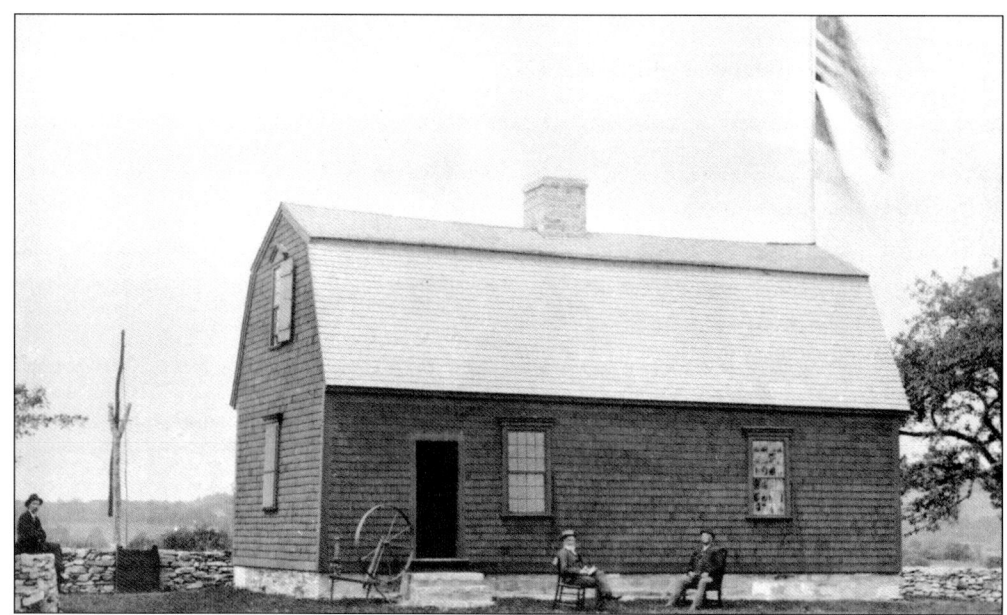

THE REVOLUTIONARY WAR OFFICE. At the outbreak of hostilities, Gov. Jonathan Trumbull turned his former store into his headquarters, leading to Lebanon's nickname, "the Heartbeat of the American Revolution." More than 500 meetings of the Council of Safety were held in this building, which is now a museum owned by the Connecticut Society, Sons of the American Revolution. The photograph was taken in 1892, shortly after the society had acquired and restored the building. (Courtesy Virginia Mullaly.)

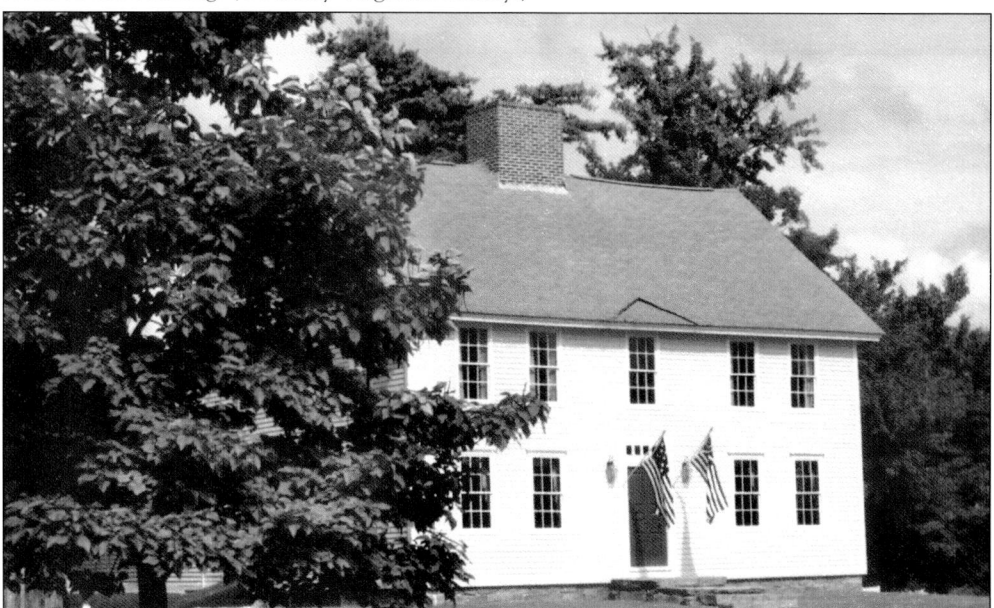

THE JONATHAN TRUMBULL JR. HOUSE, C. 1769. Governor Trumbull's four sons—Joseph, Jonathan Jr., David, and John—all served in the Revolution. Jonathan Jr. was military secretary to Gen. George Washington and later served in the first Congress elected under the Constitution in 1789. Like his father before him, Jonathan Trumbull Jr. served as governor, from 1797–1809. His house is now a museum owned by the town of Lebanon. (Courtesy LHS.)

A BOLD PATRIOT. William Williams (1731–1811) was one of Connecticut's four signers of the Declaration of Independence. He was a fiery orator and eloquent pamphleteer who tirelessly toured the state to urge support for the war and to enlist recruits. Williams served in the Continental Congress for a short period, then returned home to provide indispensable service on the Council of Safety throughout the war. (Courtesy First Congregational Church of Lebanon, special collection.)

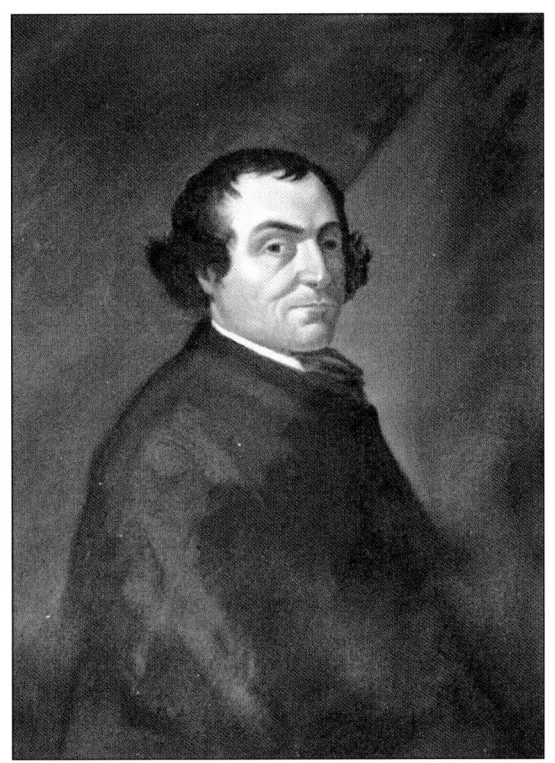

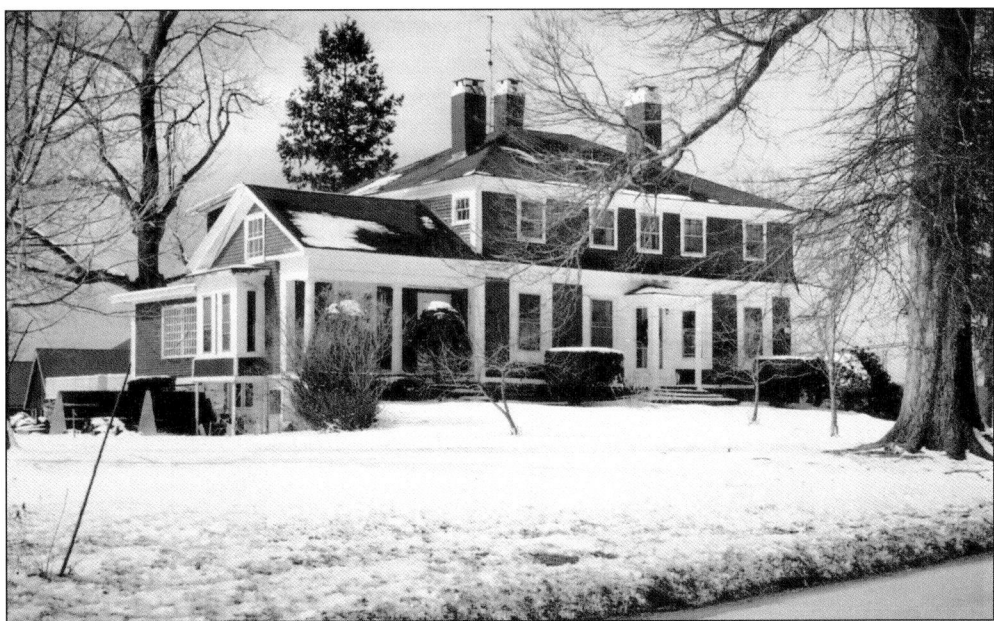

REDWOOD, 1778–1779. David Trumbull, son of the governor, commissioned Isaac Fitch of Lebanon to design and build this house. During the encampment of the French army's cavalry unit in Lebanon from 1780 to 1781, David turned over his house to their commander, the duc de Lauzun, to use as his headquarters. David's son Joseph, born here in 1782, served as governor from 1849 to 1850, the third generation of Trumbulls to head the state. (Courtesy LHS.)

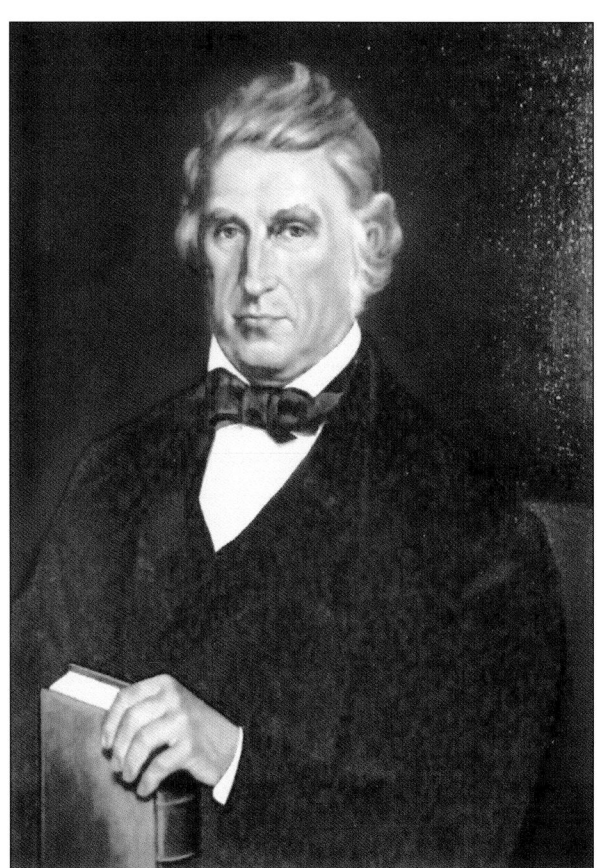

A Frontier Doctor. Dr. William Beaumont, born in Lebanon in 1785, was a pioneer medical researcher. As a U.S. Army surgeon, Beaumont was assigned to Fort Mackinac, a wilderness outpost in northern Michigan. There he conducted experiments on a wounded fur trapper that established for the first time the complex nature of digestion. He published his research in 1833 to worldwide acclaim. Nearly all of his conclusions are still studied today. (Courtesy LHS.)

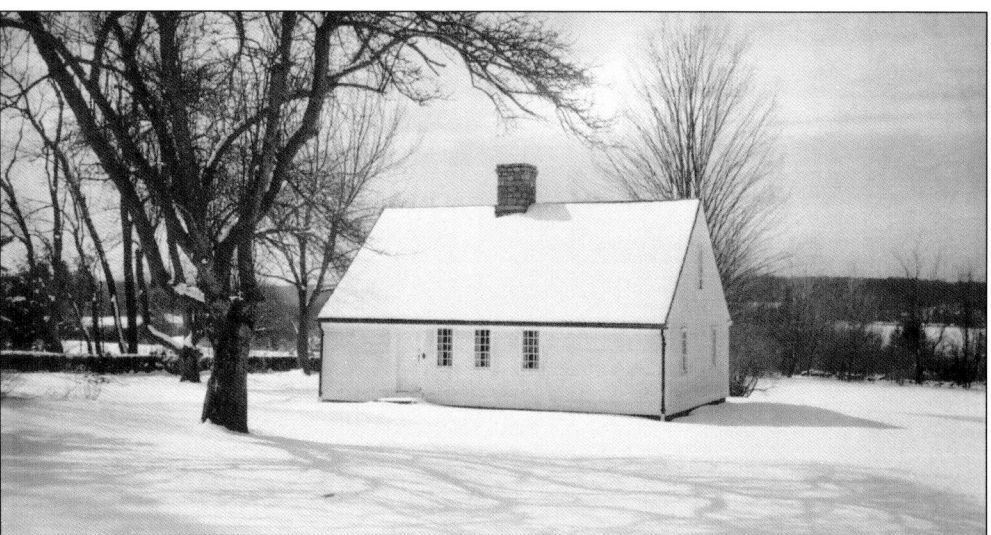

The Beaumont Homestead. Dr. Beaumont's childhood home was built by his father, Samuel, c. 1750. The Beaumont Medical Club of Yale University moved the house from its original location on Village Hill Road to a site behind the Governor Trumbull House. The house was restored, and one room was re-created as an early 19th-century doctor's office. It is now a museum owned by the Lebanon Historical Society. (Courtesy LHS.)

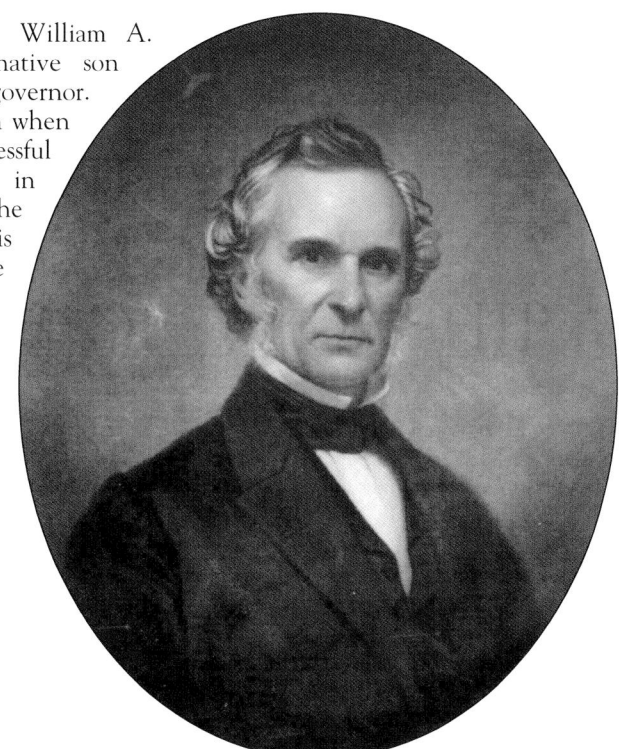

THE CIVIL WAR GOVERNOR. William A. Buckingham was the fifth native son of Lebanon to serve as governor. Buckingham moved to Norwich when he was 19 and became a successful merchant. Elected governor in 1858, he served through the Civil War to 1866. Under his leadership, Connecticut once again became the "Provisions State," producing food, textiles, machine tools, and armaments for the Union army. (Courtesy First Congregational Church of Lebanon, special collection.)

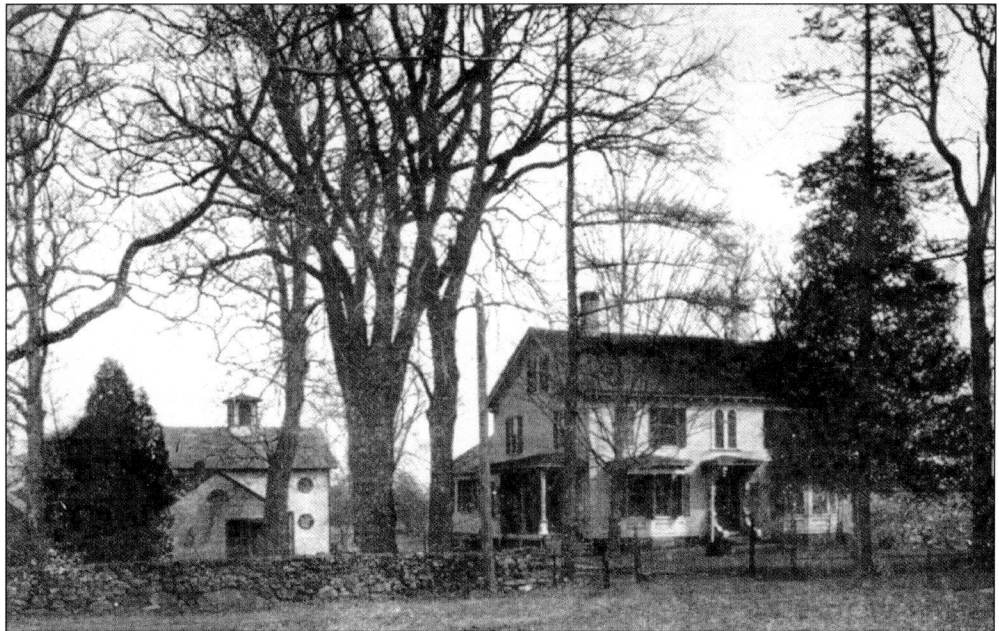

THE SECOND BUCKINGHAM HOUSE. Governor Buckingham, born in Lebanon in 1804, grew up in this house, built by his father, Samuel, sometime after 1808. That year, the proprietors of the still-undivided land sold Samuel a strip from the highway on which to build a new house. This 1907 photograph shows the mid–19th century dairy barn with its circular windows and cupola. The building now houses a veterinary clinic. (Courtesy Charles H. Baldwin, D.V.M.)

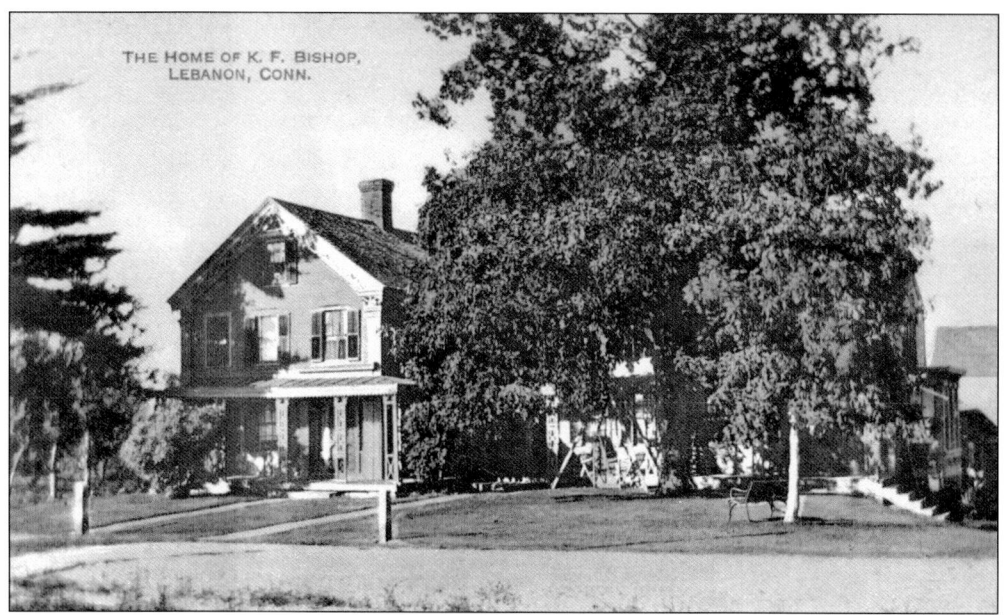

DR. SWEET'S HOUSE, C. 1850. Charles Sweet (1810–1896) was known as "Bonesetter Sweet," famous for his ability to set broken or dislocated bones. His office was located on the green where the library now stands. Patients boarded at his "remedial institution" (on the site of the present community center) for treatment of various diseases. Selectman Karl Bishop lived in the house when this early 20th century postcard was made. (Courtesy Ed Tollmann.)

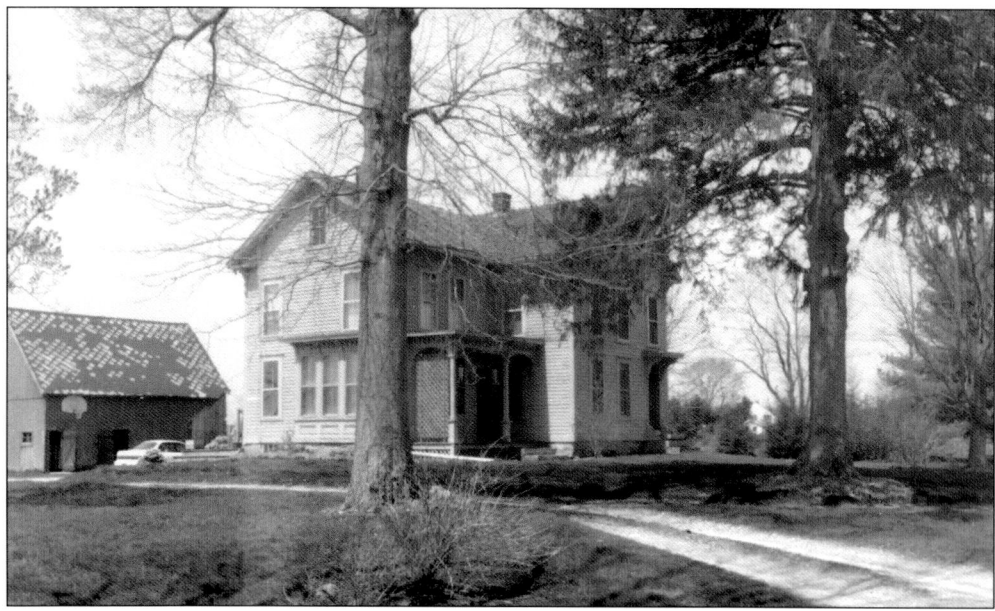

THE CONSTITUTION OAK. This Eastlake-style house on West Town Street was built by Isaac Gillette c. 1880. Gillette was Lebanon's delegate to the state's 1902 Constitutional Convention. Each delegate received a pin oak sapling as a memento. The saplings were planted statewide, in both public and private locations, the first mass commemorative tree planting in the state. Gillette planted his sapling on his front lawn, where it still flourishes. (Courtesy LHS.)

Two

Houses of Worship

Lebanon's houses of worship have evolved from the single established Congregational church of the Connecticut colony to a diversity of denominations to meet the spiritual needs of the town's residents. The First Congregational Church of Lebanon was organized on November 27, 1700. In 1706, the first meetinghouse was erected, at the intersection of the two main roads in the town center. A new meetinghouse was built on the site of the present church in 1732.

The meetinghouse was the focal point of the community. Town meetings, elections, and Sabbath services took place in the same building. Here, too, the stirring events of independence and the Revolution were debated.

The Rev. Solomon Williams, the third minister, served the society for 54 years, from 1722 to 1776. He was a strong influence during the formative years of the town and left money in his will for the support of the Revolution. He was the father of William Williams, signer of the Declaration of Independence.

The brick meetinghouse was designed by John Trumbull, son of Governor Jonathan Trumbull. Built from 1804 to 1809, it is the only surviving example of the artist's architectural work.

The town was soon divided into several ecclesiastical societies because of the difficulties of traveling by foot or horseback to the town center. In 1715, the inhabitants of the northern section of town were granted permission to form the Second, or North, Society, now the town of Columbia. The North Society's best-known pastor was its third, Eleazar Wheelock, who served from 1735 to 1769.

The third society was organized as the Goshen Congregational Church in 1729. It originally served the neighborhoods of Goshen and Exeter, but Exeter was split off as a separate society in 1773. The Goshen church has served the community for 275 years, making it the second-oldest extant church in Lebanon.

The Lebanon Baptist Church, at the north end of the town green, was organized in 1805, the result of a long-simmering controversy over the location of the Congregational meetinghouse, a mile distant at the south end of the green. After much thought and study, many parishioners left the Congregational church to unite with the Baptist church. Their first meetinghouse was built in 1805. Hard feelings over the split must have died down early, because both meetinghouses were used as sites for town meetings until the town hall was built in 1848.

The Lebanon Jewish Congregation was formed in 1903, meeting in the homes of members. By 1920, Lebanon had nearly 100 Jewish families. The congregation purchased the vacant Levita Street Schoolhouse in 1933 to use as a synagogue. When this burned in 1955, the congregation built a new synagogue on Goshen Hill Road. After World War II, the congregation dwindled, and the synagogue was sold to the Lebanon Bible Church in 1995.

The German people of Lebanon arrived from the Ukrainian village of Karlswalde, where their parents and grandparents had settled as farmers. Karlswalder immigrants, arriving between 1911 and 1928, settled in the Village Hill area. The Redeemer Lutheran Church, built entirely by the volunteer labor of members, was completed in 1944. The intricate woodwork was carved by Godfrey Laibrandt, who also carved the woodwork in the First Congregational Church when it was restored after the 1938 hurricane.

The St. Francis of Assisi R.C. Church began as a mission church in a converted residence on the east side of the green in 1943. Expanded membership led to the need for a larger building. In 1965, the church purchased a large parcel on West Town Street as the site for a new building and set about raising money for construction. Construction finally began in 1979 and was completed the following spring. St. Francis became a parish in its own right in December 1980.

The Andover, North, and Exeter Ecclesiastical Societies, the Scott Hill Baptist Church, the Methodist Episcopal Church, the St. Mary Mission Chapel, the Liberty Hill Church, and the Jewish synagogue are no longer with us. They were among the spiritual roots of the community that provided the moral foundation that sustains us today.

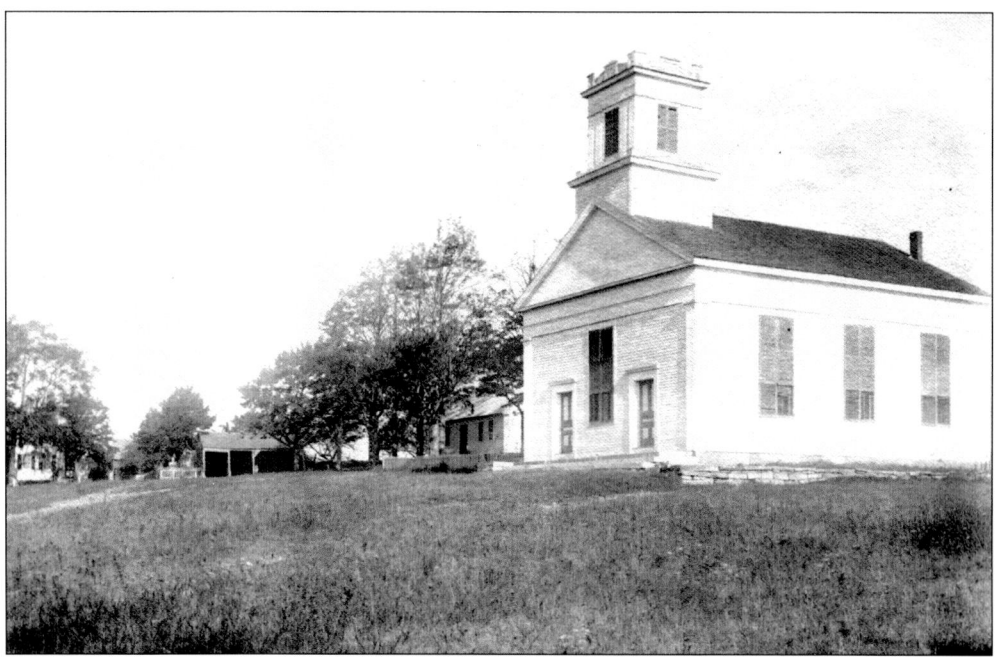

THE EXETER CONGREGATIONAL CHURCH. The Exeter section of Lebanon was served by the Goshen church until it was set off as a separate society in 1773. In 1844, Exeter's meetinghouse was replaced by this new church on Olenick Road. Because of declining membership, the church merged with Liberty Hill in 1919 and finally dissolved in 1945. The vacant building deteriorated over the years and was demolished in the early 1960s. (Courtesy LHS.)

THE BRICK MEETINGHOUSE.
The First Congregational Church of Lebanon was formally organized in November 1700. The first meetinghouse, used for both town meetings and religious services, was built in 1706, and the second was built in 1732. The third meetinghouse was designed by John Trumbull, an artist of the Revolutionary War period, and was constructed between 1804 and 1809. Its graceful spire rising over the hilltop is a local landmark. It is the only surviving example of Trumbull's architectural work. (Photograph by Grant Huntington; courtesy town of Lebanon.)

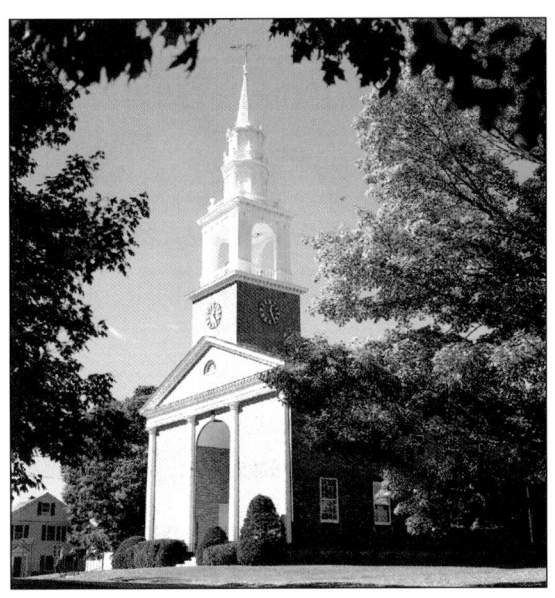

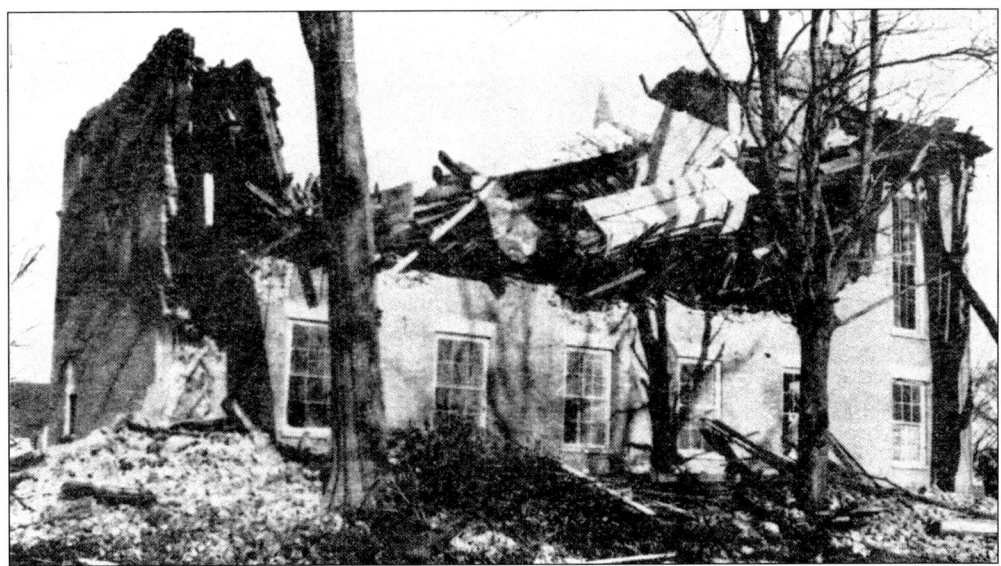

DEVASTATION. The church stood directly in the path of the 1938 hurricane. High winds toppled the steeple, sending it crashing into the nave. The interior lay in ruins. Rebuilding, interrupted by World War II, was completed in 1950, except the steeple. In 1954, the finished steeple was dedicated to the memory of William Williams. The church was restored to John Trumbull's original design. (Courtesy Virginia Mullaly.)

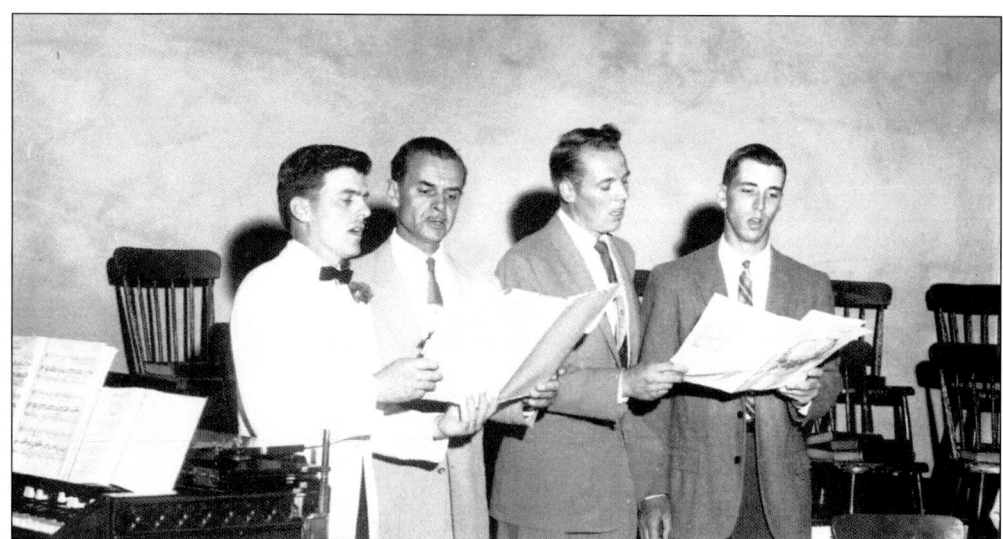

WEDDING SONGS. Henry Grabber, Walter Jakoboski, Russell Blakeslee, and Robert McCaw, shown from left to right, sang at the wedding of Kenneth Lathrop and Gretchen Grabber in 1955. The wedding was performed at the First Congregational Church. (Courtesy Russell Blakeslee.)

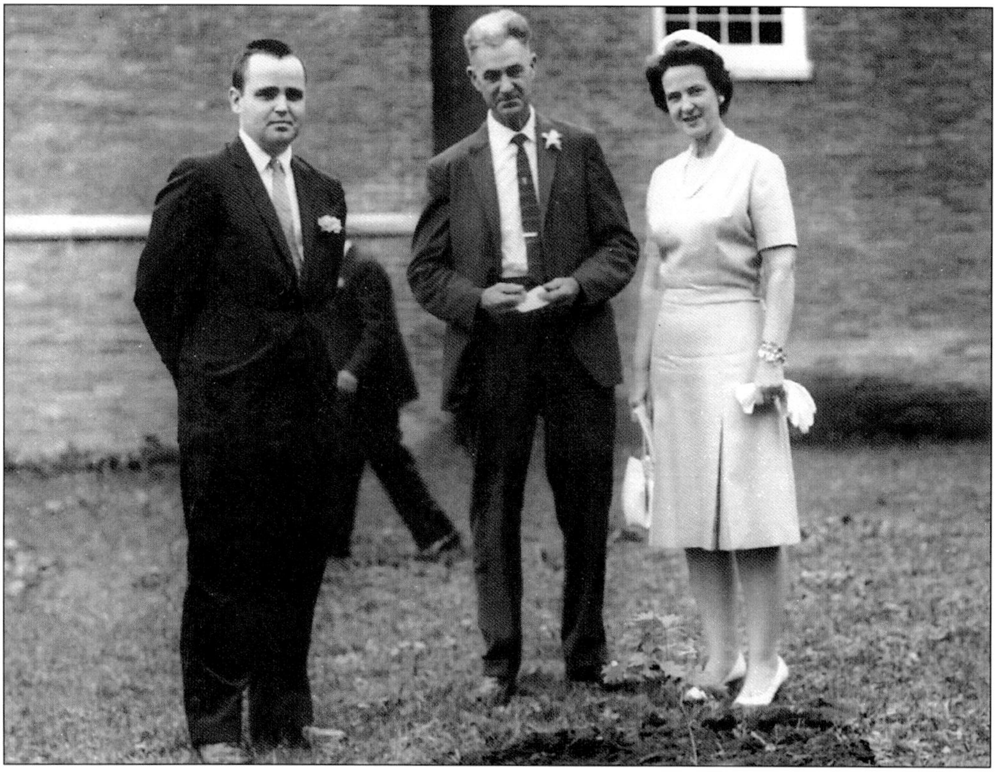

TREE PLANTING. A Charter Oak sapling was planted at the dedication of the new fellowship hall at the First Congregational Church in June 1962. Admiring the sapling donated by Dr. William Jahoda are, from left to right, Rev. Richard L. Rush, Leslie Clarke Sr., and Alison McBride. The tree, a direct descendant of Connecticut's famed Charter Oak, now towers over the lawn behind the hall, providing welcome shade during outdoor events. (Courtesy William Jahoda.)

THE 300TH ANNIVERSARY CAKE. A Colonial worship service on November 26, 2000, concluded a year of activities celebrating the 300th anniversary of the First Congregational Church. Attending the reception afterward were Art Wallace (in period clothing at the far left), Neil Whitehead, and Ellen Lathrop. Rose Pogmore made the anniversary cakes, which were decorated with replicas of the brick meetinghouse. (Courtesy William Jahoda.)

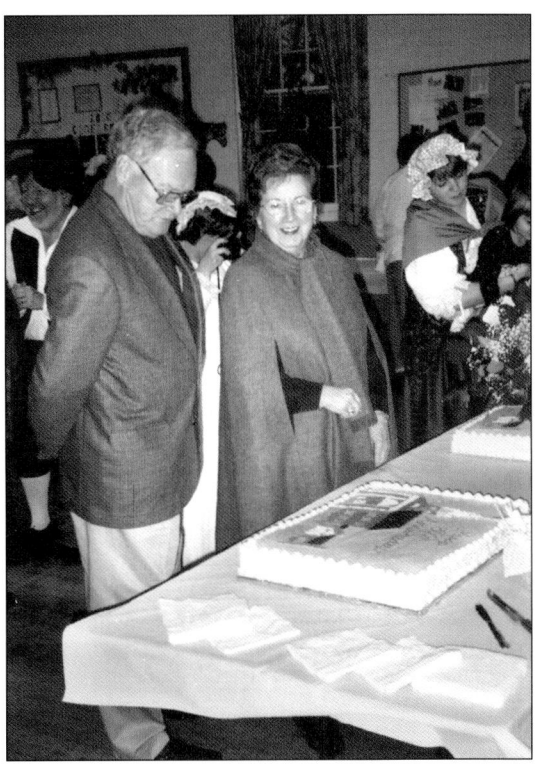

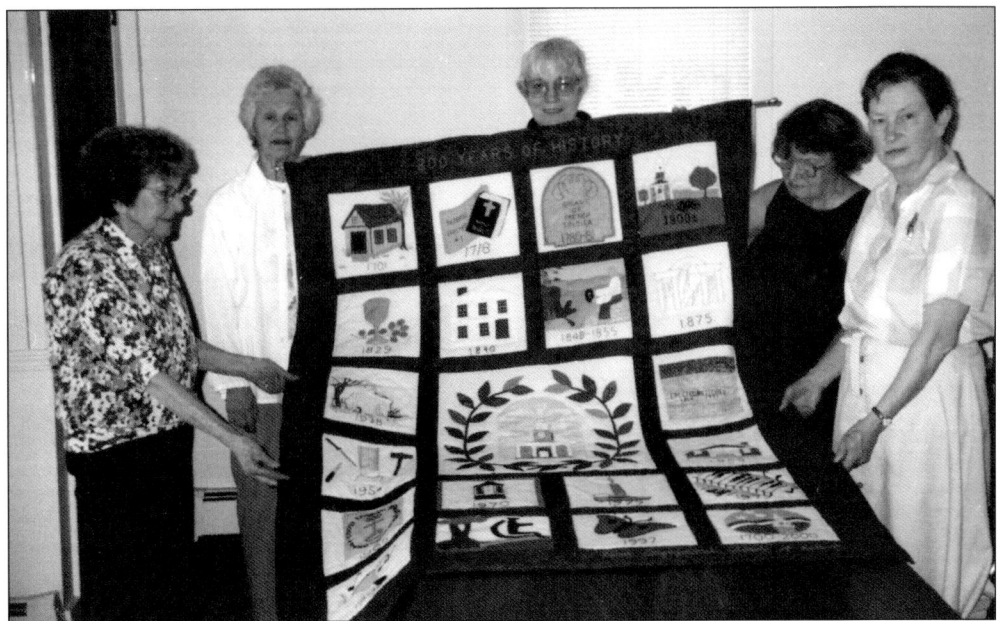

A GIFT OF FAITH. Displaying the wall hanging made in 2000 for the tercentennial of the First Congregational Church are, from left to right, Phyllis Bartizek, Margery Jahoda, Sylvia Ryan, Helen Szajda, and Evelyn Lathrop. A committee designed the quilt and organized 21 people to make the squares. Members were chairwoman Margery Jahoda, Helen Szajda, Sylvia Ryan, Iola Jakoboski, Lucia Day, Evelyn Grabber, and Beverly York. (Courtesy William Jahoda.)

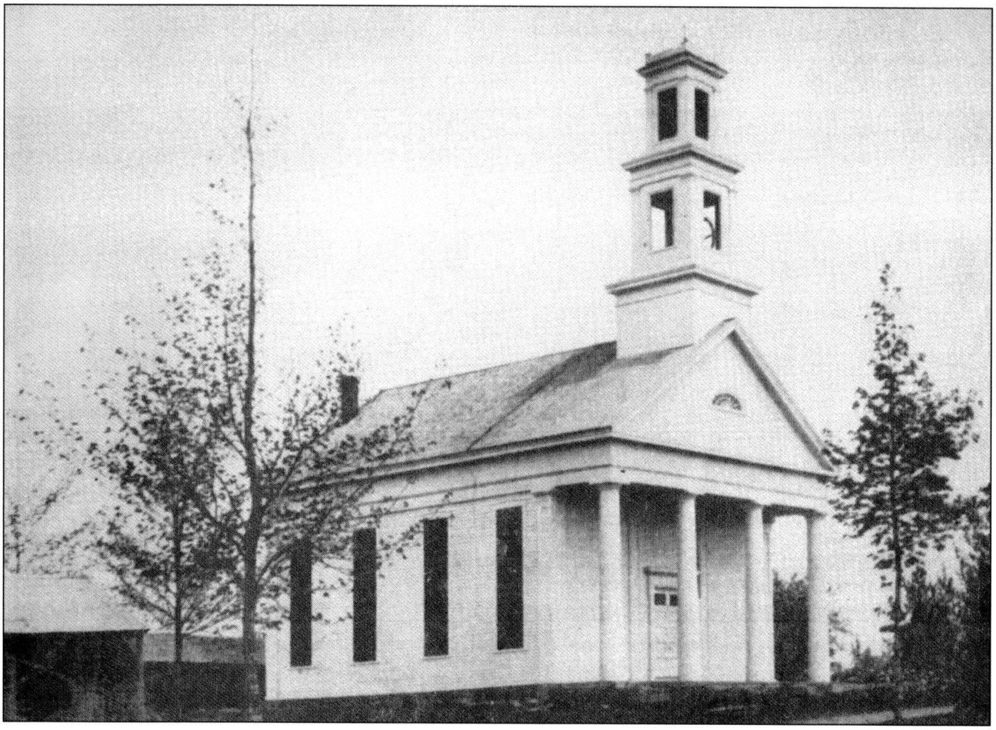

THE OLD GOSHEN CONGREGATIONAL CHURCH. The Goshen church was organized in 1729 to serve the Goshen Hill and Exeter neighborhoods. The original site was on Goshen Hill Road near the McCall Road intersection. After the Exeter members separated in 1773, the Goshen congregation built a new meetinghouse on Church Road in 1801. It was significantly remodeled in the Greek Revival style in 1852. The church burned to the ground in 1898. (Courtesy LHS.)

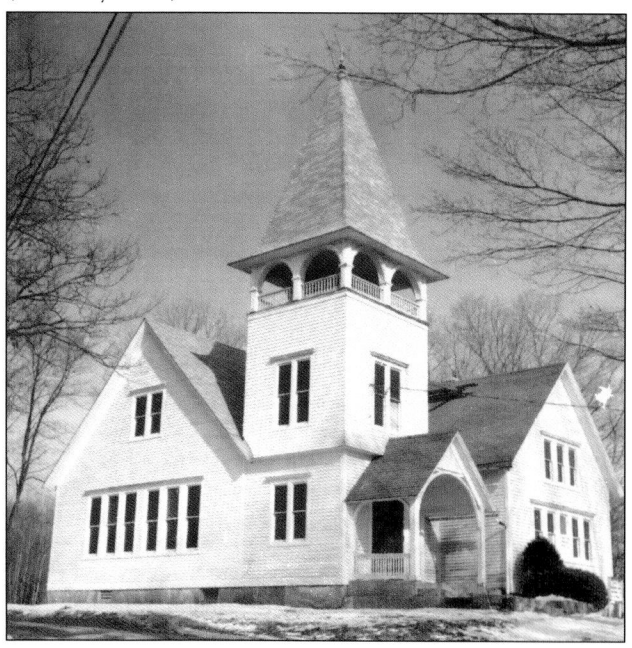

A VICTORIAN GEM. After the fire, the Goshen congregation built a new church in the Victorian style. The kerosene chandelier saved from the fire hangs in the sanctuary, and the church bell was recast from the melted remains of the bell hanging in the old church. A fellowship hall was added in 1997. The Goshen Congregational Church has been a central part of the surrounding community for nearly three centuries. (Courtesy LHS.)

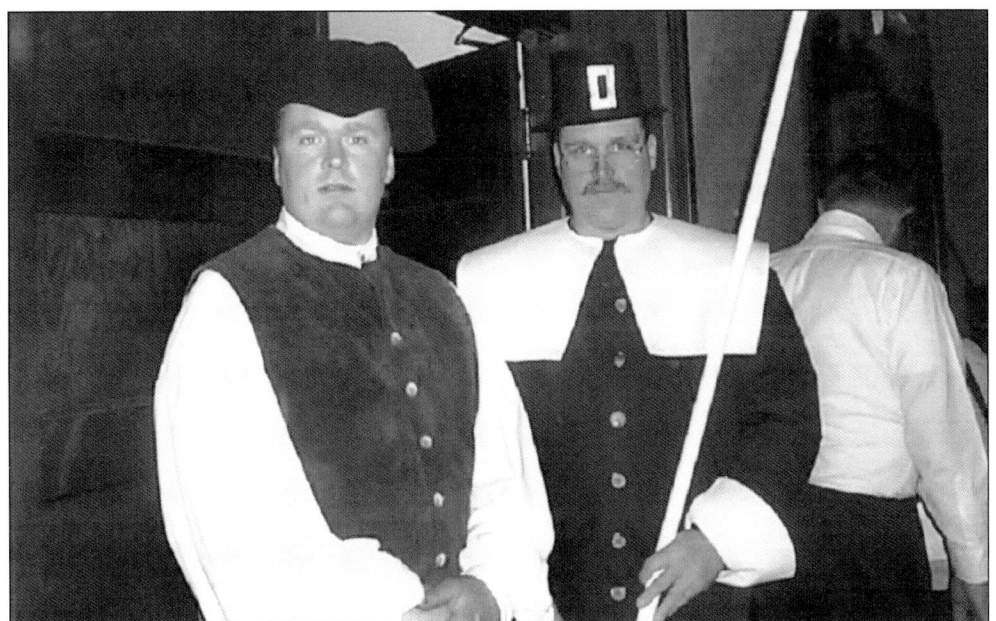

A PURITAN WORSHIP SERVICE. The Goshen Congregational Church celebrated its 275th anniversary in 2004. A Puritan worship service on January 11 was the first of many events held throughout the yearlong celebration of the church's rich history in the community. Brothers Frank (left) and Kevin Blakeslee were among the many parishioners who attended the service in period attire. (Courtesy Russell Blakeslee.)

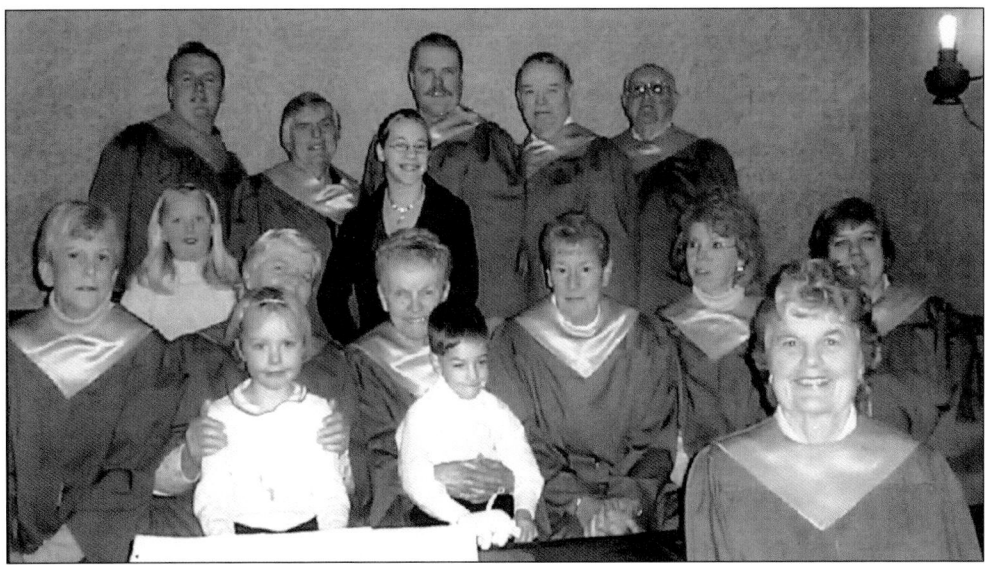

THE GOSHEN CHURCH CHILDREN'S AND SENIOR CHOIRS. Gathered here, from left to right, are the following: (first row) Alicia Watson, Gretchen Lathrop (holding Emelia Blakeslee), Gloria Corbett (holding Charlie Weinsteiger), Ann Dorflinger, Alison Palshaw, and Maureen McCall; (second row) Lillian Blakeslee and Heather Weinsteiger; (third row) Frank Blakeslee, Henry Grabber, Kevin Blakeslee, Russell Blakeslee, and Kenneth Lathrop. Missing are Diane Gray and children Mae and Tony Santillo and Joene Tomick. Organist and choir director Jonica Blakeslee appears in front, at the far right. (Courtesy Russell Blakeslee.)

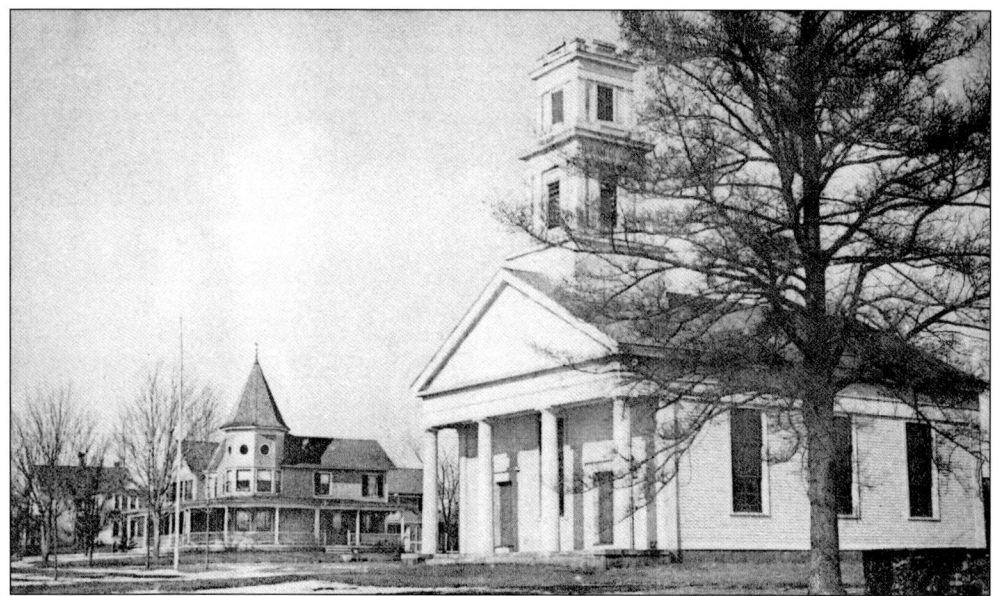

THE FIRST BAPTIST CHURCH. The first meetinghouse of the Lebanon Baptists dates from the founding of the church in 1805. This Greek Revival church replaced it in 1841. A chapel, built from lumber from an old cheese factory, was added in 1907. The deteriorated second stage of the steeple was removed in the 1930s. This photograph, taken before 1900, shows the Joseph Abel house next door, which burned in 1910. (Courtesy LHS.)

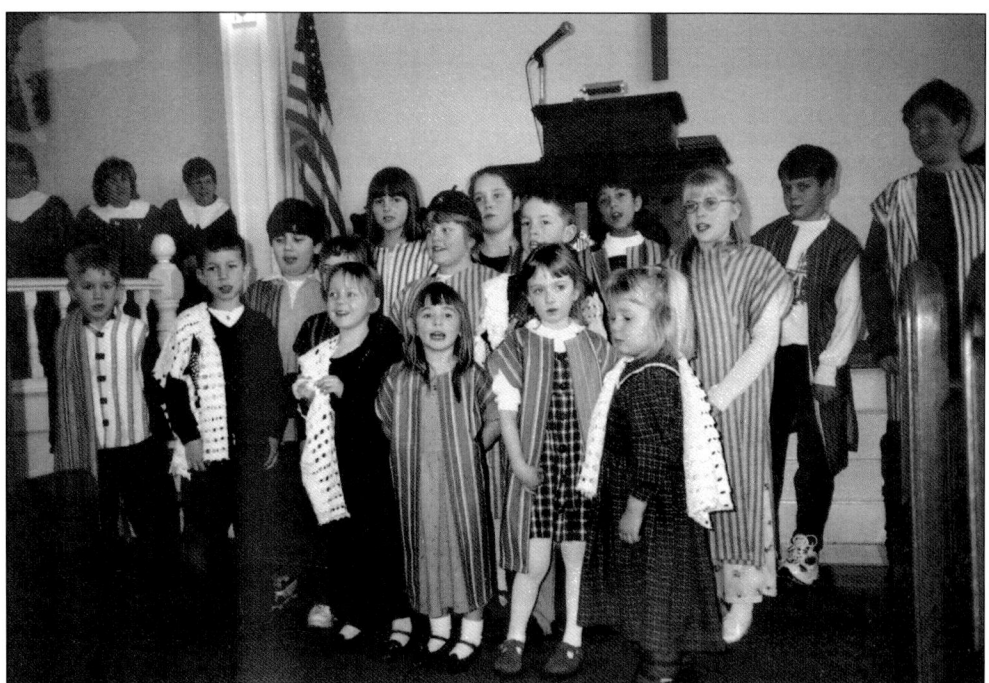

SUNDAY SCHOOL. Sunday school children at the First Baptist Church take part in the regular Sunday worship services on a monthly basis. Here, the children are dressed in Biblical costumes as they present a Bible story to the congregation in March 2000. (Courtesy Beverly Duntz.)

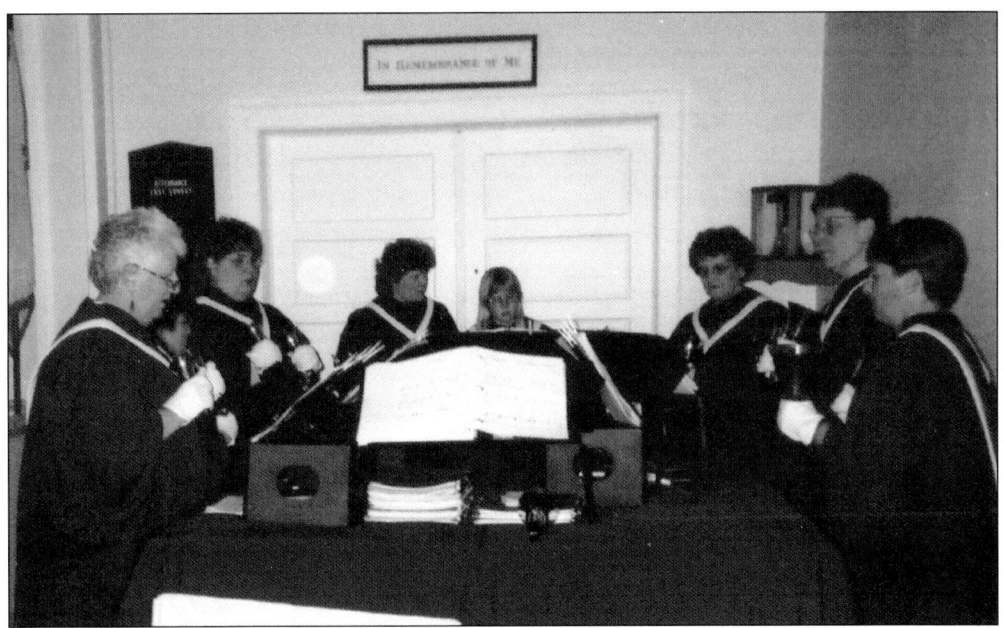

THE BELL CHOIR. The bell choir of the First Baptist Church plays at almost every Sunday worship service. Members seen here are, from left to right, Joyce Kelly, Shirley Deflaviis, Sue Lyon, Molly Lathrop, Bonnie Lathrop, Beverly Duntz, Deborah Martin, and Lynn Littlefield. Their musicianship is highly regarded, and the bell choir also performs at many community events. (Courtesy Beverly Duntz.)

THE LIBERTY HILL CHURCH. Built in 1838, this building became a Congregational mission in 1892 and a full church in 1912. In 1919, the Exeter church was joined to Liberty Hill. In 1945, its assets were transferred to the First Congregational Church. The building was used by the Liberty Hill Men's Club and the Lebanon Guild of Arts and Crafts for many years before being sold to a private party in the 1970s. Once a vital part of the Liberty Hill community, it has now collapsed. (Courtesy Ed Tollmann.)

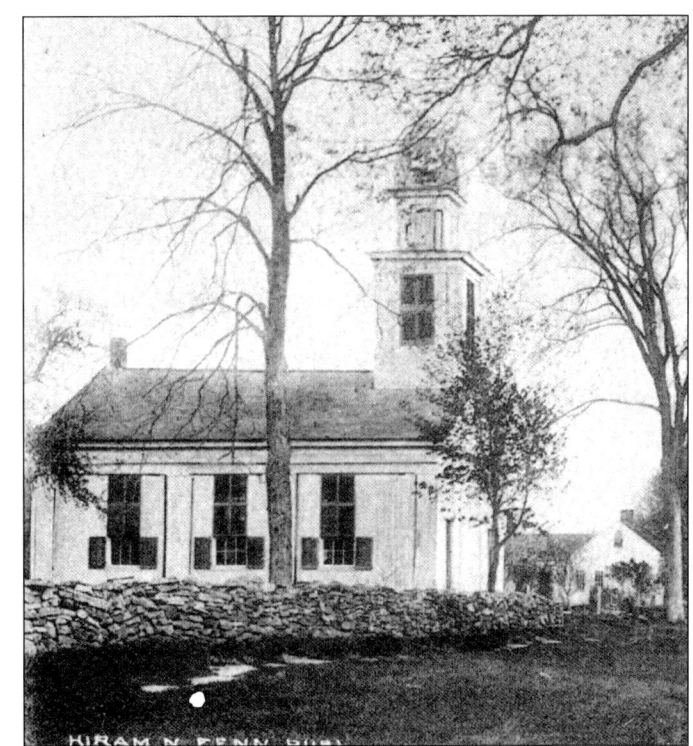

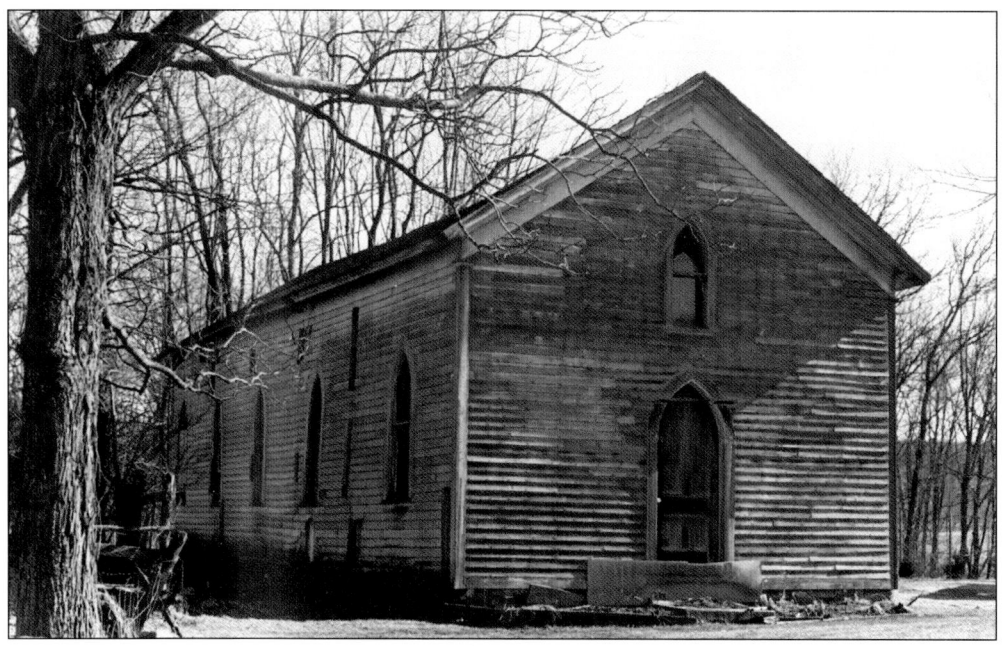

THE ST. MARY MISSION CHAPEL. Sometime between 1860 and 1870, Irish Catholic immigrants built this chapel on McGrath Lane as a mission church under the Colchester parish. The Irish settlers worked in the rubber and paper mills on the Yantic River. When the mills failed, many moved to the cities to find work, and the congregation dwindled. The church was finally closed in 1921. The old building is now used for storage. (Courtesy Barbara Wengloski.)

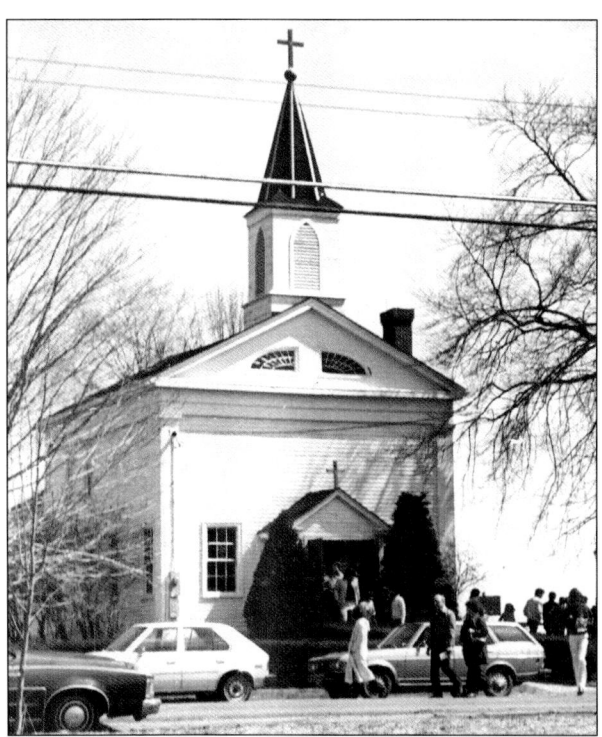

THE FORMER ST. FRANCIS OF ASSISI CHURCH. This house, located at 812 Trumbull Highway, was built by Leonard Hebard c. 1840. It was purchased and converted for use as a mission church for Lebanon Catholics in 1943. A steeple was installed on the roof. When the new St. Francis church opened in 1980, the house was sold and converted back to a residence. (Courtesy Barbara Wengloski.)

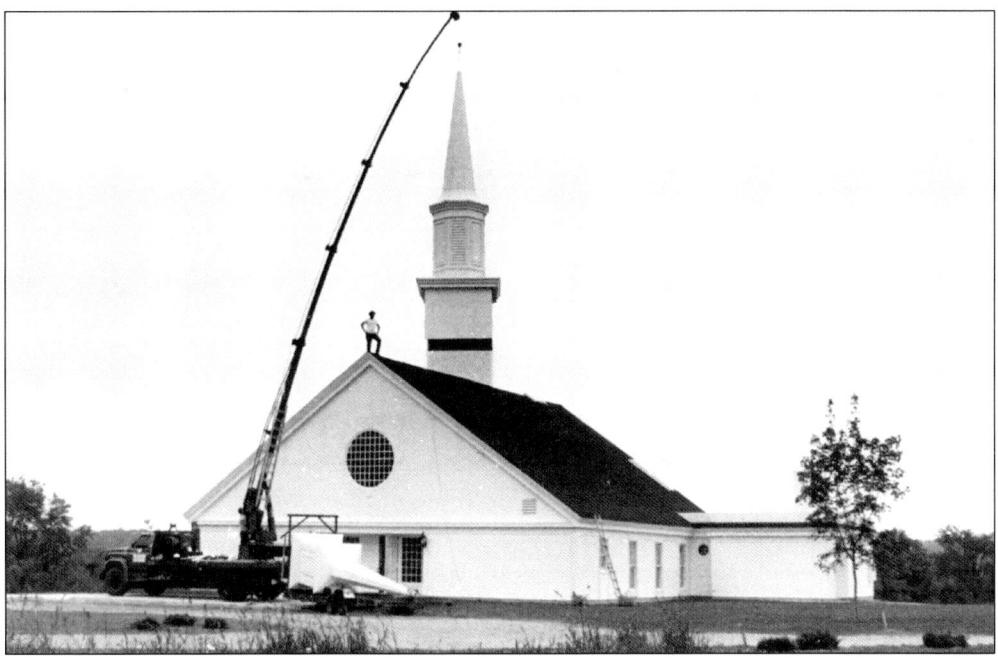

THE ST. FRANCIS OF ASSISI CHURCH. Expanding membership led to the need for a new church building for local Roman Catholics. In 1965, the church purchased a large parcel on West Town Street, and parishioners began raising funds for a building. Construction finally began in 1979 and was completed the next spring, when the steeple was set in place. In 1985, St. Francis added a parish hall and rectory. (Courtesy Barbara Wengloski.)

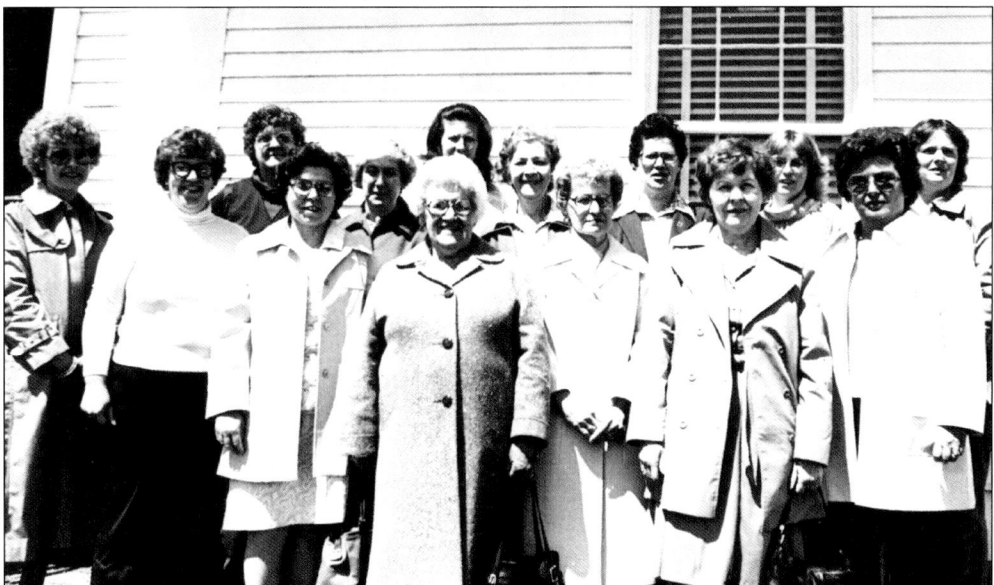

THE LADIES GUILD. The St. Francis Ladies Guild was organized in 1949 and celebrated its 50th anniversary in 1999. For over half a century, the members have carried out a large number of service activities and projects to benefit both their church and the community. They also participate in events that foster the ecumenical movement. This photograph was taken in 1980; the guild members are unidentified. (Courtesy Barbara Wengloski.)

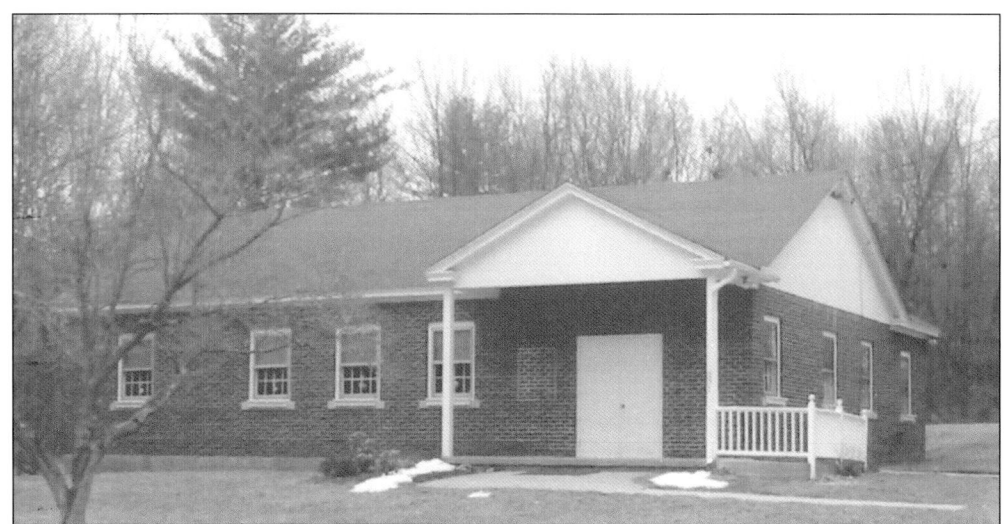

THE LEBANON BIBLE CHURCH. This church began as a mission of the Scotland Christian Fellowship Church in 1987, with the members meeting in each other's homes in Lebanon. In 1991, it was incorporated as the Lebanon Bible Church and began renting the Jewish synagogue on Goshen Hill Road. The Lebanon Jewish community no longer had the necessary quorum for services and did not need the building. The church purchased the building in 1995. (Courtesy LHS.)

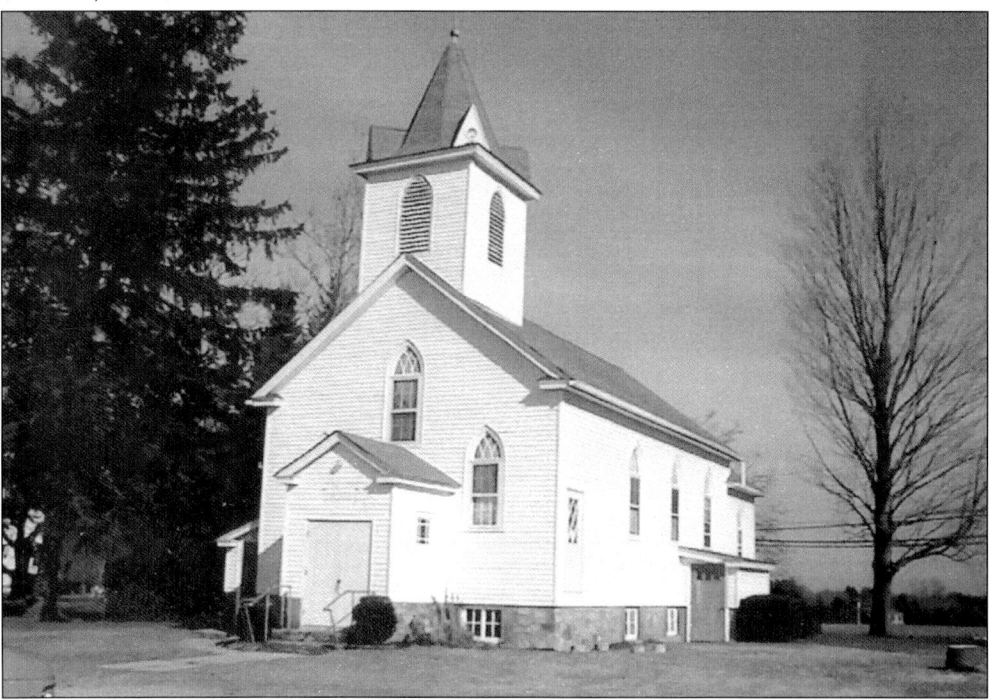

THE REDEEMER LUTHERAN CHURCH. German immigrants began arriving in Lebanon from Ukraine in 1911. At first, they traveled to Willimantic to attend church services. In 1937, they purchased the vacant Village Hill Schoolhouse for a church, but the 1938 hurricane weakened the building. The salvaged lumber was used in the construction of this church, designed by Gottlieb Laibrandt and built entirely by volunteer labor. (Courtesy Claire Krause.)

Three

THE LIBERTY HILL NEIGHBORHOOD

The road leading into Liberty Hill from Chestnut Hill (Columbia) was known as the Hartford to New London Stage Coach Road. Horse-drawn coaches traveled the highway carrying passengers, freight, and mail. Liberty Hill had its own post office and received mail three times a week. The post office was housed in a general store, the second building south of the present Swyden's Store. Until a fire in 1906, Liberty Hill contained two general stores. Liberty Hill was a regular stop, with the general store on the west and Gay's Tavern on the east side of the highway. Passengers were able to secure lodging, food, and supplies in Liberty Hill. Locals would also gather at the tavern and discuss the happenings of the day. The organization papers for the Liberty Hill Church were written in Gay's Tavern, with George Gay as clerk, in 1837.

A gristmill situated on the west side of the highway was the first building on Liberty Hill's boundary with Columbia. This mill was operated with waterpower from a millpond fed by the Ten Mile River, which served as the boundary line between Lebanon and Columbia. Local farmers brought their grain to the mill to be ground. Across the street was a blacksmith shop.

In 1873, with the arrival of the Boston & New York Air Line Railroad, Liberty Hill changed. The mail was now delivered by rail. A train station and store were built just over the town line in Chestnut Hill to accommodate passengers and freight. The station served as the post office for Chestnut Hill, with Liberty Hill's post office still at the general store in the village. When Eva Dimon was appointed Chestnut Hill postmistress in 1905, she moved the post office into her house in Liberty Hill. The residents of Chestnut Hill complained bitterly that they would now have to enter another town to get their mail. Worse yet, they would be crossing from Tolland County to New London County. The complaints fell on deaf ears. Instead of moving the post office back or combining it with Liberty Hill's, the postal service left it named the Chestnut Hill Post Office even though Chestnut Hill was not in the town of Lebanon. In 1907, the Liberty Hill Post Office was eliminated, leaving the Chestnut Hill Post Office to serve both Chestnut Hill and part of Liberty Hill. This change caused considerable confusion, for everyone who lived in Lebanon from the town border south to the Route 87 and 207 intersection had a Chestnut Hill address. Remember that Chestnut Hill is in the town of Columbia. The village of Liberty Hill runs from the Ten Mile River to Pease Brook.

School No. 4 was at the corner of Cook Hill Road and Trumbull Highway. This school served Cook Hill and Liberty Hill students. Across from the school to the west was a magnificent granite quarry where foundation stones and large step stones were cut and sold. Before you entered the village, a peat moss bed could be observed to the left of the highway. As you entered the village, the stately homes of such families as Loomis, Gay, Babcock, Clarke, Kingsley, and Fuller dotted both sides of the highway.

The Liberty Hill Church served as the center of activity, with a very active congregation until the 1940s. Leaving the village, the last home on the left was known as the Chestnut Hill House. There, water from a mineral spring was advertised as a life-extending elixir. Folks would come and stay to relax and partake of the mineral water.

Liberty Hill was once a vibrant, active community with beautiful homes, granite sidewalks, two general stores, a gristmill, a blacksmith shop, a school, and its own house of worship. But the 1940s witnessed the decline of the village. The church was consolidated with the First Congregational Church in Lebanon Center, and the schoolhouse was sold to the Liberty Hill Men's Club in 1936, when the new elementary school was opened. All photographs in this chapter are from Ed Tollmann's personal collection.

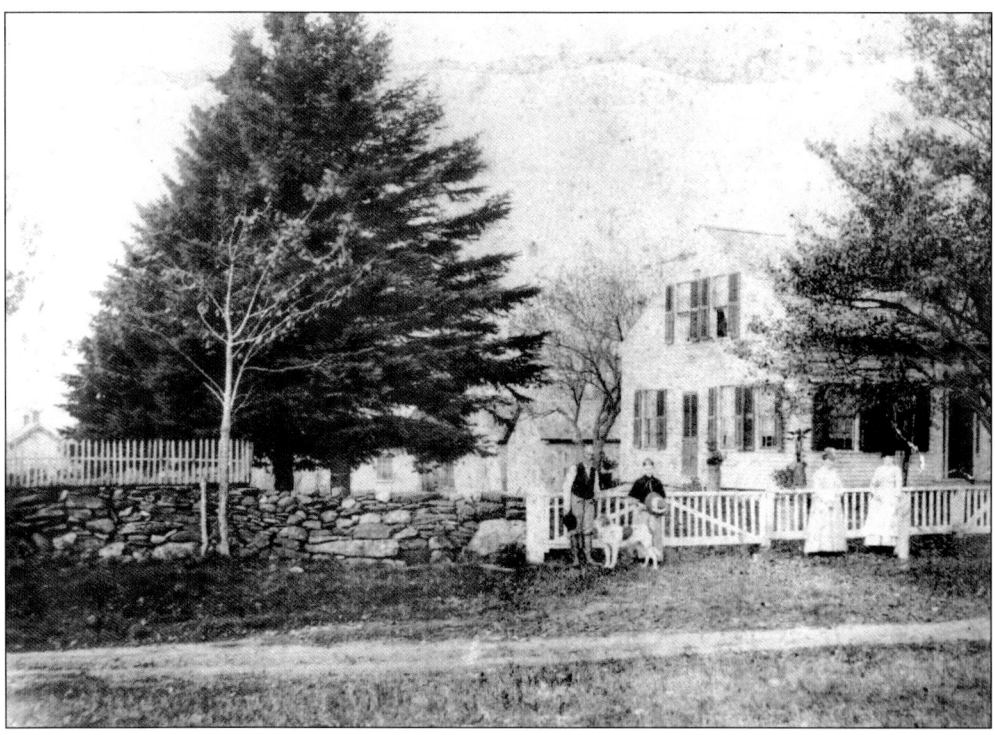

THE WHITE FEATHER FARM. When this photograph was taken, the White Feather Farm, on Cook Hill Road, was the first farm on the left from Trumbull Highway. A white feather weathervane identified the farm for many years. There, the Goodrich family hatched and sold chicks. Charles and Nancy Goodrich (left) and their daughters Abbie and Flora were photographed in front of their farmhouse in 1889.

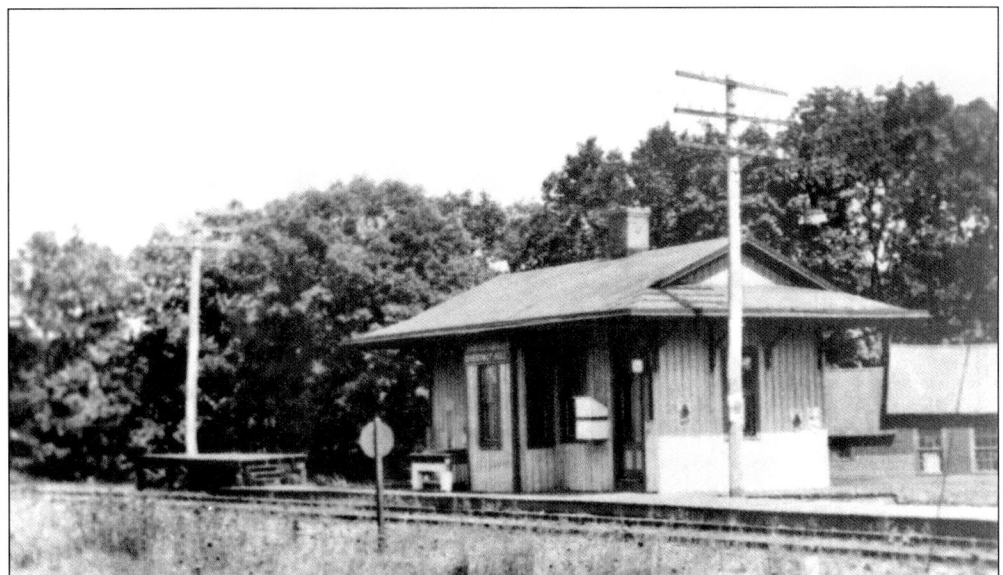

THE CHESTNUT HILL STATION. This railroad station was located just before the Lebanon town line in Columbia, and served the village of Liberty Hill. Students rode the "airline" to and from Windham High School, and families took it to Willimantic and other cities. Special reduced-price tickets, as seen at the right, were provided for high school students.

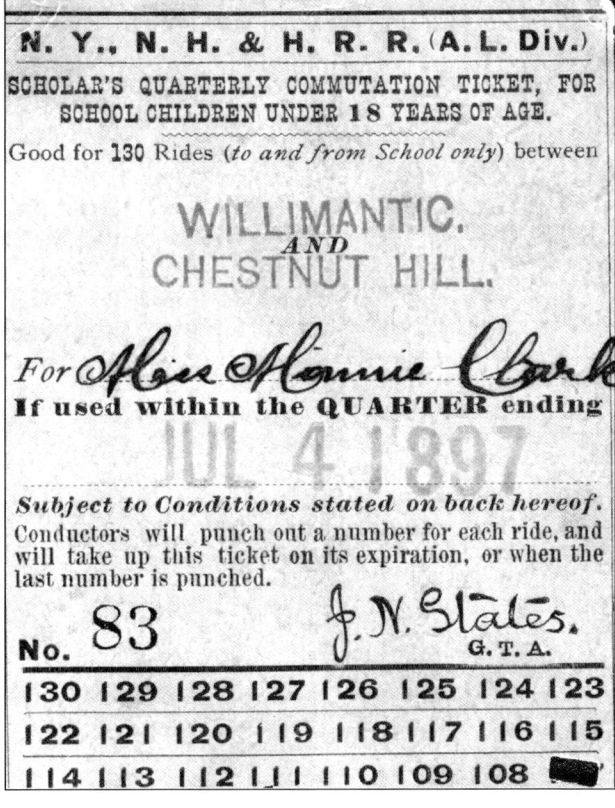

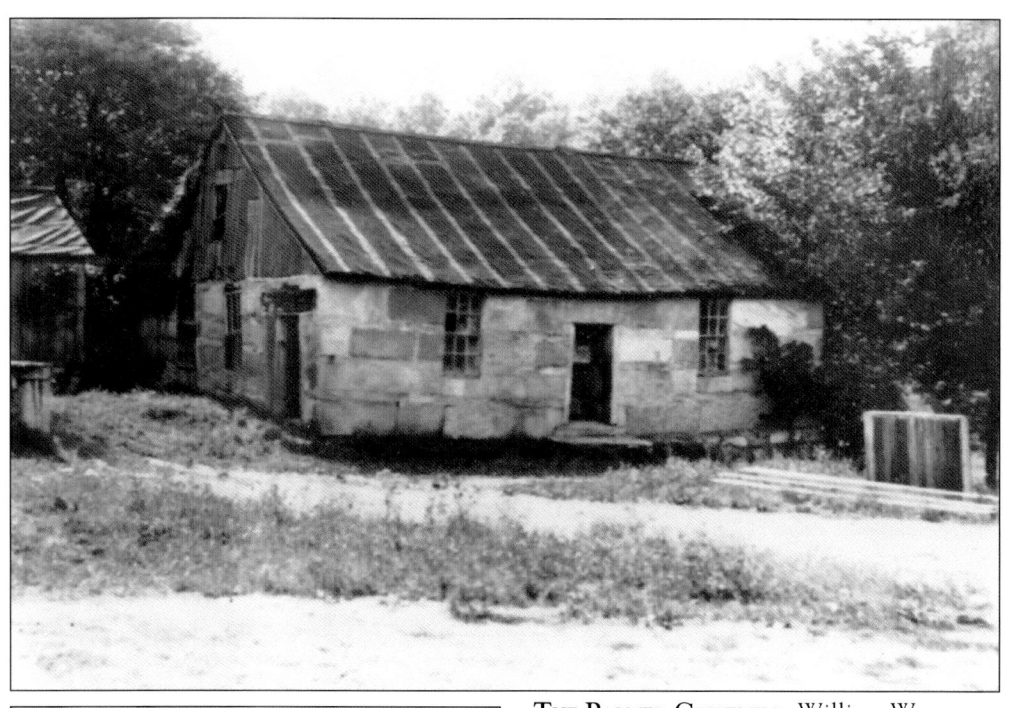

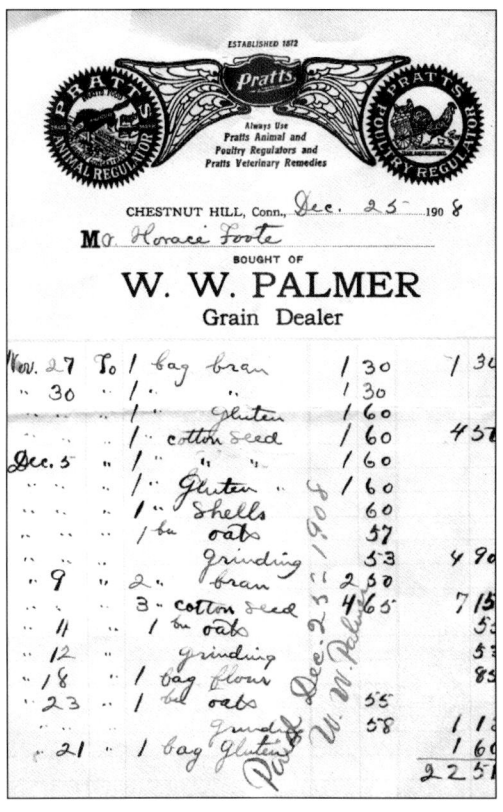

THE PALMER GRISTMILL. William W. Palmer ran this gristmill for many years, grinding grain for local families. The mill was built in 1829 and was run by waterpower from an upstream millpond on the Ten Mile River. It was torn down in the 1950s, and a house was built on the site, the first on the right when coming into Liberty Hill.

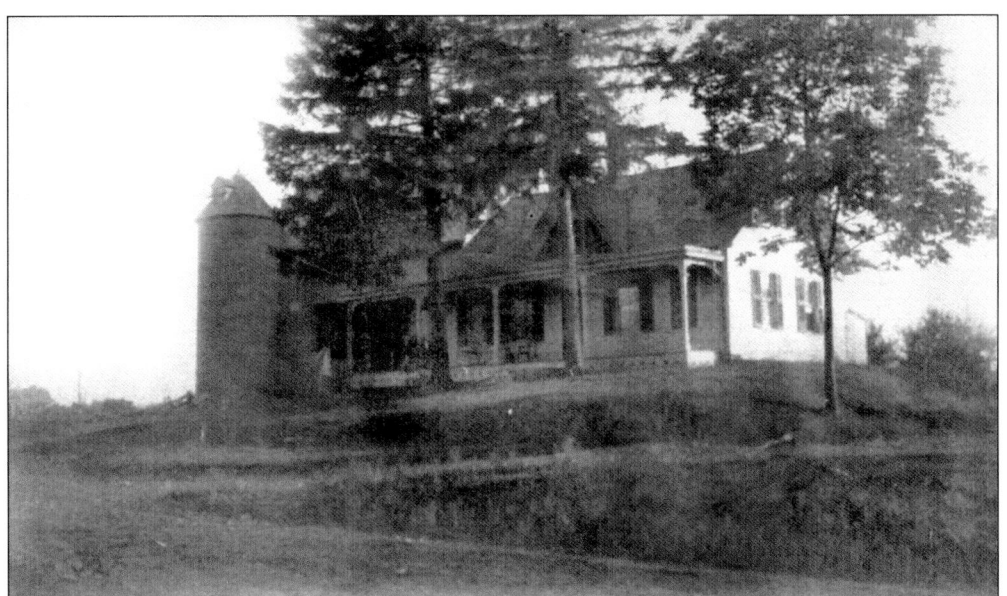

THE HOME OF WILLIAM W. PALMER. Located to the south of the gristmill, this house was electrified by the mill. In 1924, a fire originating in the attached barn destroyed the house as well.

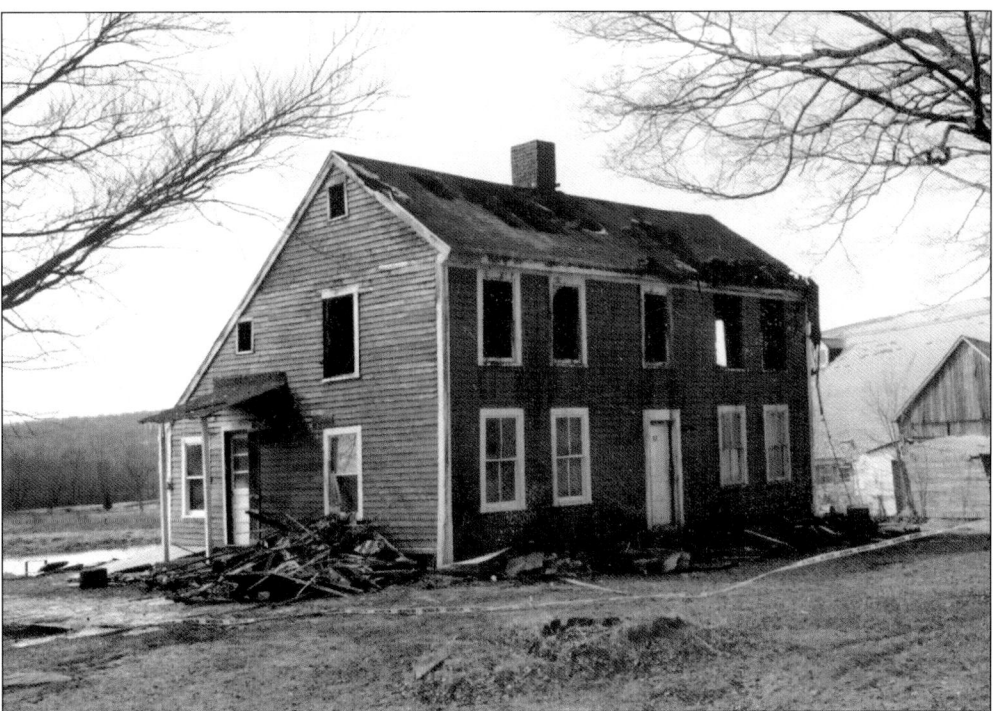

AN OLD SALTBOX HOUSE. This house, one of the oldest saltbox homes in Lebanon, was located just south of the Ten Mile River on Trumbull Highway. It was torn down after being partially destroyed by fire in 1990.

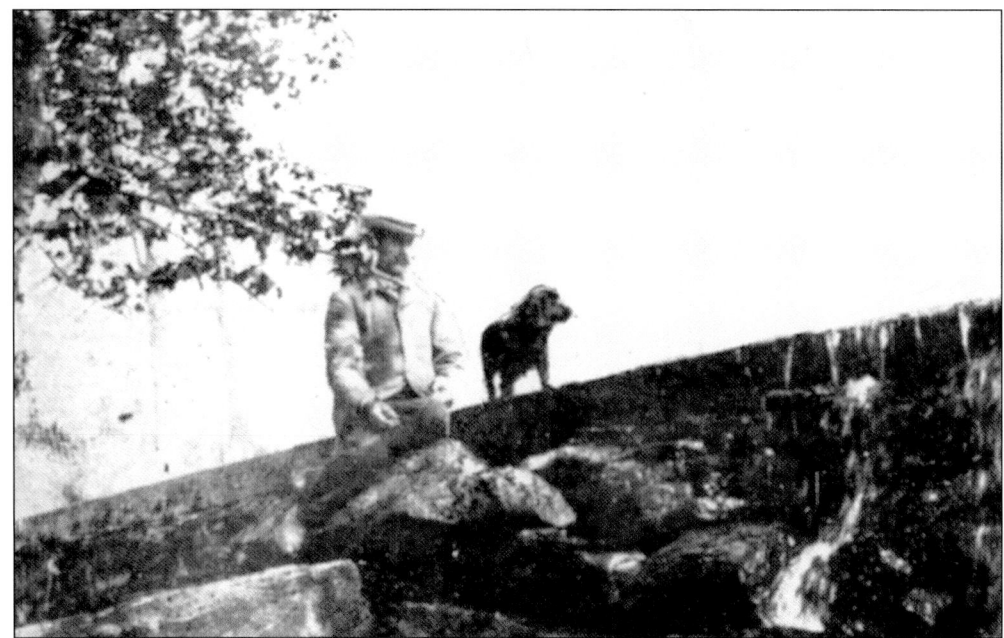

THE MILLPOND. G. R. Dimon stands atop the millpond dam behind Palmer's gristmill with one of his cocker spaniels. Dimon ran Nomid Kennels, a clever backward spelling of his name.

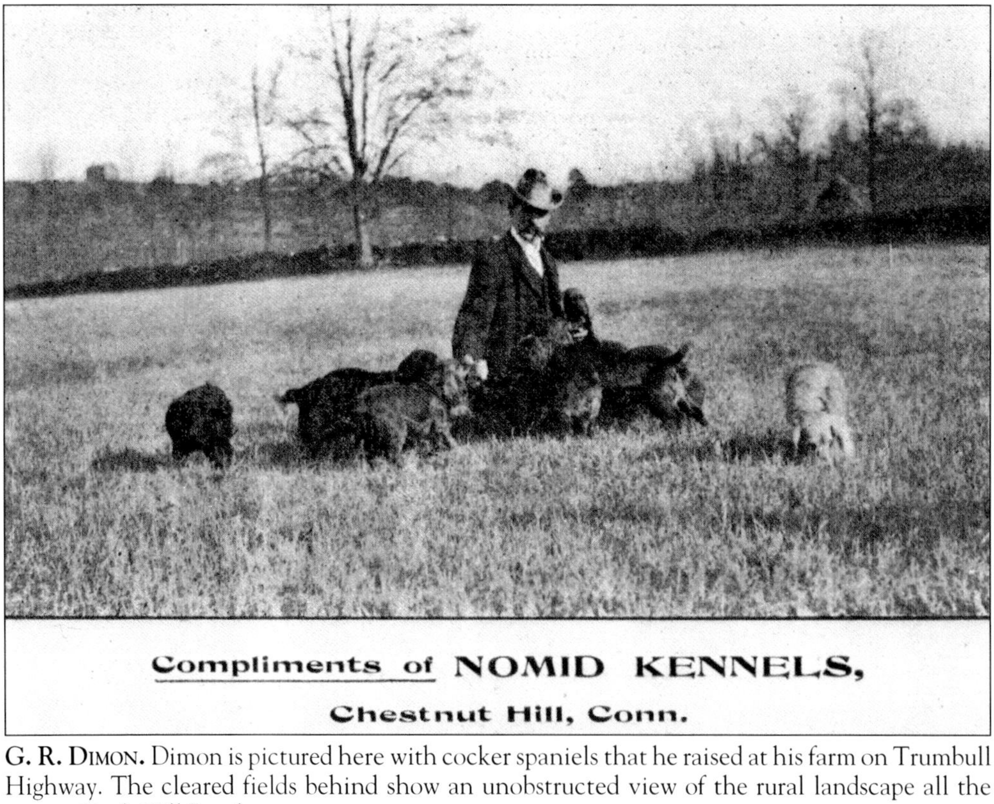

G. R. DIMON. Dimon is pictured here with cocker spaniels that he raised at his farm on Trumbull Highway. The cleared fields behind show an unobstructed view of the rural landscape all the way to Cook Hill Road.

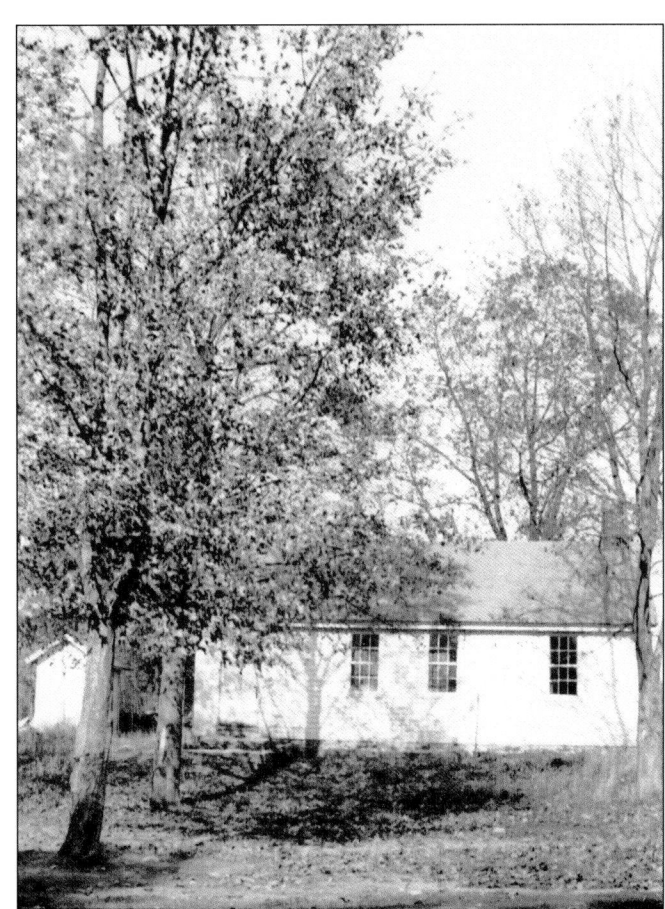

THE LIBERTY HILL SCHOOL. Located on the corner of Cook Hill Road and Trumbull Highway, School No. 4, shown at the right, served Cook Hill Road and Liberty Hill. Teacher Flora (Bruce) Williams is pictured below in the middle of her students; the group is posing in front of a ledge north of the school. Williams taught first through eighth grades in one room.

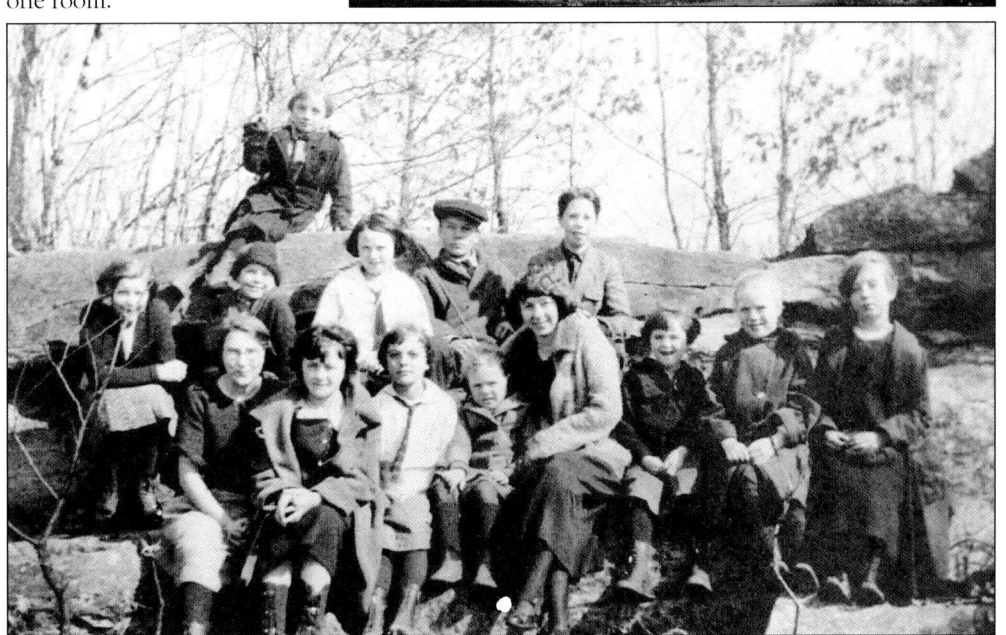

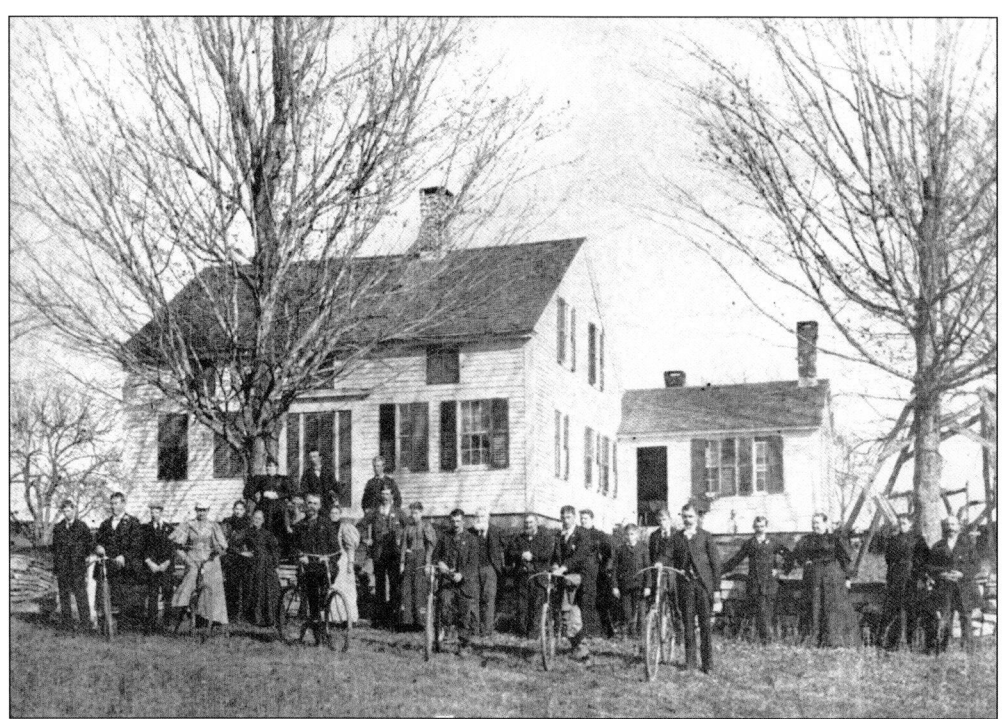

THE FARM ON COOK HILL. The Clark family enjoys a gathering c. 1880. This farm is on Cook Hill Road and has not changed much over the years. Everett Payson owned it from 1916 to 1947, when Russ Tollmann purchased the farm. Payson and Tollmann both served Lebanon as selectmen.

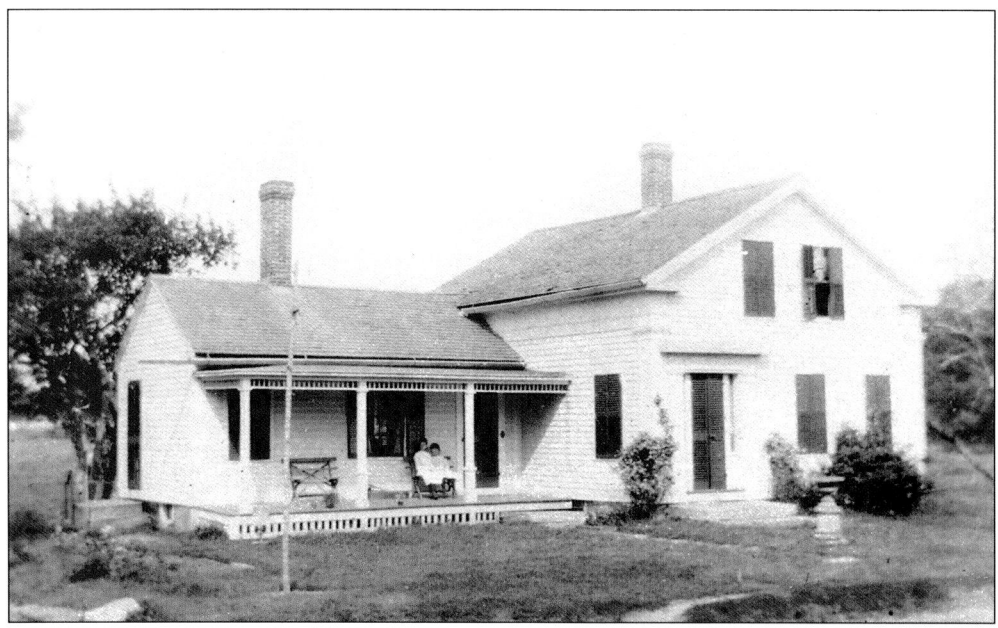

THE HARVEY HOUSE. This home is situated on the northern corner of Clarke Road and Trumbull Highway. It was owned by the Harvey family, which was very active in the Liberty Hill community.

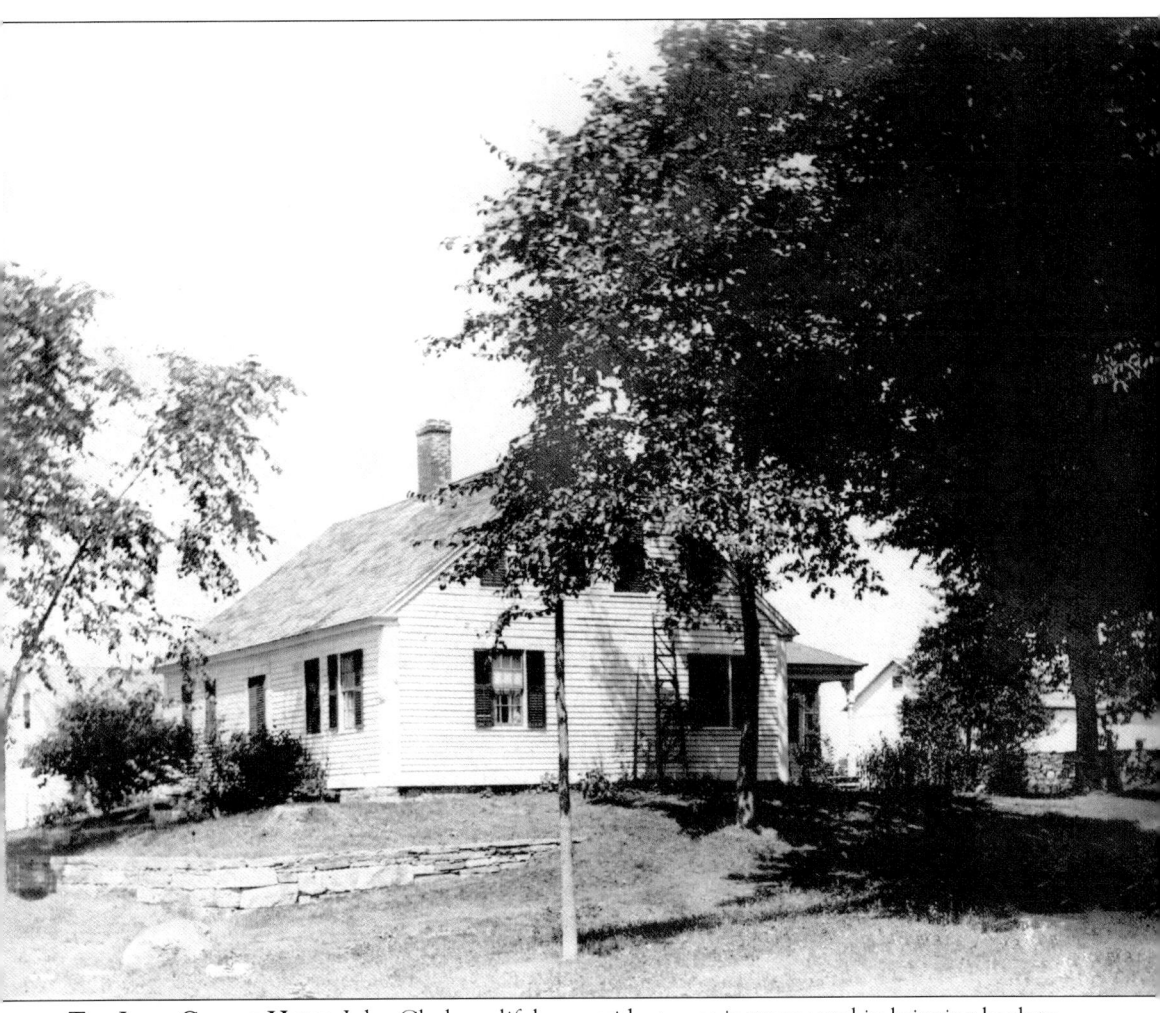

THE JOHN CLARKE HOME. John Clarke, a lifelong resident, was instrumental in bringing back to life the "village of Liberty Hill" in the early 1900s. His home stands on the northern corner of Burnham Road and Trumbull Highway.

ATTENTION!

If you want any Second-hand Goods come to Clarke's Great Auction Mart.

We can supply you with anything, it makes no difference what.

We have OX CARTS, OX WAGONS, PLOWS, HARROWS, and various kinds of Farming TOOLS, TWO-HORSE TEAM WAGONS, BUSINESS WAGONS, BUGGIES, CARRIAGES, ONE and TWO HORSE SLEDS and SLEIGHS, HARNESS, Heavy and Light, Single or Double, BLANKETS, ROBES, ETC., ETC.

Revolvers, Guns, Bicycles, Watches, Clocks, Furniture, Stoves, Crockery, Glass and Tin Ware, and a thousand and one things to numerous too mention.

If you have any articles of any kind that you wish to dispose of, bring them to me, or send me a discription of them, and I will sell them for you.

If you have any Old Fashioned Furniture or Crockery, let me know and I will make it worth your while.

AUCTION SALE
—OF—
Horses, Cattle, Etc., Every Month.

Articles sold at private sale every day except sundays.

If you have any work for an Auctioneer, let me do it, and I will guarantee you satisfaction.

Respectfully,

J. H. CLARKE,
LIBERTY HILL, CONN.

Baldwin Printing & Mfg. Co., 501 Main St., Willimantic, Conn.

JOHN CLARKE, AUCTIONEER AND ENTREPRENEUR. Pictured here is an advertisement for John Clarke's auction business. John, a shrewd businessman, was involved in many land and estate transactions.

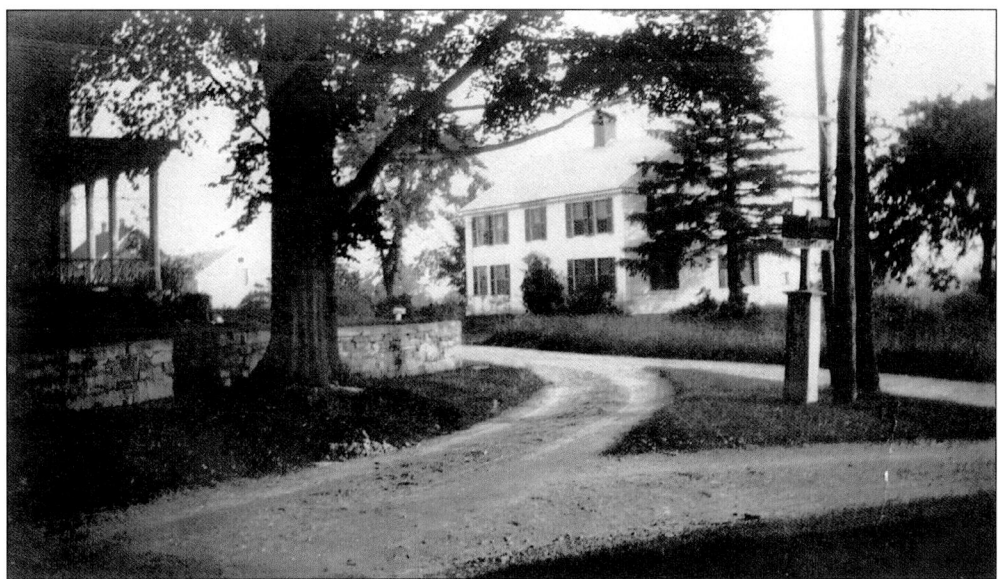

THE PARSONAGE. This home was purchased by the Liberty Hill Church in 1918. The downstairs was used to house the pastor, and the upstairs was used for church meetings and dinners. The Liberty Hill Men's Club, formed in 1928, met upstairs for many years and was a very active civic group. The signpost at the intersection of Burnham Road and Trumbull Highway points the way to Colchester by way of Clarke Road.

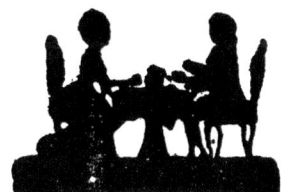

Liberty Hill Men's Club
Ladies' Night

Lebanon Baptist Chapel, Wed., Oct. 23, 1946

Supper at 7 o'clock

admits two   not transferable

Contribution $1.50

Frank Bartizek

LADIES' NIGHT. Once a year, a ladies' night was held by the Liberty Hill Men's Club.

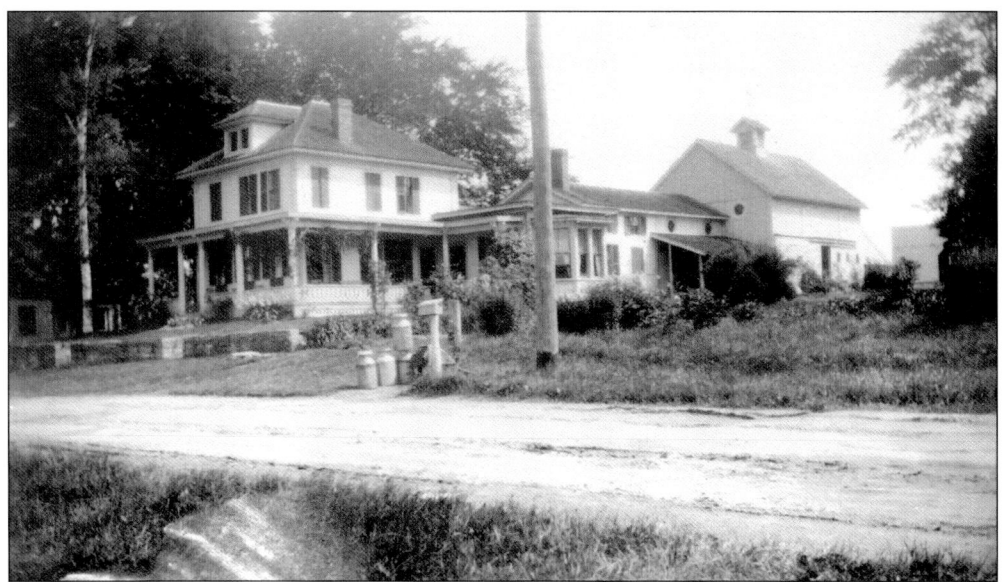

THE FOOTE FARM. This beautiful farm is a great example of a "joined" New England farm where the farmhouse and outbuildings are all connected. Horace and Lizzie Foote operated it from 1889 until the 1940s. The house is still standing on the southern corner of Burnham Road and Trumbull Highway.

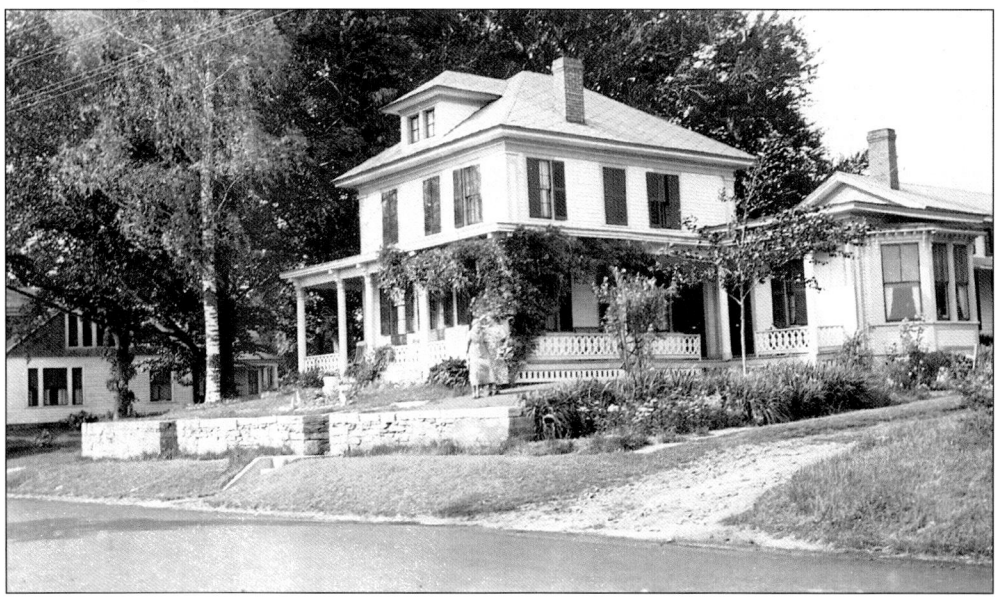

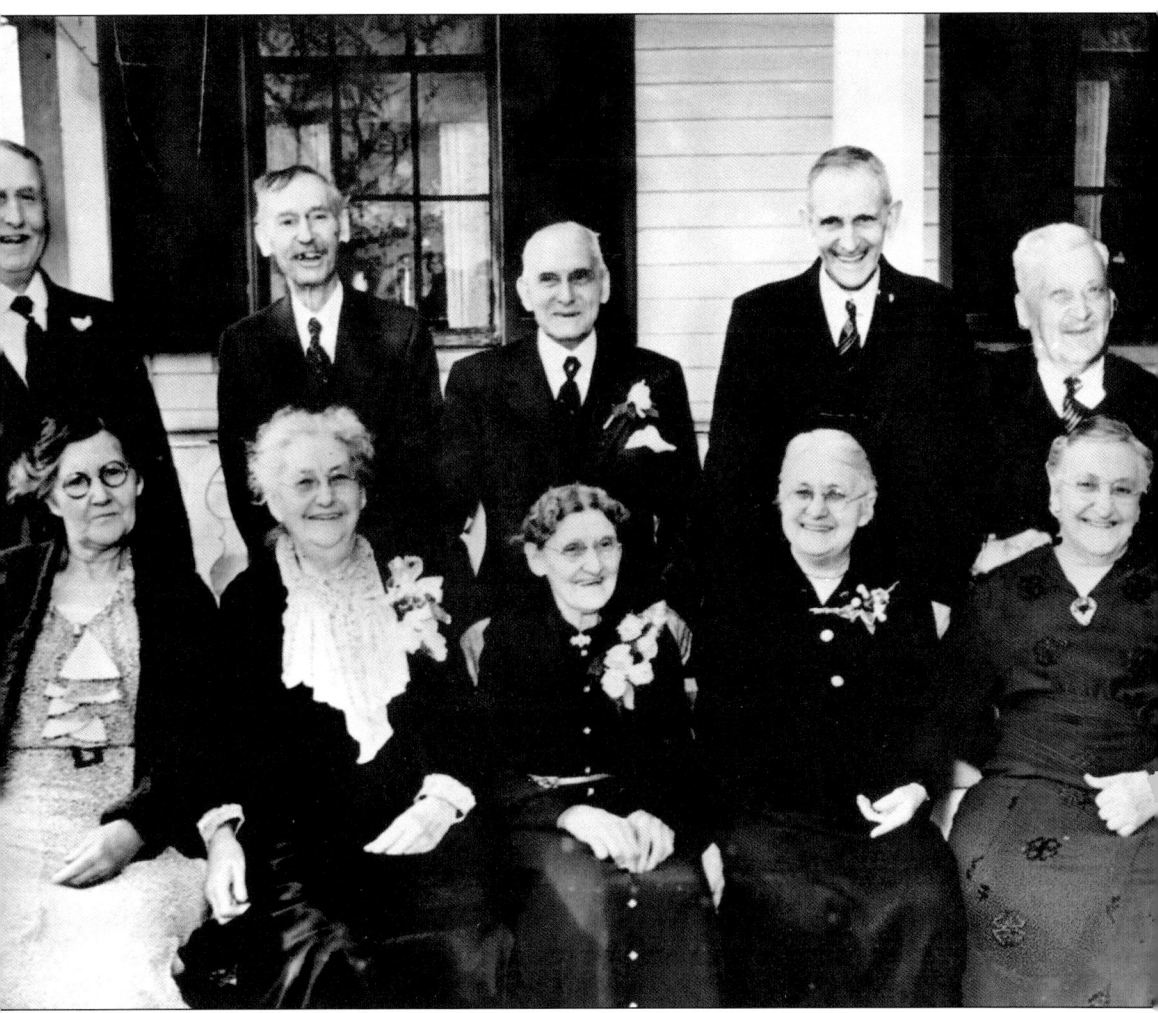

THE FOOTES' ANNIVERSARY. Attending the 50th wedding anniversary of Horace and Lizzie Foote in 1938 are, from left to right, Mr. and Mrs. Milo Davoll, Mr. and Mrs. Albert Peckham, Mr. and Mrs. Horace Foote, Mr. and Mrs. John Clarke, and Mr. and Mrs. James Choquette. The couples pictured here were the movers and shakers of the village. Mr. and Mrs. Choquette operated the general store.

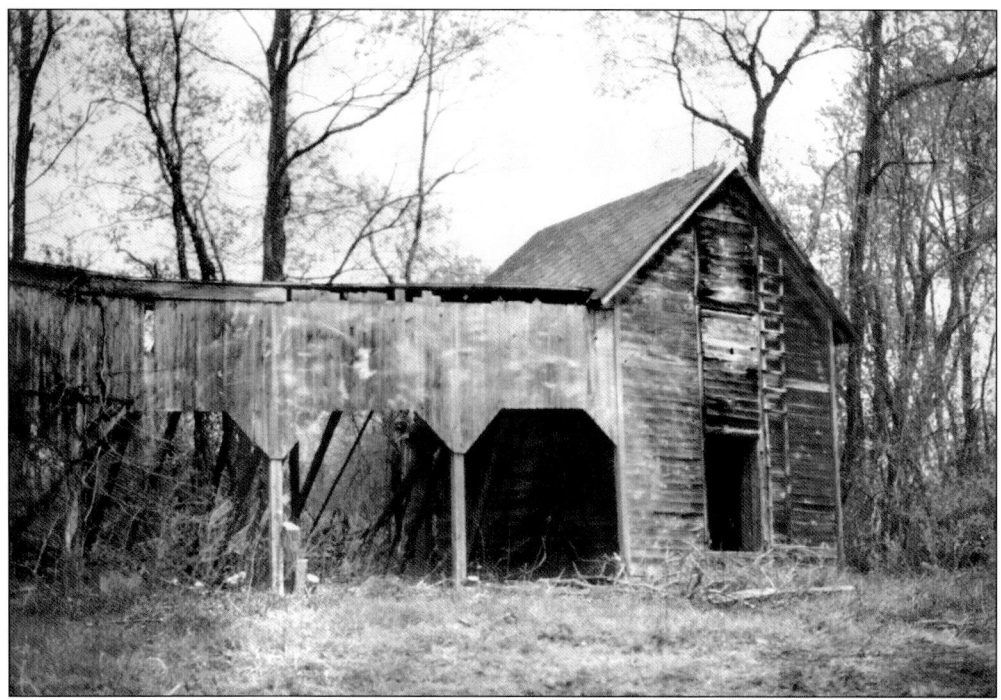

THE LAST ICEHOUSE IN LIBERTY HILL. This icehouse, part of the Foote farm, is a great example of one found in New England. Icehouses were a vital part of life before electricity.

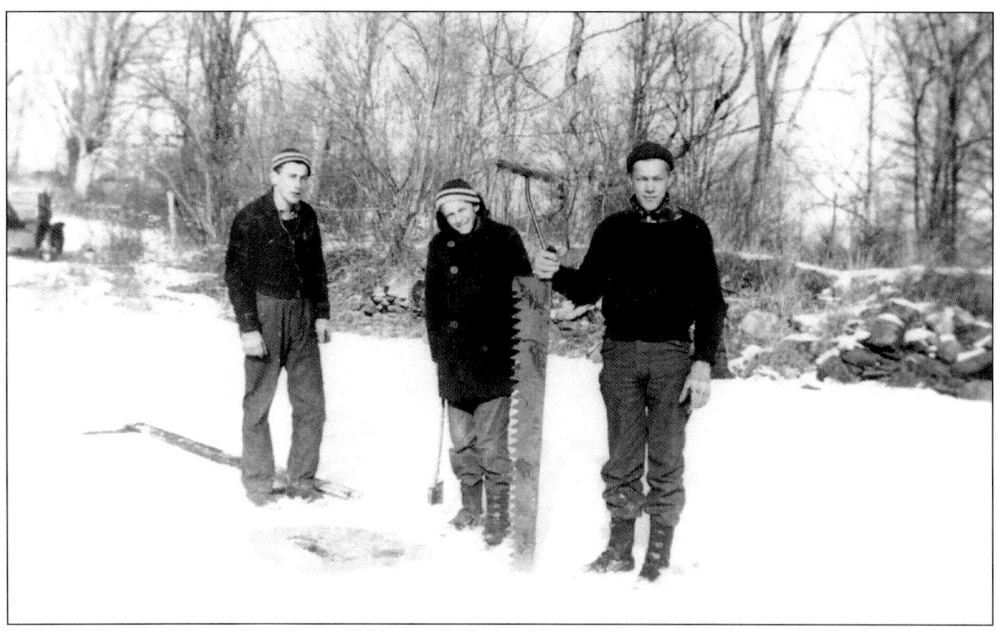

ICE CUTTING. Fred, Walter, and Matt Arson, seen here from left to right, prepare to cut ice on Flumes Pond on Tobacco Street.

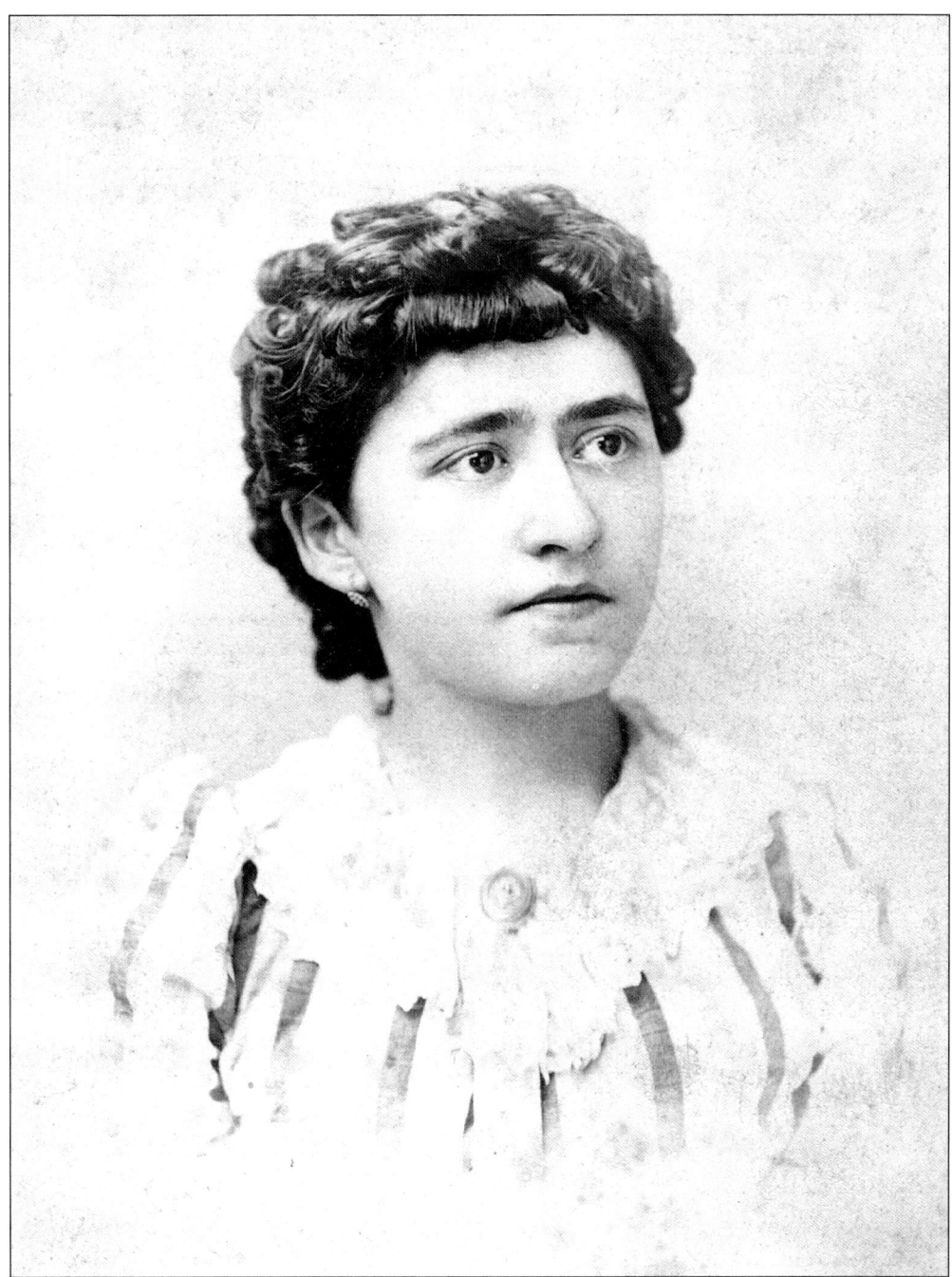

FLORA CAPLES. Flora Caples and her husband, Elmer, a carpenter by trade, came to Liberty Hill in the early 1900s. They purchased a piece of property that had been left vacant by a disastrous 1906 fire, which had destroyed three homes, a barn, and the Farnham Store, which also housed the Liberty Hill Post Office. Elmer and Flora built a house and soon became an integral part of the village. Elmer, known as a topnotch carpenter, built the upstairs addition to the local general store. Flora was postmistress and ran the post office out of her home for many years in the 1940s.

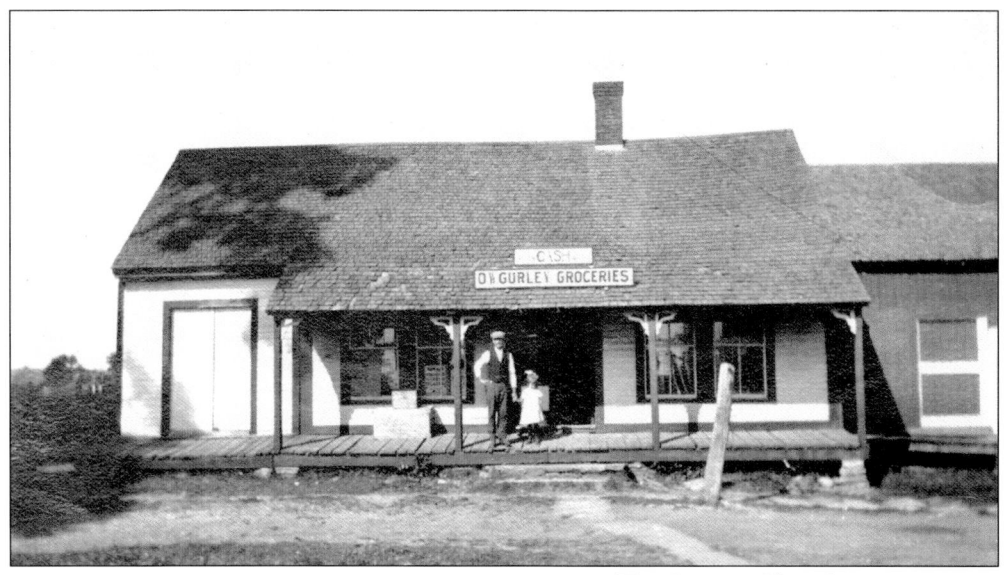

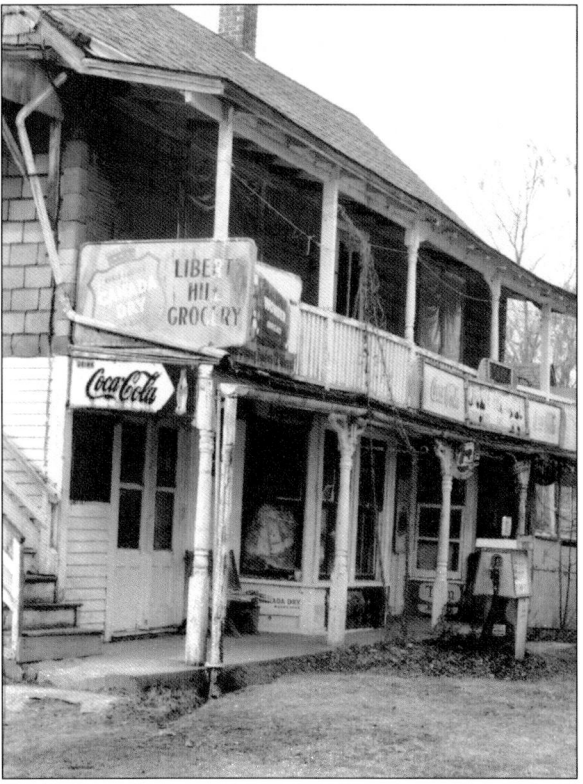

THE LIBERTY HILL STORE. Orville Gurley owned the Liberty Hill Store, shown above, from 1918 to 1925. He is seen above with his daughter Mildred. In 1925, James and Lena Choquette purchased the store and hired Elmer Caples to add a second story, shown at the left, where they then lived. In 1943, the property was sold to the Assad Swyden family, which ran the store and service station into the late 1980s.

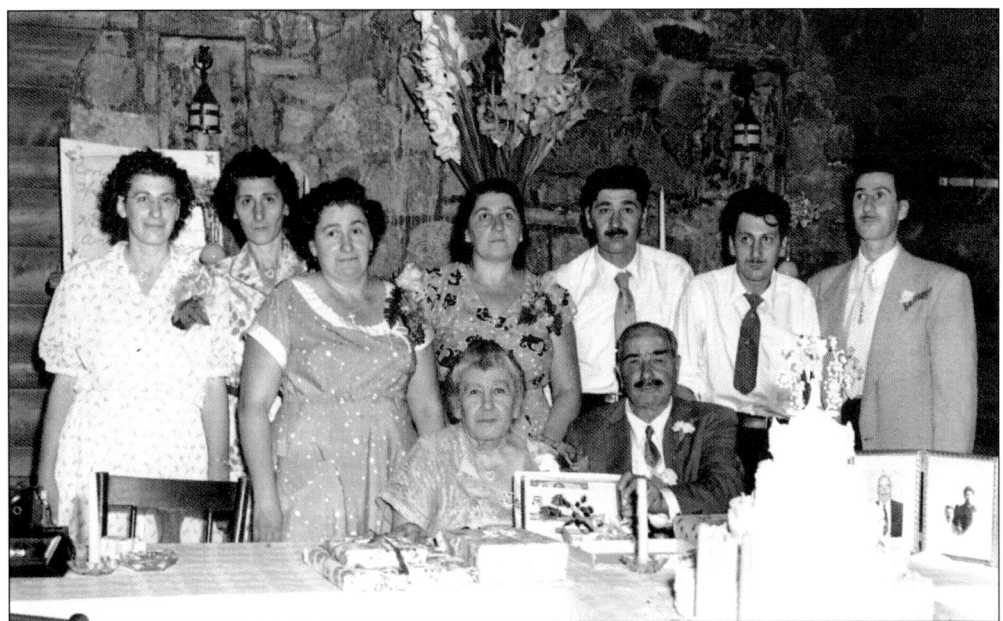

THE SWYDENS' ANNIVERSARY PARTY, 1955. Assad and Mary Swyden's 50th wedding anniversary party was held at the Log Cabin Restaurant. The couple is seated at the table. Pictured behind them, from left to right, are their children, Julia, Olga, Minerva, Sophie, David, Sammy, and Louis. The Swyden family ran the general store and owned numerous pieces of property in Liberty Hill.

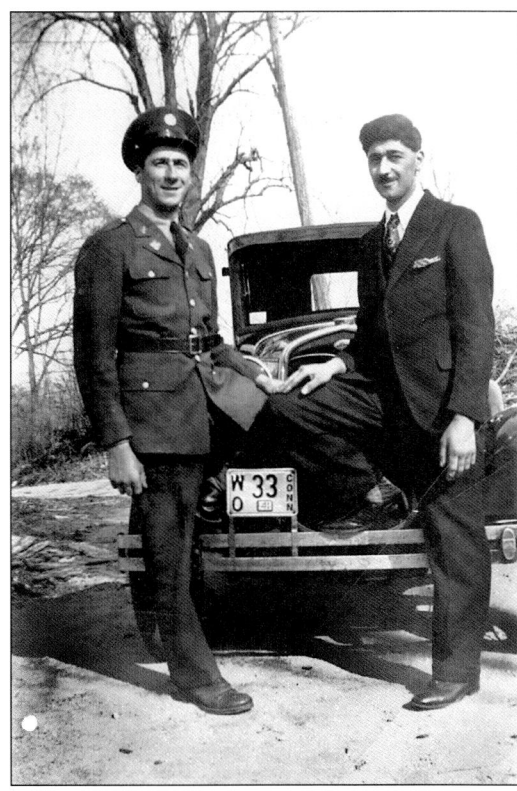

HOME DURING WORLD WAR II. While home, Louis Swyden enjoys a visit with his brother David Swyden.

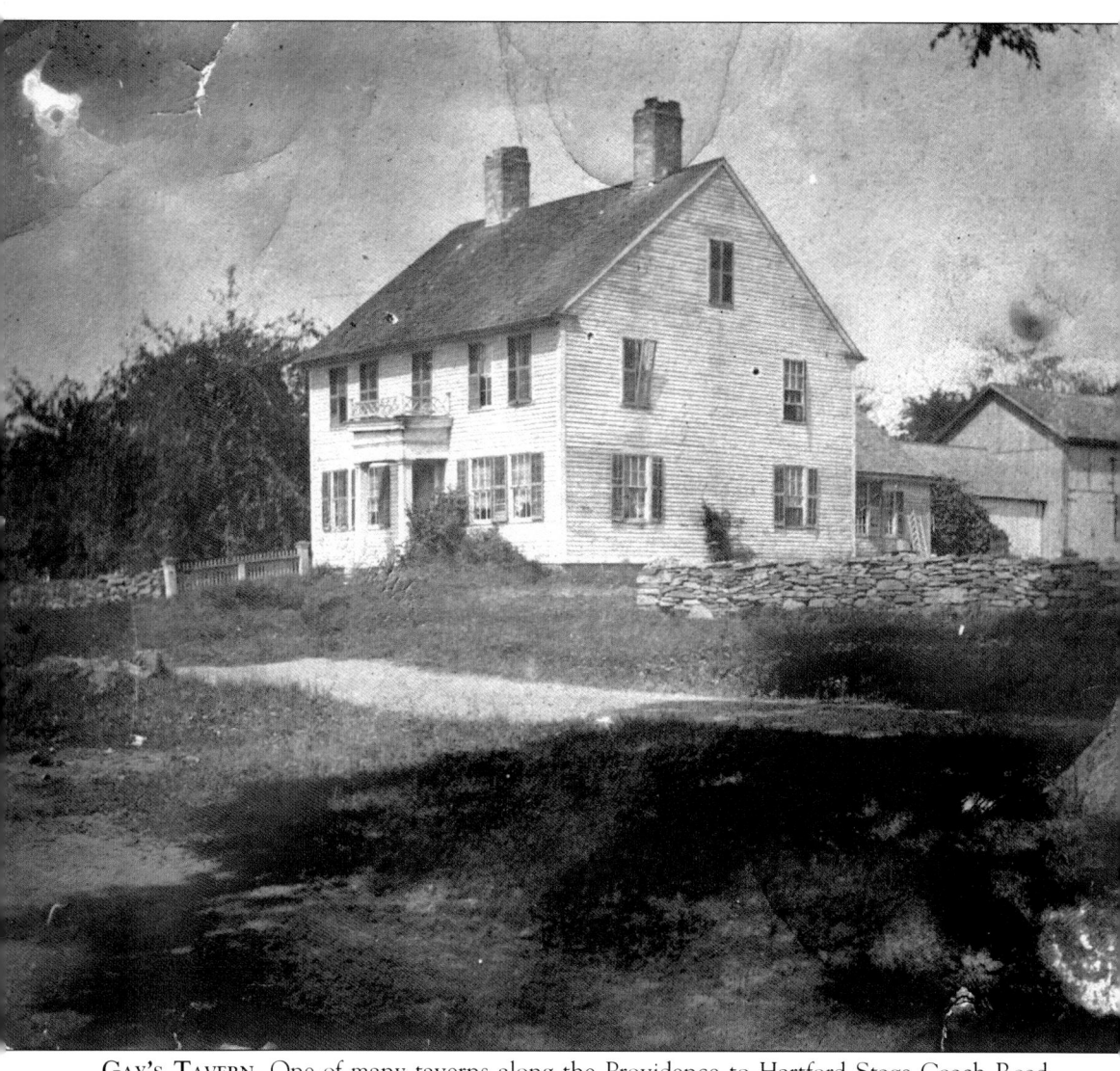

GAY'S TAVERN. One of many taverns along the Providence to Hartford Stage Coach Road, Gay's Tavern was named for George Gay, who owned it while the stagecoaches were running. The tavern was purchased by the Loomis family. After the roof blew off in the 1938 hurricane, the building was bought by the Schweitzer family and turned into a Cape-style house.

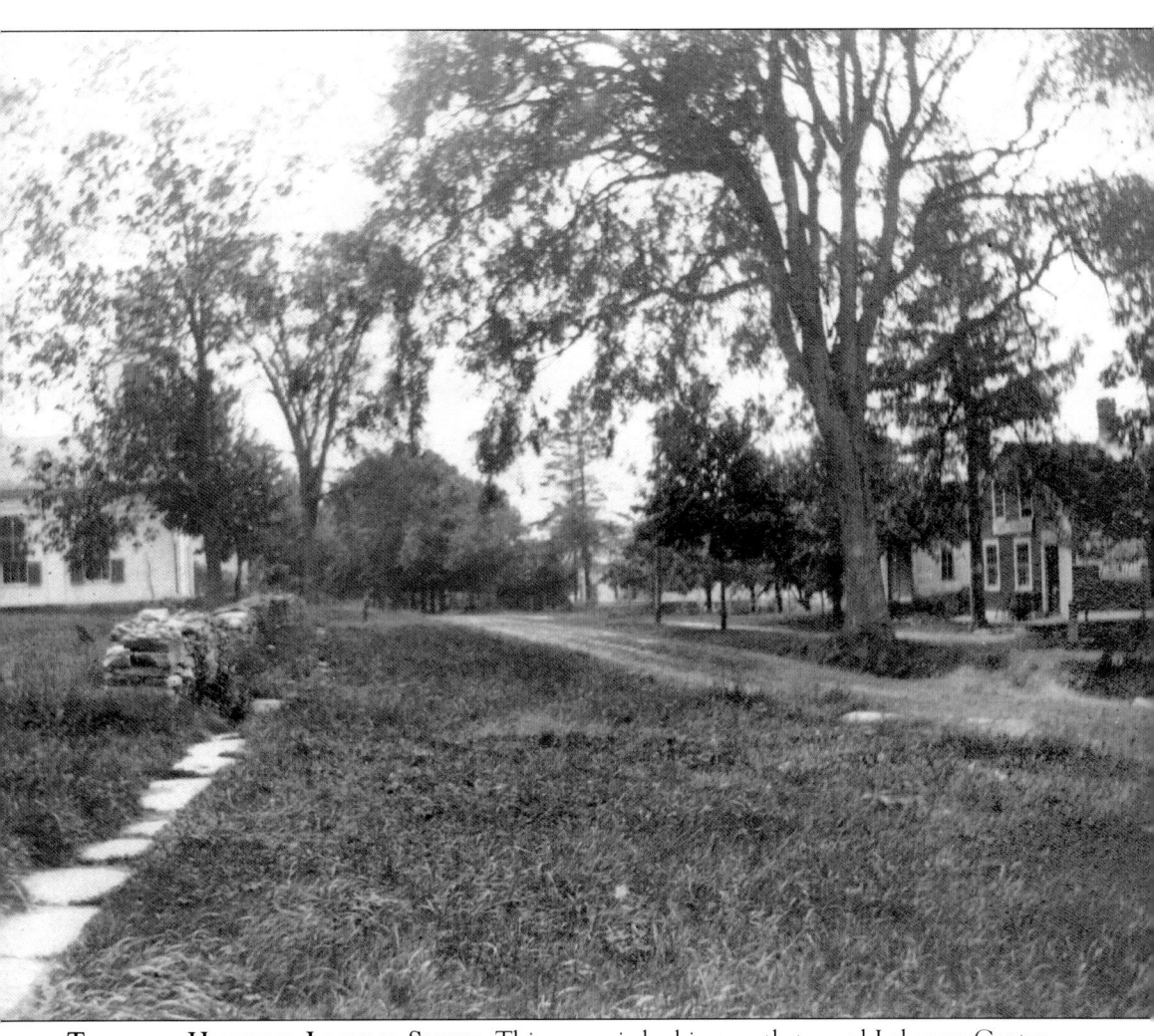

TRUMBULL HIGHWAY, LOOKING SOUTH. This scene is looking south toward Lebanon Center. On the left is the Liberty Hill Church. To the right is the Farnham General Store, which was owned by John Farnham and housed the Liberty Hill Post Office for many years. The house, store, barn, and woodshed owned by John Farnham all burned to the ground in an early morning fire on November 12, 1906.

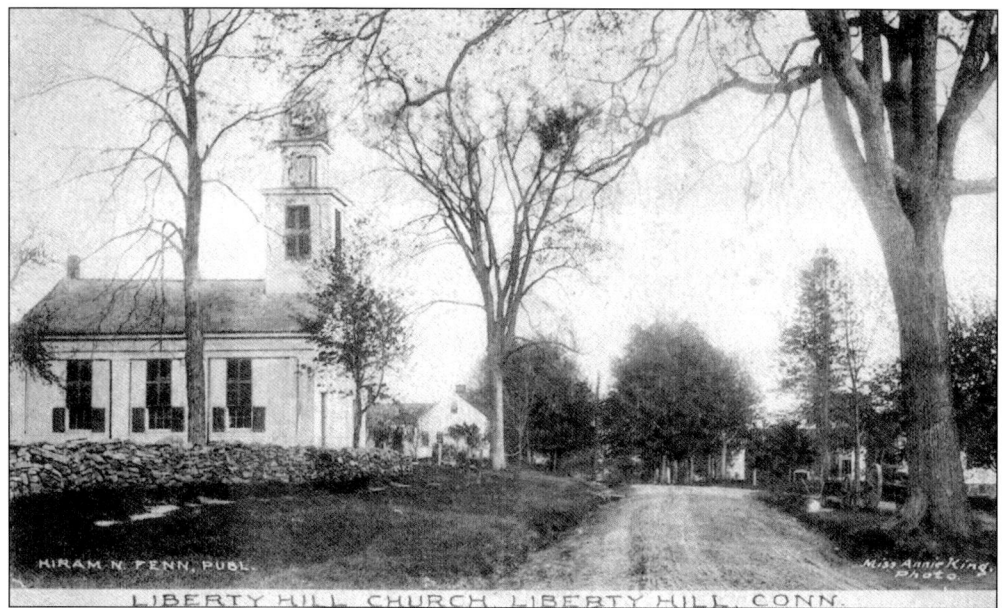

THE LIBERTY HILL CHURCH. This church was built in 1838 and was a First Christian Church for many years. It became a Congregational mission church in 1892 and a full church organized as the Liberty Hill Church in 1912. The congregation bought and maintained a parsonage and was very active until the early 1940s, when, due to a dwindling membership, the church was deeded over to the Lebanon First Congregational Church in 1945.

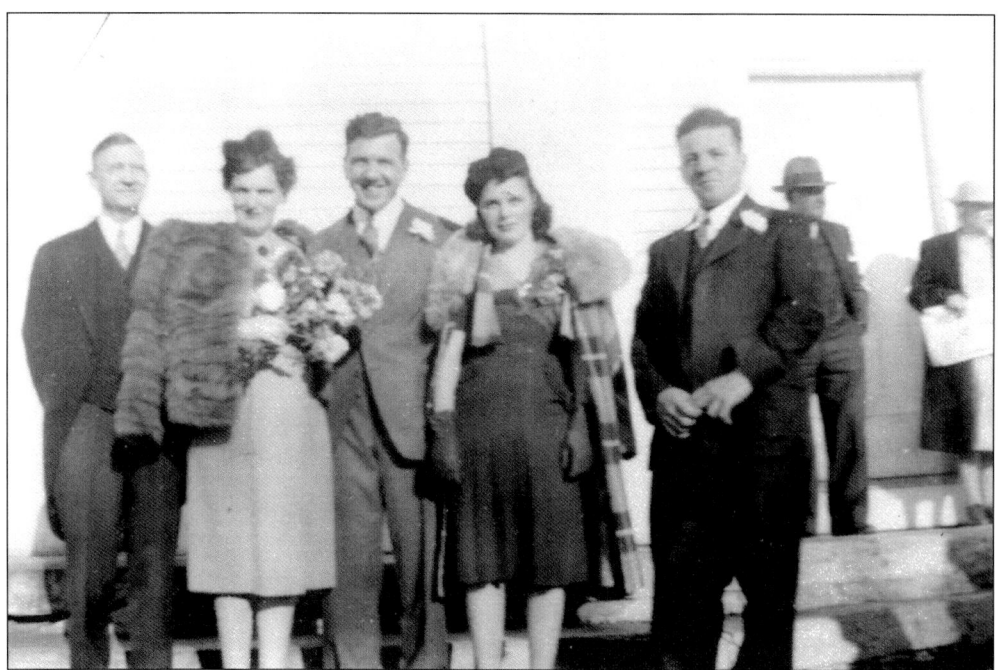

A WEDDING AT LIBERTY HILL. Isabelle and Henry Haddad married in 1942. Pictured from left to right are Pastor Howard C. Champe; Isabelle; Henry; Hazel Wood, sister of the bride; and Fred Haddad, brother of the groom.

THE HOME OF JAMES AND MARY CLARKE. The Clarke family was a very active and a vital part of Liberty Hill.

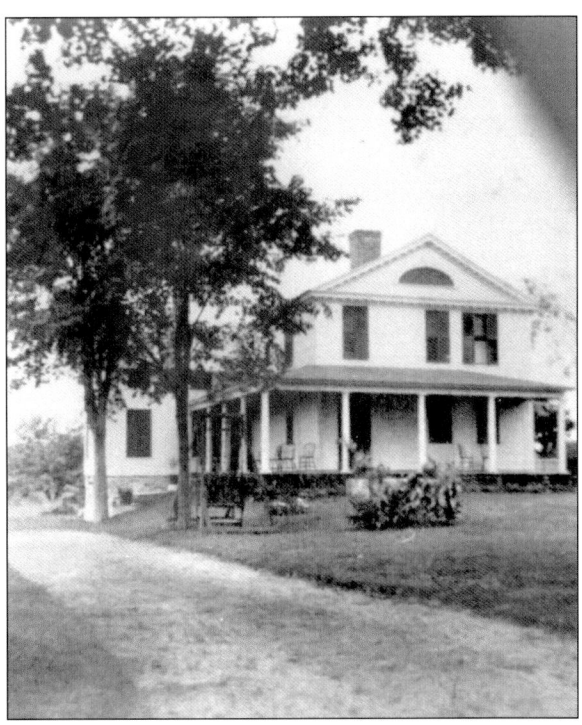

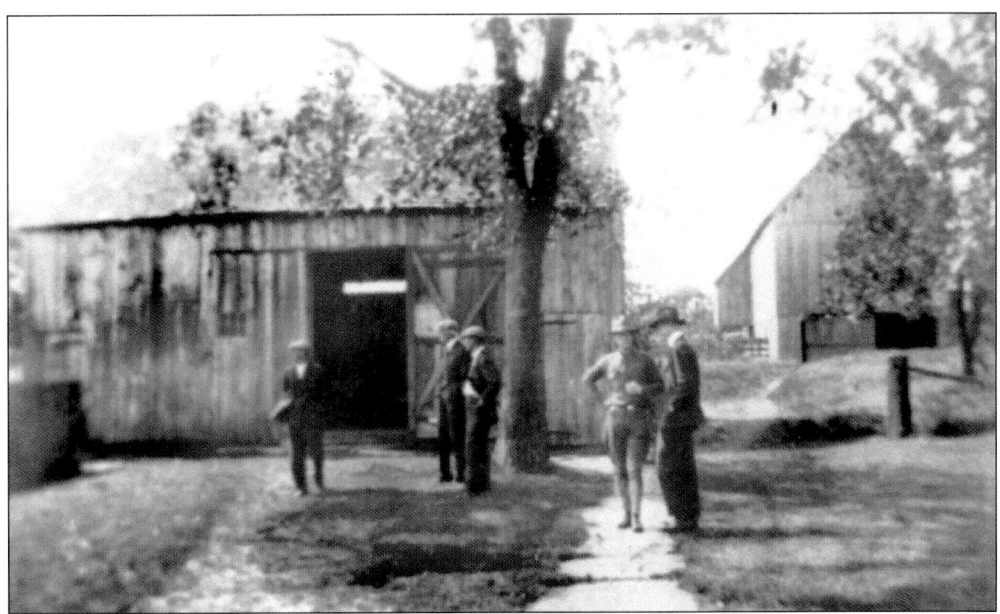

A CLARKE FAMILY GATHERING. This photograph was taken during World War I, probably at a gathering for an unidentified family soldier (second from the right). The barn to the right was destroyed by the 1938 hurricane and was rebuilt by Leslie Clarke Sr. It is now an antique shop.

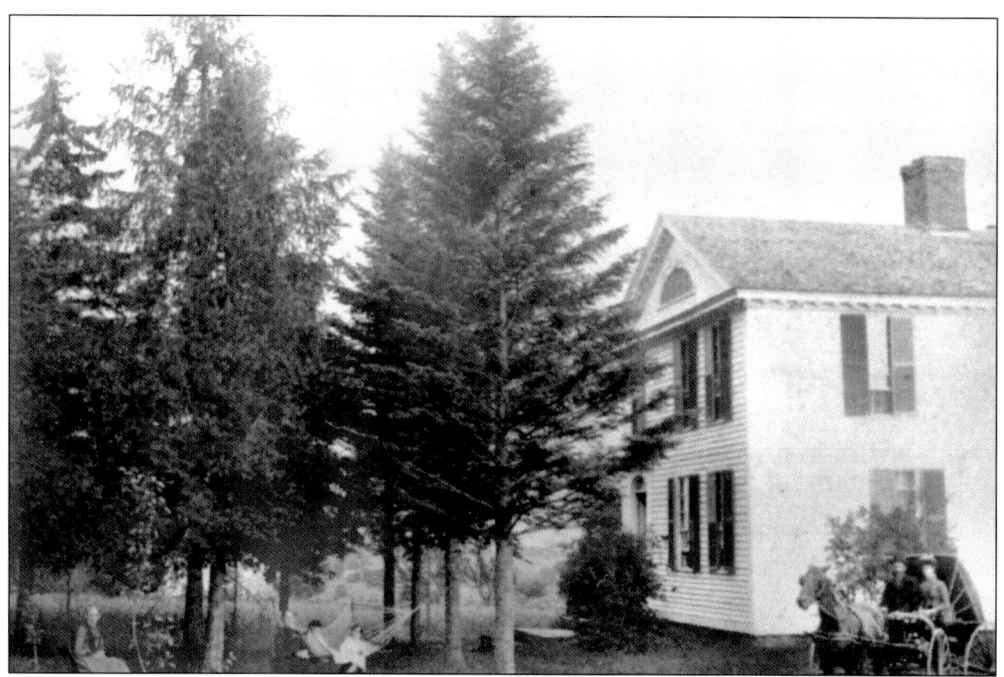

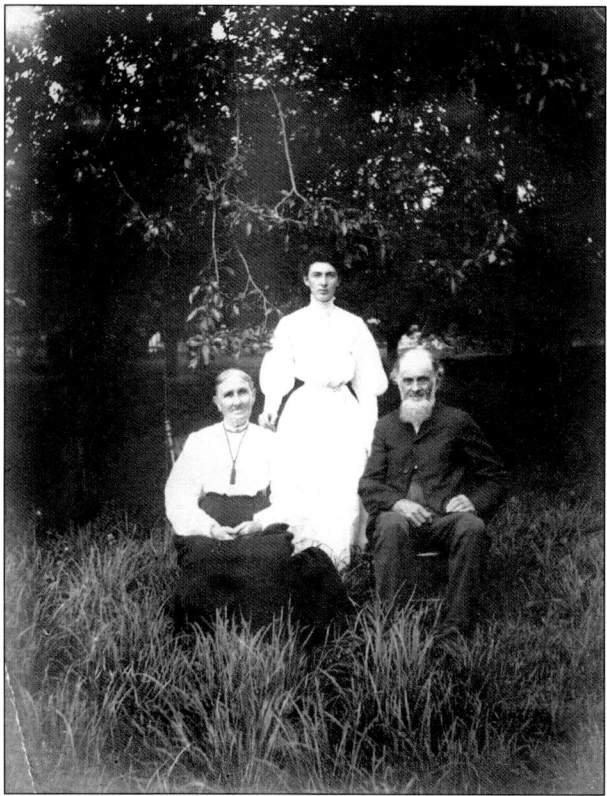

THE JAMES CLARKE HOUSE. In the above photograph, the Clarke house is shown before the Victorian porch was added. The structure still stands on Route 87, just north of the Liberty Hill Farm greenhouses. At the left, James and Mary Clarke and their daughter Minnie are shown at the house in the mid-1880s.

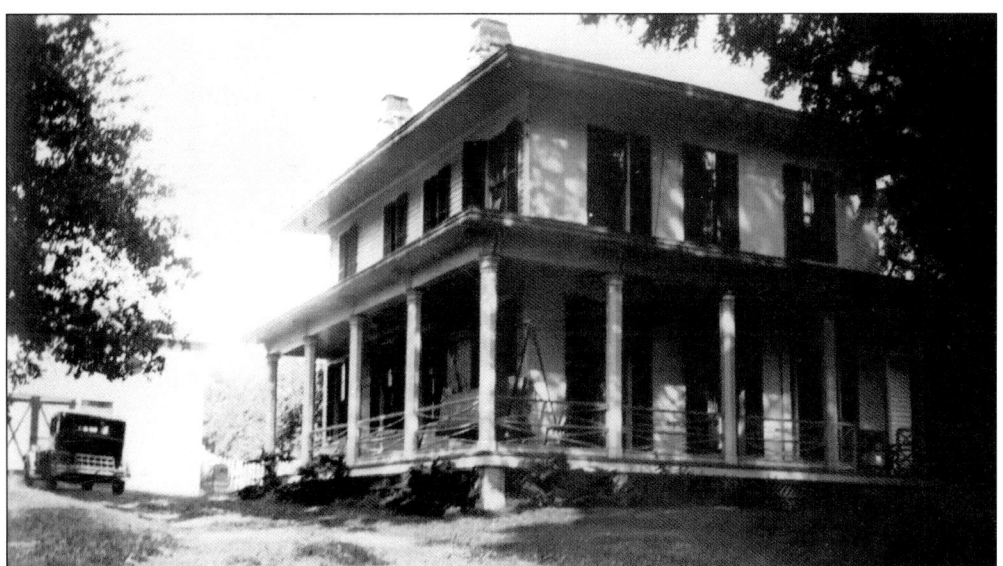

THE HOME OF CAPT. SLUMAN GRAY. Captain Gray, skipper of a whaling vessel, died at sea. His wife, Sarah, was aboard the *James Maury* when he passed away. She demanded that he be brought back to Liberty Hill to be interred. In order to preserve his body, she had it placed in a barrel of rum until he could be laid to rest. He was buried in the Liberty Hill Cemetery. His gravestone is shown at the right. Some of the names are misspelled on the gravestone

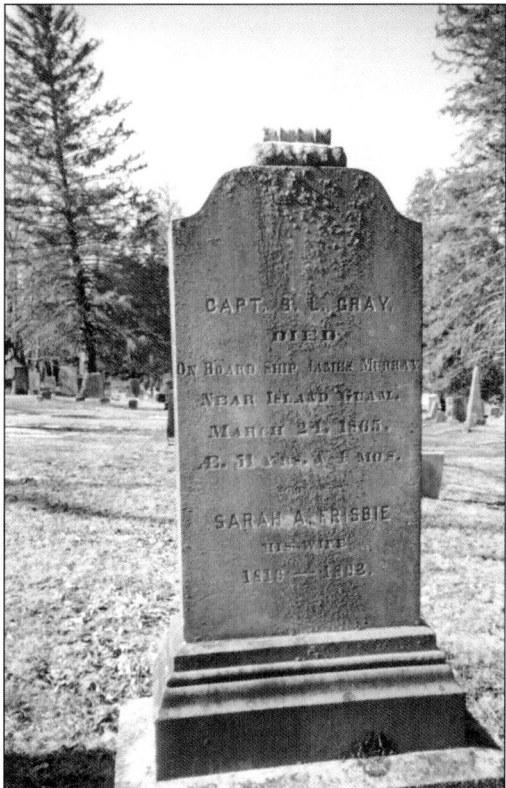

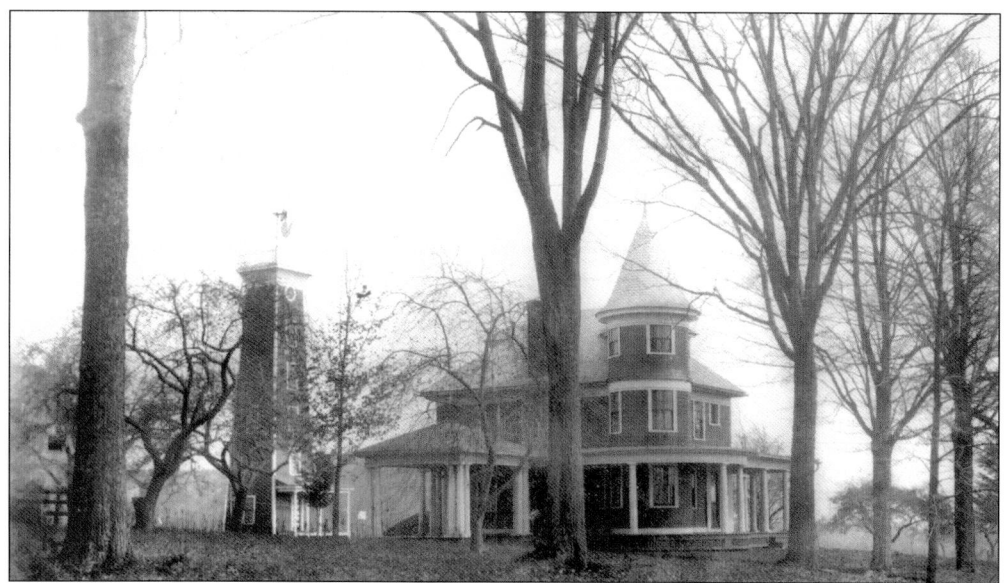

THE HOME OF HENRY AND MINNIE OHLERS. This home was remodeled in Victorian fashion by Paul McCormac. Mr. and Mrs. McCormac were killed in an automobile accident on Boston Post Road on December 7, 1907, in Norwalk. In 1908, Henry and Minnie Ohlers purchased the home from the McCormac estate. The property stayed in the Ohlers family until the 1990s. Note the windmill next to the house; it was said that Long Island Sound could be seen from the top. The windmill was destroyed by the 1938 hurricane, leaving just the first two stories.

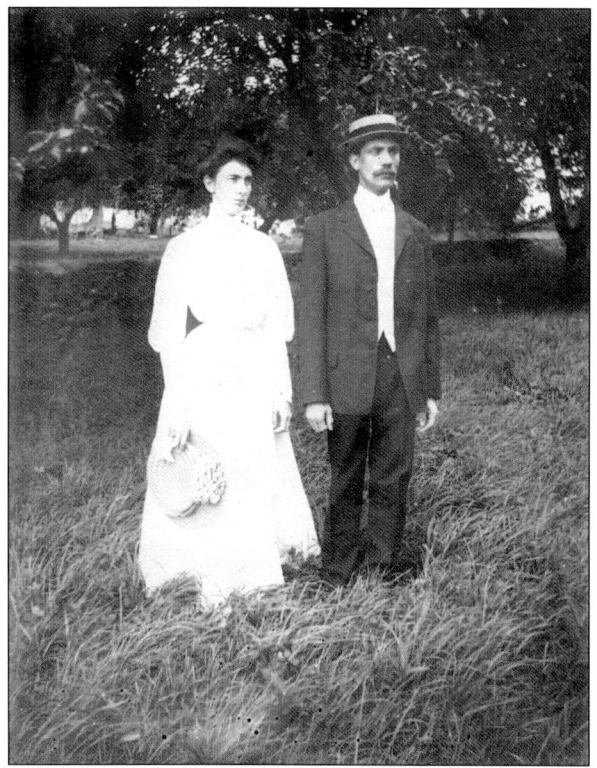

HENRY AND MINNIE CLARKE OHLERS. Henry and Minnie were married in 1902. Many people still remember their son Homer, who delivered mail from the Chestnut Hill Post Office until it closed. He then delivered mail from the Lebanon Post Office.

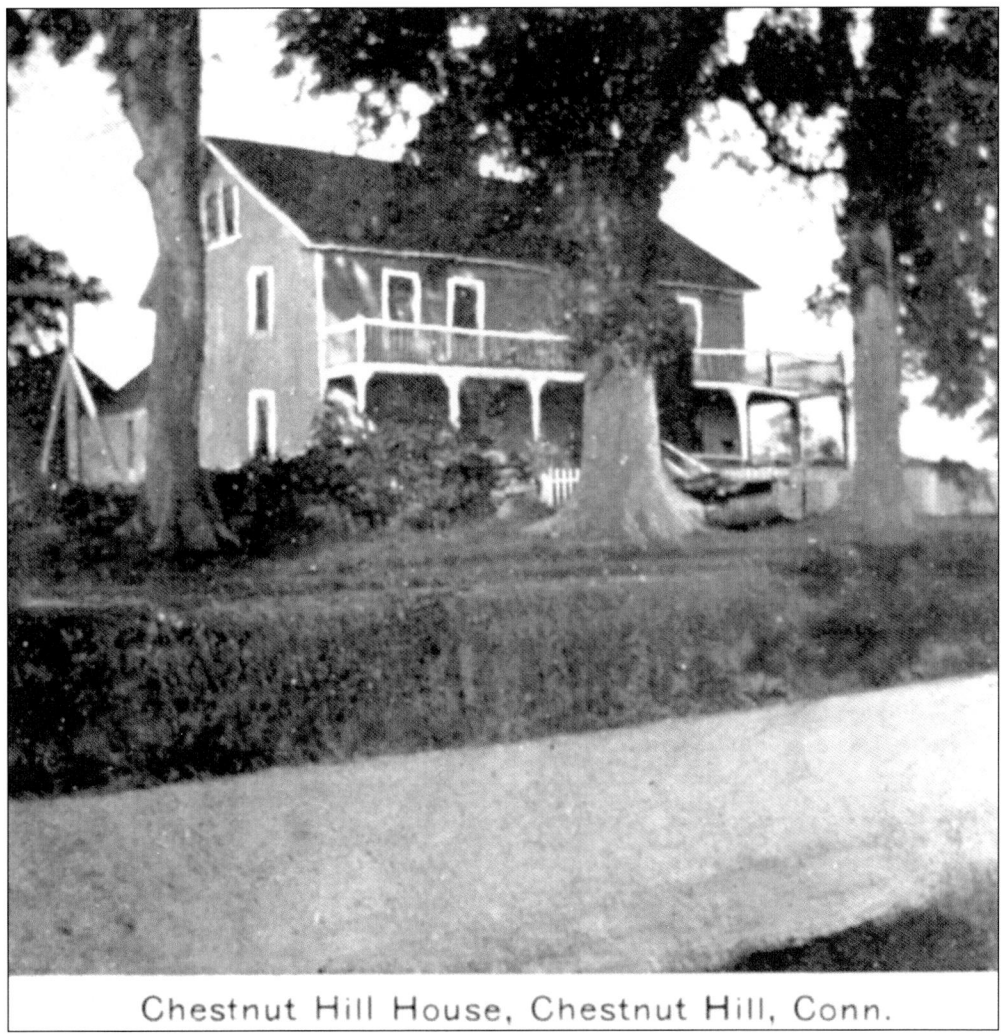

Chestnut Hill House, Chestnut Hill, Conn.

THE CHESTNUT HILL HOUSE. This home, situated on the east side of Trumbull Highway across from the Liberty Hill Plant Farm, was a bed-and-breakfast and spa of its day. Water was bottled from the mineral spring on the property and sold as a youth elixir. People would travel to Liberty Hill to partake of the water and stay at the Chestnut Hill House.

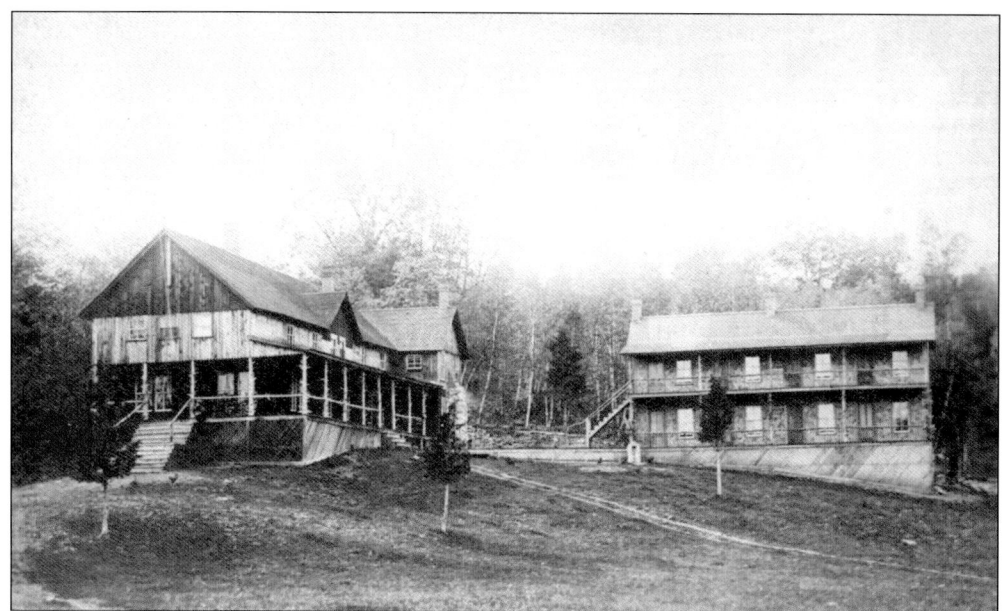

THE LIBERTY CLUB. In 1888, a group of Boston sportsmen formed the Liberty Club for the purpose of hunting and fishing. Frank Barnes and Joseph Scott had been staying in Lebanon off and on with E. A. Stiles to enjoy the hunting in the area. It was their idea to form the club. From Stiles, they bought the property on Clubhouse Road where the present-day Camp Laurel Girl Scout camp is located. The clubhouse, pictured here, was erected by Barnes, Scott, and 13 other men from Boston. It burned on June 2, 1925. The only part of the building that is still intact is the stone fireplace, around which a new structure was constructed.

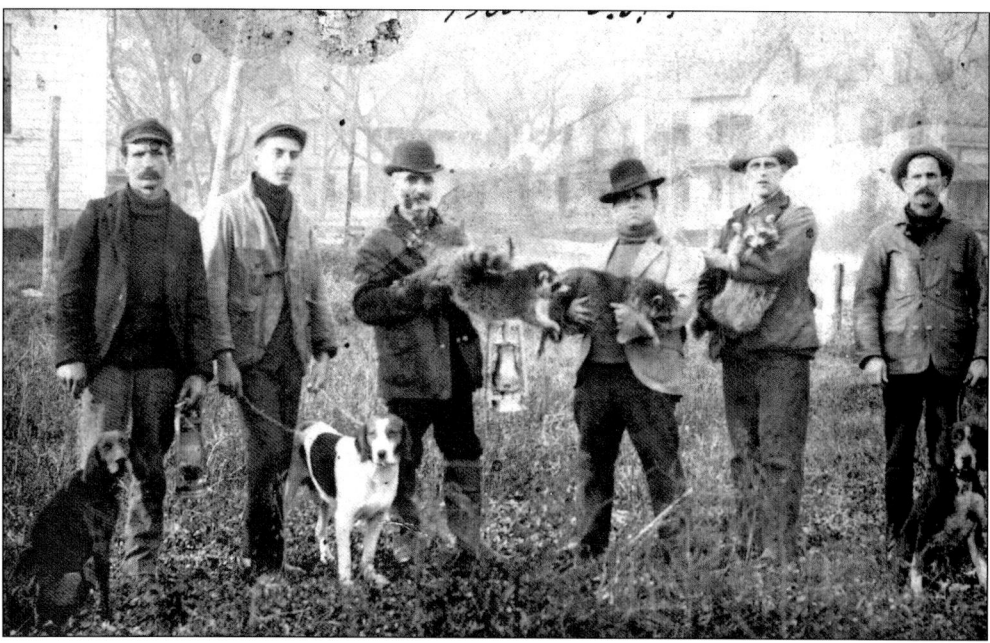

A SUCCESSFUL HUNT. Liberty Club members return from a coon hunt in 1912.

Four

THE FARMING COMMUNITY

Livestock raising brought early prosperity to Lebanon. Joseph Trumbull, who moved here from Simsbury in 1704, was a merchant who bought cattle from farmers in Lebanon and neighboring towns. The cattle were driven to markets in Boston and Norwich, where Trumbull exchanged the herds for manufactured goods to sell in his store.

The trades that developed were necessary adjuncts to agriculture. Tradesmen made boots, saddles, harnesses, furniture, axes, hoes, knives, and other tools for farmers. Millers ground the grain, and fulling mills processed wool. But these were for local use and were not part of the export trade.

Lebanon gradually evolved into a major stock-raising center. This growth was largely due to Joseph's son Jonathan Trumbull, the future governor, who greatly expanded the business when he joined his father, probably in 1730. Jonathan soon took over as the principal operator of the business, which became the largest meat-packing business in the colony.

Local farmers produced livestock, lumber, barrel staves, barreled meat, butter, and cheese for the export market. Live animals could be driven to distant cities, but barreled staples and lumber products were carted to Norwich because of the poor roads. These products were shipped overseas, to larger towns along the coast, and to the West Indies.

The growth in livestock production meant that farmers needed to keep large acreage for pasture. The population was expanding rapidly, and there was less land available for sons to inherit or purchase; all public land in the colony was taken by 1750. In the 1760s, many young families moved to western Massachusetts, New Hampshire, and Vermont, where land was available. By 1797, more than 13,000 acres were listed as pastureland on Lebanon tax lists.

In the early 19th century, stock raising declined with the growth of cheaper imports from the Midwest. Lebanon farmers concentrated on dairying, first in butter and cheese and then in whole milk. The increase in dairy production also brought changes to the landscape. Because dairy cattle have to be confined, fencing increased dramatically to enclose pastures. Where the farmer's product—primarily livestock—had formerly "walked out" to market, now the product had to be carried out. This necessitated the construction of new roads for horses and wagons to carry dairy products to market, further changing the landscape.

Barn designs also changed from the English style, with openings on the broad side, to the New England style, with openings on the gable end. Dairying also called for new businesses to handle these products. The opening of the Lebanon Creamery on Exeter Road in 1885 reflects the new trend in agriculture. The cream for the butter was furnished by local farmers, who installed cooling tanks chilled by ice stored in icehouses.

The railroads expanded the market for dairy farmers, providing quick transport to the cities. Refrigeration using block ice in the cars allowed the creamery to send its butter far and wide.

The new markets helped keep farmers in business. In the 20th century, dairy farmers switched to whole-milk production, and the Lebanon Creamery, once the largest in the state, closed in 1933. Farmers now send their milk by trucks to large cooperative milk plants, but the railroad still brings fertilizer and feed to dairy and egg farmers.

In the 20th century, gasoline-powered mechanical equipment and the advent of electricity revolutionized agriculture. While easing the burden of manual labor, these developments also changed the face of agriculture in Lebanon. Many of the smaller dairy farms have gone out of business, while the dairies that do remain are run on a larger and more intensive scale. Modern agribusinesses include a major egg-production factory, a large nursery-stock operation, and a compost business. There are also a number of small farms providing maple syrup, fresh produce, fruit, beef cattle, horses, and llamas.

Today, the economy of Lebanon is still primarily agricultural, although it faces increasing pressures from suburban development. Only time will tell if the ancient roots of agriculture will vanish into history as town life continues to unfold in the 21st century.

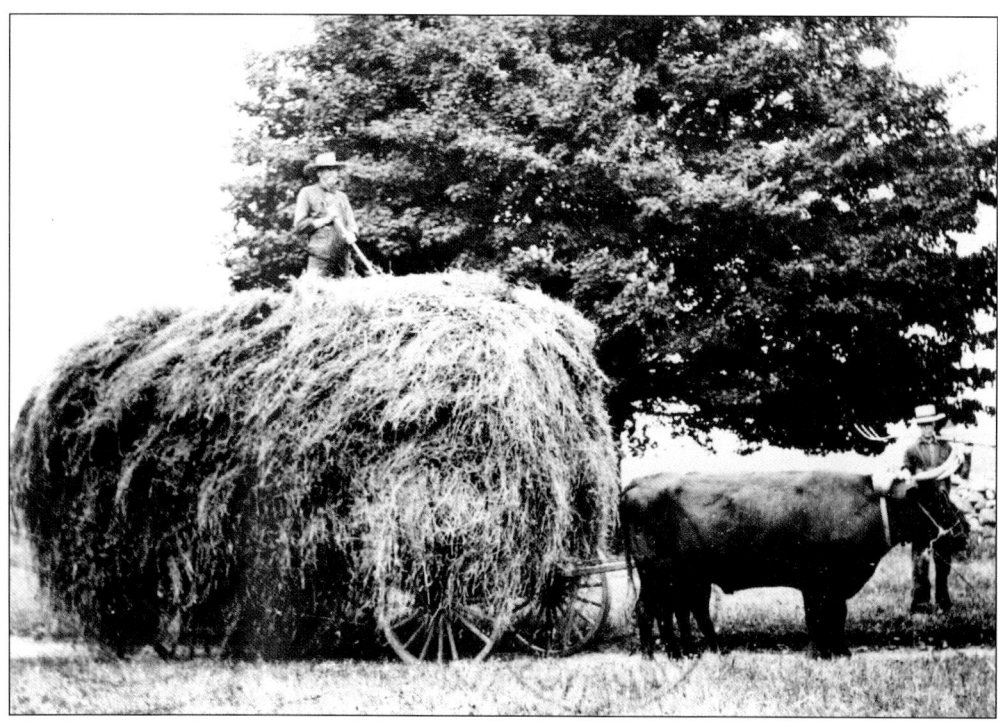

THE GEER FARM. J. Nelson Geer, on top of the load, and Elmer N. Geer, standing by the oxen, have just completed loading a wagon with hay c. 1905. The Geer farm was located on Exeter Road, near the present high school. (Courtesy Harold Geer.)

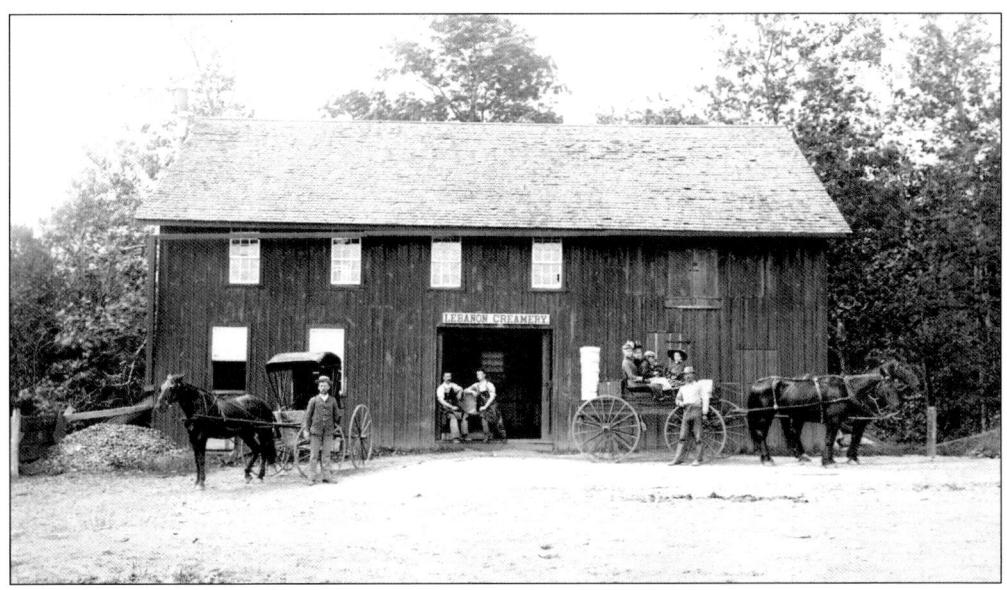

THE LEBANON CREAMERY. The Lebanon Creamery opened for business in 1885 on Susquetonscut Brook, below the present elementary school on Route 207. Cream was gathered from local farmers and brought here to be churned into high-quality butter. Creamery butter won a gold medal at the 1893 World's Fair in Chicago. Although the Lebanon Creamery was once the largest creamery in the state, business fell off as markets changed. The assets were sold at auction in 1933. (Courtesy LHS.)

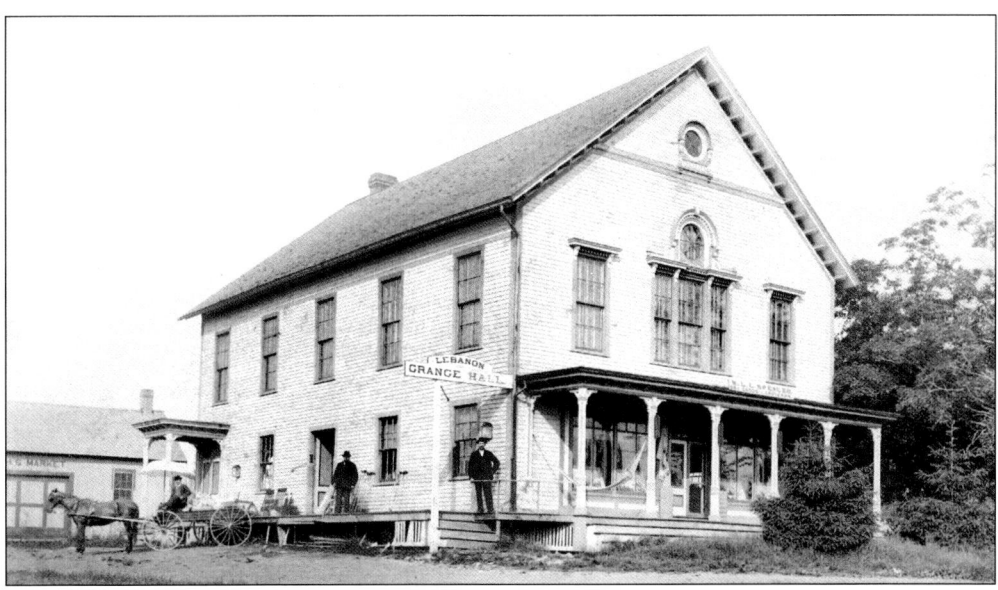

THE LEBANON GRANGE HALL. The Granger Movement began after the Civil War as a national association to advocate for issues important to farmers. It also became a strong social force wherever local Granges were established. The Lebanon chapter, organized in 1884, built this meeting hall and store in 1885. The center of community activities for many years, it is now the Lebanon Green Market. (Courtesy LHS.)

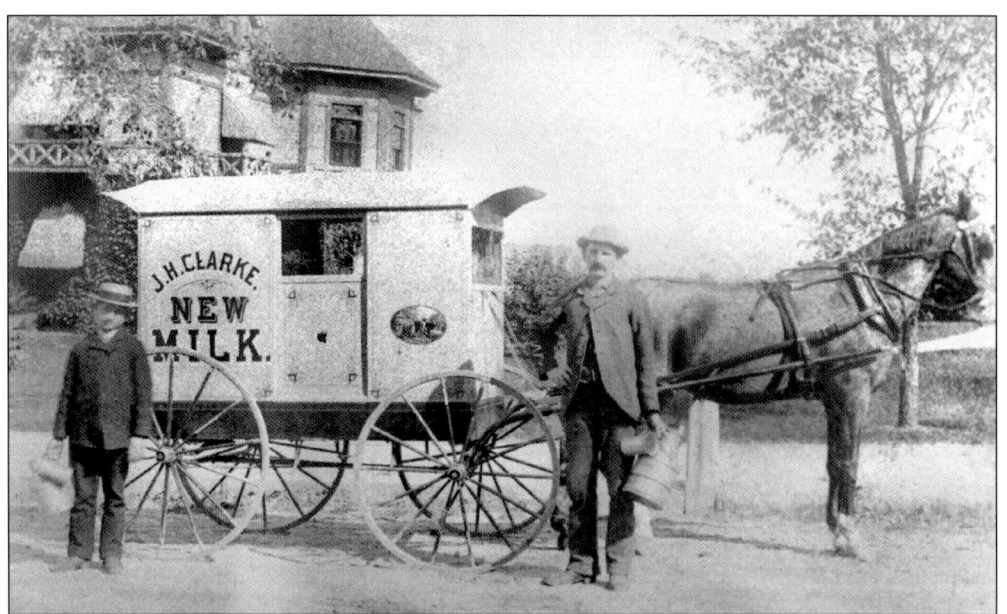

THE MILK ROUTE. John Clarke is shown here with his milk wagon sometime in the early 1880s. He sold his milk route in 1892 but continued operating his farm in the Liberty Hill section of town for many years. The area covered by his milk route is not known but was probably in the nearby city of Willimantic, since local people normally had ready access to fresh milk. (Courtesy Ed Tollmann.)

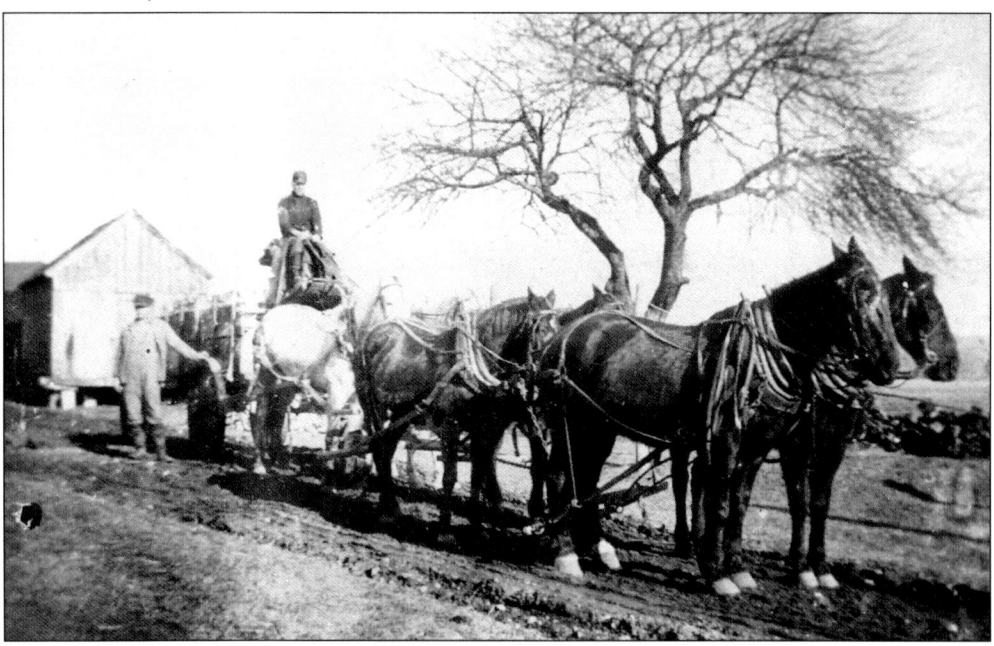

A SIX-HORSE TEAM. In this early 1900s photograph, Reuben Manning drives a six-horse team, with a load of milk cans, to the train station in South Windham. Each pair of horses—the pole horses, the middle pair, and the lead pair—had to have a pair of heavy leather reins. The weight of all those long reins equaled 25 to 30 pounds pulling on each arm throughout a drive. (Courtesy Harold Geer.)

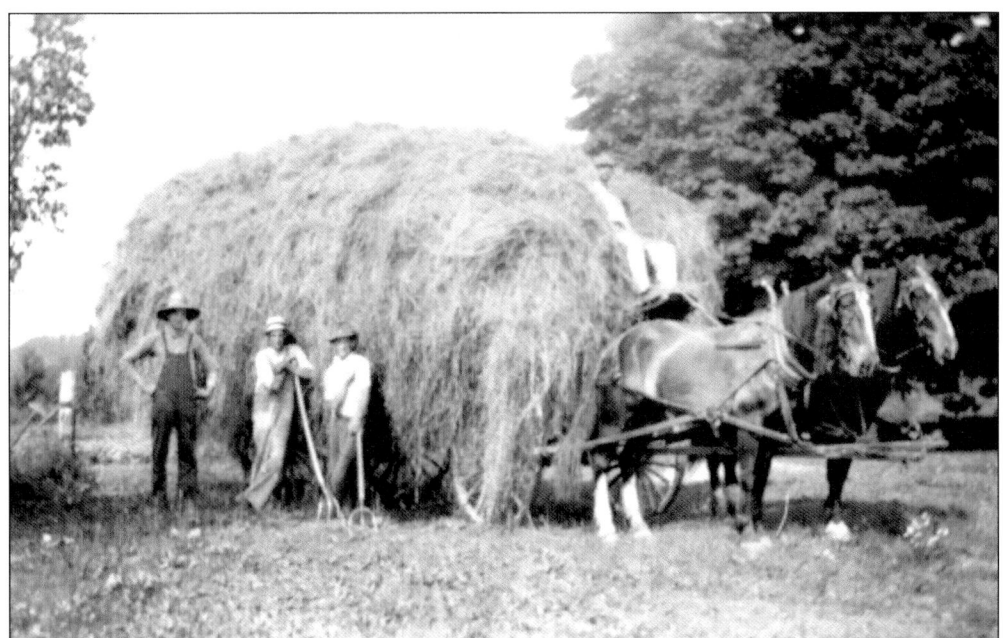

THE HOXIE FARM. Everett Hoxie had a large farm on Waterman Road. This photograph, taken c. 1913, shows Everett atop the hay load, driving the horses. His three sons stand next to the wagon. Everett Hoxie also owned oxen but preferred to use the faster horses for haying. (Courtesy Phyllis Bartizek.)

A SMOKEHOUSE. Dating from c. 1820, this stone smokehouse was located on a farm on Tobacco Street. Most farms had smokehouses to preserve food before the advent of modern canning methods and refrigeration. This smokehouse is one of the few surviving examples in New England. Although it was missing its roof, the smokehouse was purchased by the Lebanon Historical Society and was moved to the museum grounds. It was restored by Glenn Pianka. (Courtesy LHS.)

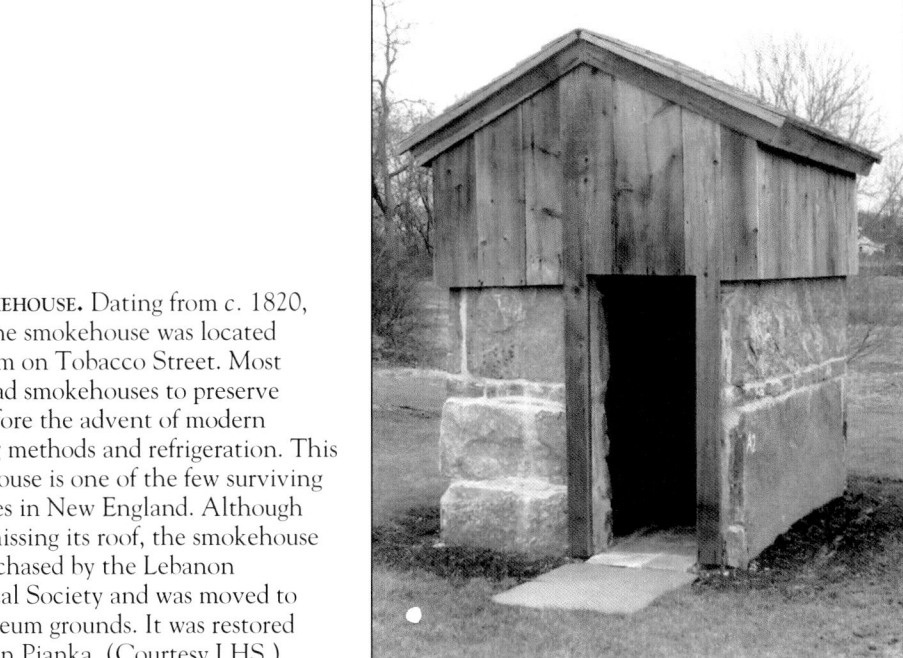

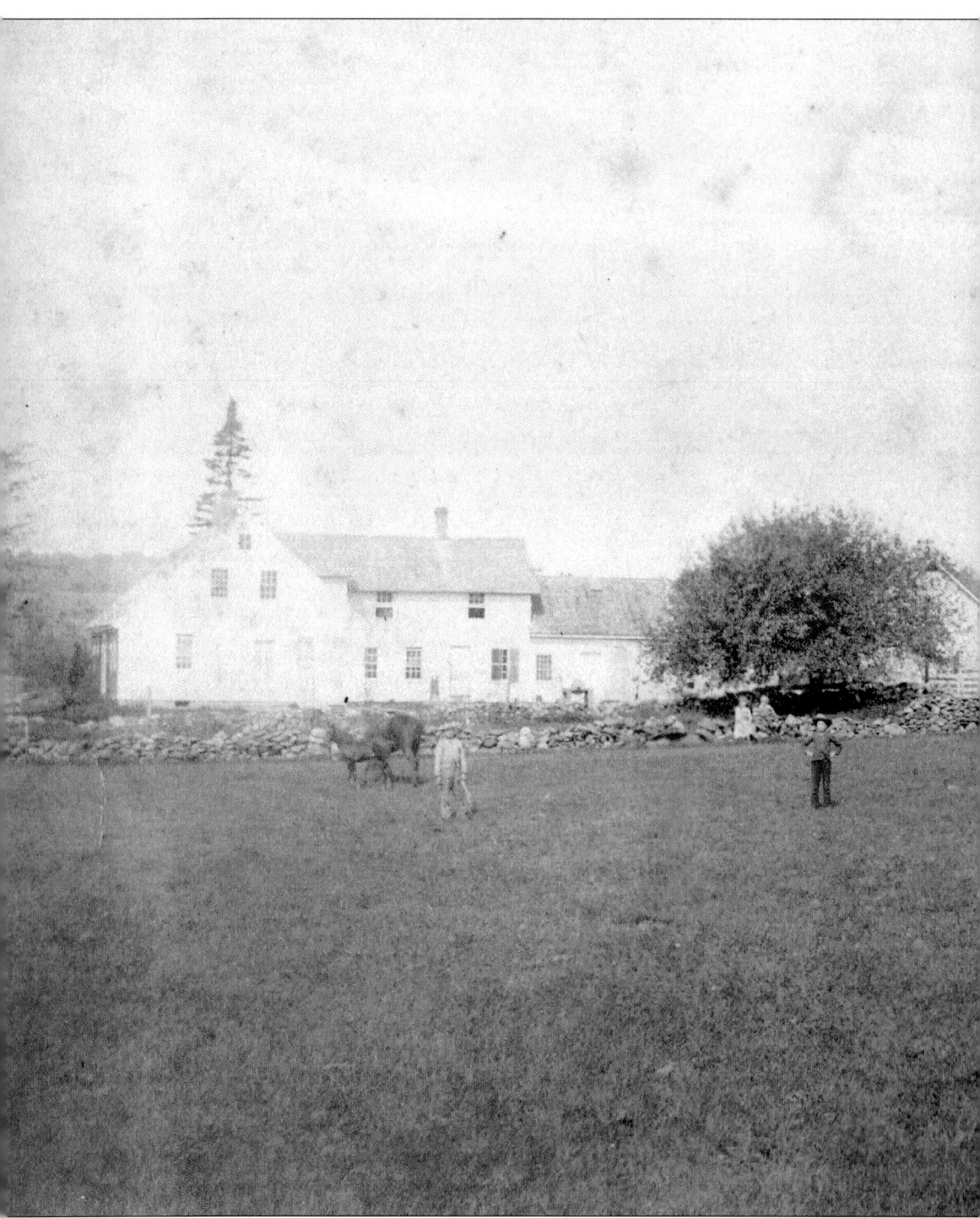

THE MANNING HOMESTEAD. Nathaniel Manning and his family pose for an itinerant photographer in the late 1880s. The Manning farm was located on Exeter Road (Route 207), just north of the intersection with the present Industrial Park Road near the Franklin town line. Families often posed with their prized possessions when the photographers came around. In this

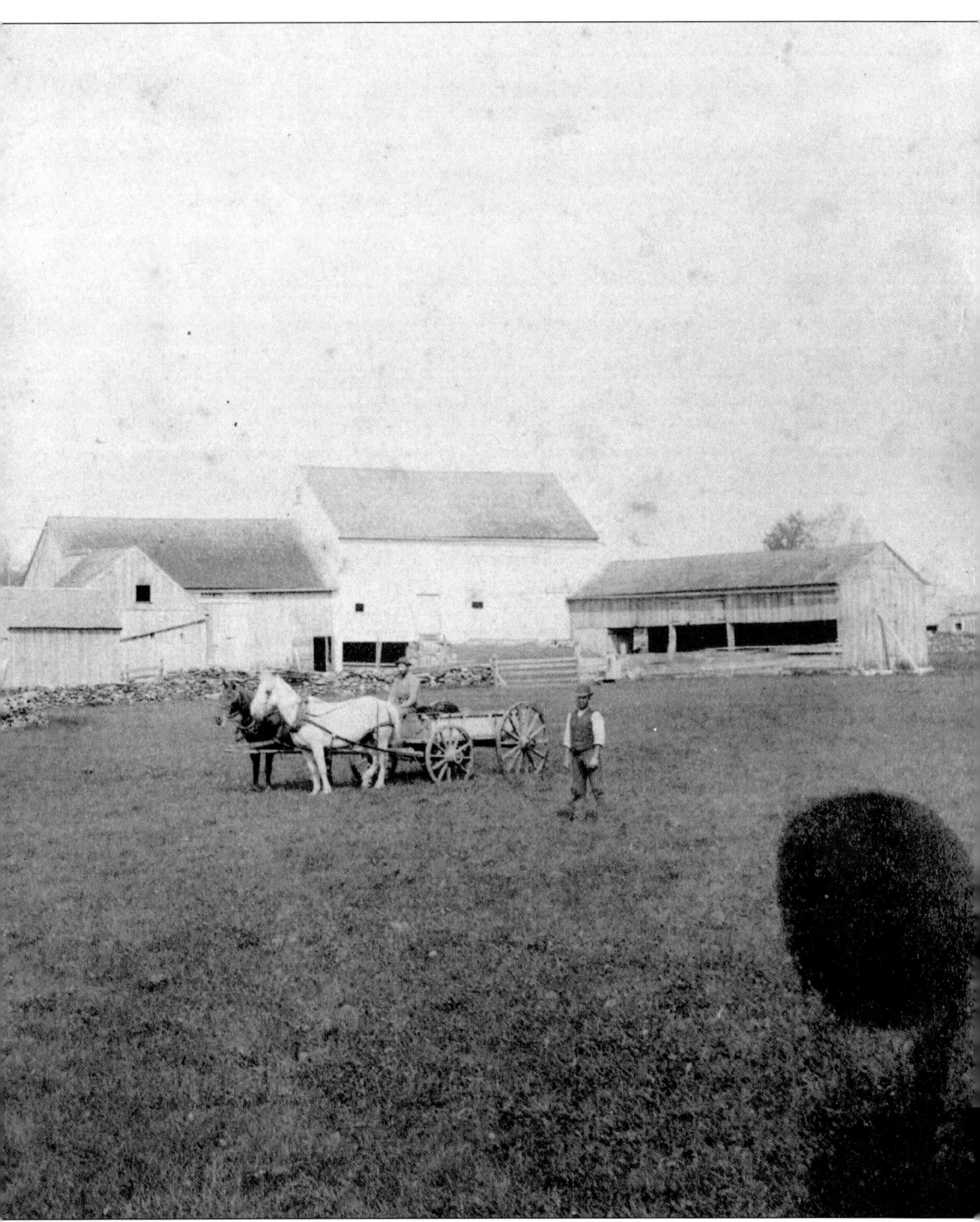

case, Nathaniel shows off his horses. This photograph is unusual for its time, however, because it shows the entire layout of a 19th-century farm, including the house, barns, and numerous outbuildings. Only the house stands today. (Courtesy Harold Geer.)

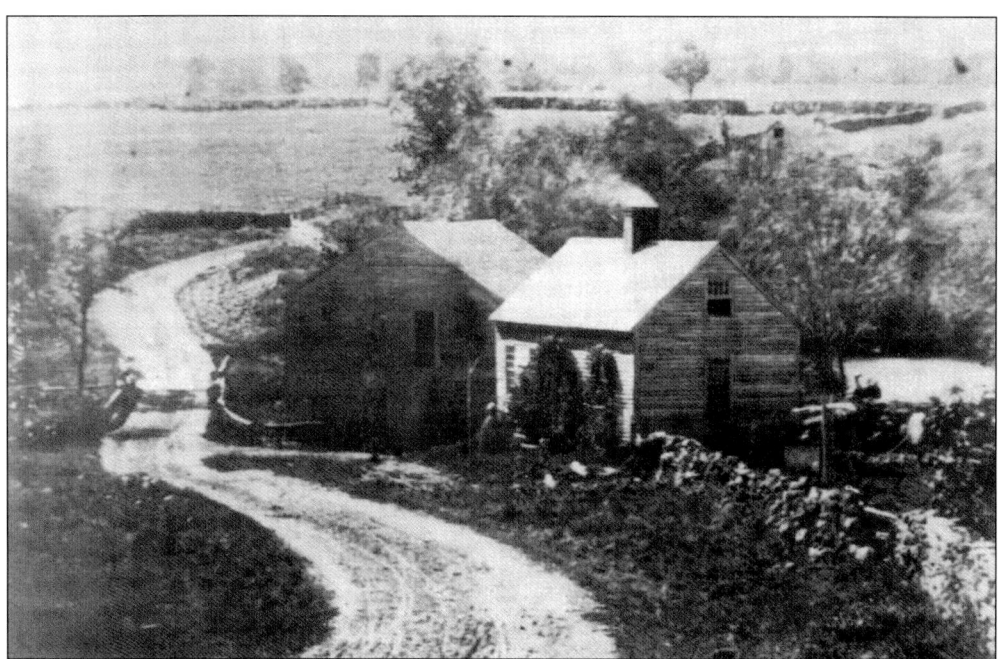

THE OLD GRISTMILL. This pre-1880 view of the old gristmill looks west over Exeter Road (Route 207) down to the bridge over Pease Brook. A gristmill was first located on this site in early settlement days. The miller's house is in the foreground, and the mill is behind it. Besides providing power to grind grain for farmers, the millpond was a source of ice. (Courtesy LHS.)

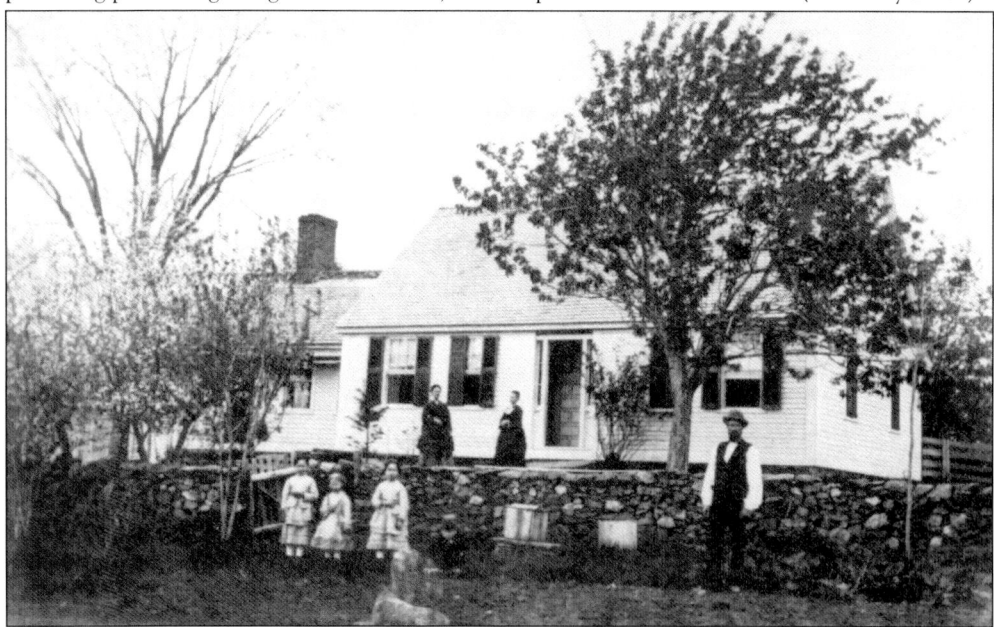

THE PECKHAM-BLAKESLEE FARM. The Peckham and Blakeslee families have lived in this farmhouse at 453 Kick Hill Road since it was built c. 1790. Here, William Peckham, at the right, poses with his family c. 1874. At the left, his twin daughters stand on either side of their cousin Lillian (Peckham) Blakeslee, Russell Blakeslee's grandmother. In front of the doorway are William's wife (left) and Mrs. Asa Peckham. (Courtesy Russell Blakeslee.)

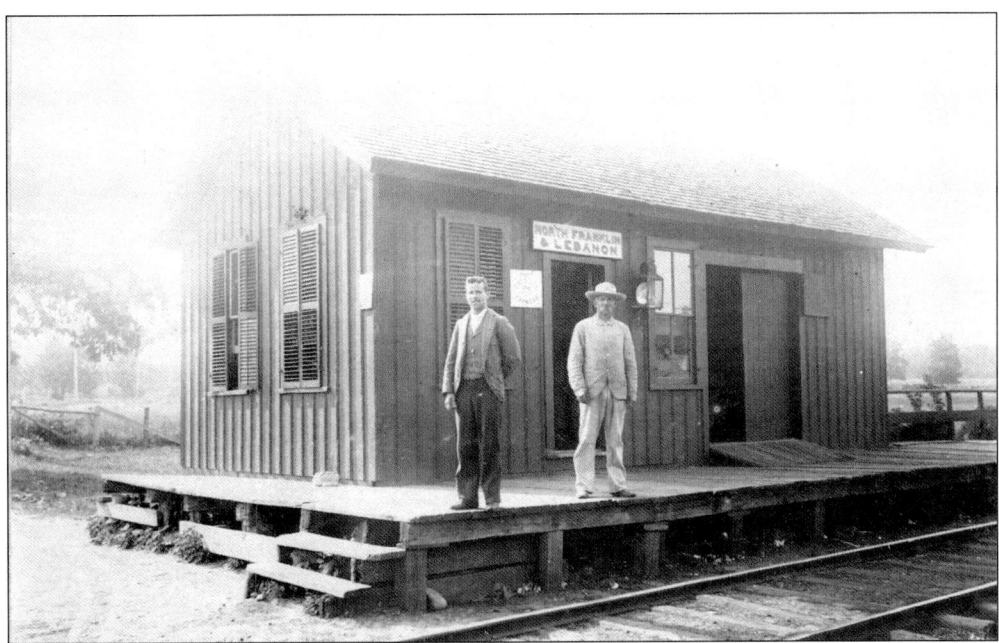

THE RAILROAD ARRIVES. The first railroad to serve Lebanon was the New London, Willimantic & Palmer Railroad, which began operations in 1849. This undated photograph shows the Lebanon–North Franklin freight house at the local station. The railroad was a boon to travelers but especially to Lebanon dairy farmers, who found a much larger market for their products in the big cities. (Courtesy LHS.)

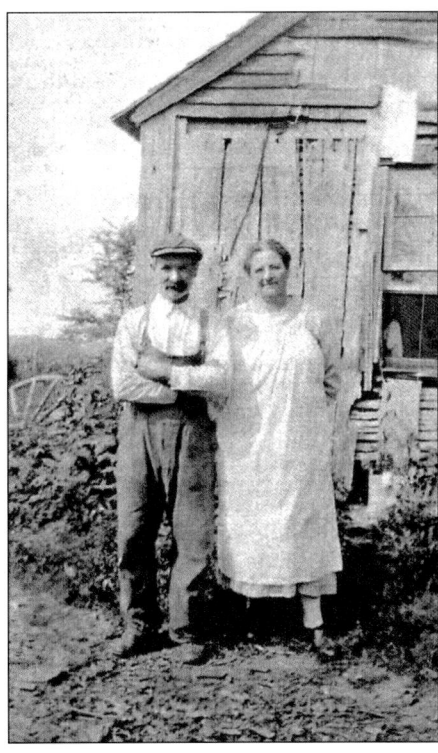

JEWISH SETTLERS. Morris Valinsky, who bought a farm in 1890 on what is now Valinsky Road, was the first Jewish settler in Lebanon. Thus began a wave of Jewish immigrants to Lebanon, people who transformed their worn-out farms into productive dairy and egg farms and laid the foundation of the large poultry industry in New London County. Morris and his wife, Anna, appear here in 1919. (Courtesy LHS.)

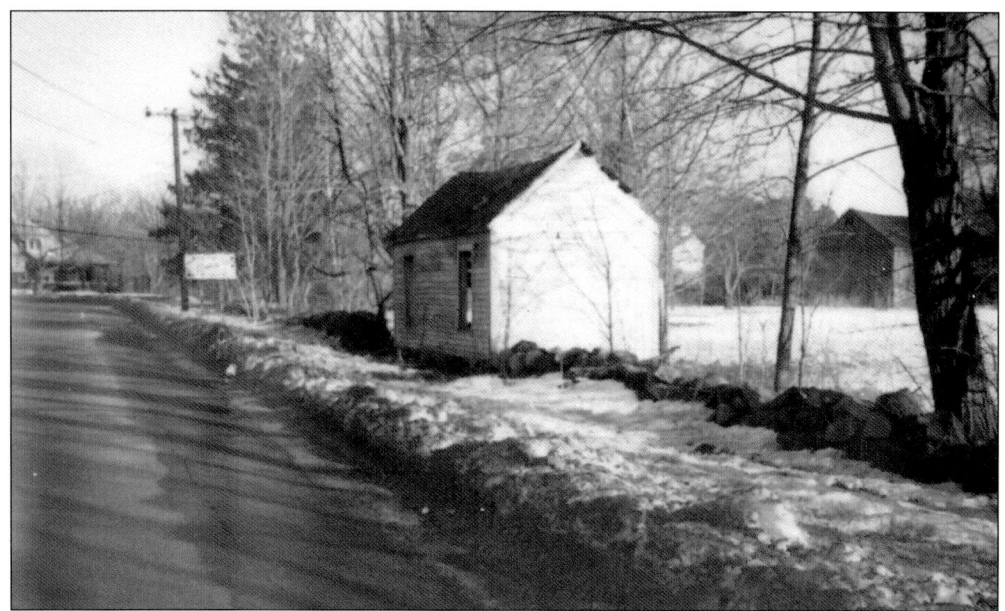

THE BROOM SHOP. From his broom shop at the north end of the town green on Route 87, Eugene Lyman provided farm families a wide variety of brooms—from small whisk brooms to large, sturdy barn-cleaning brooms. The broomcorn was raised by local farmers from seed supplied by Lyman. Members of the Lebanon Historical Society restored the dilapidated building in 1974 and furnished it with broom-making equipment. It was later moved to the museum grounds. (Courtesy LHS.)

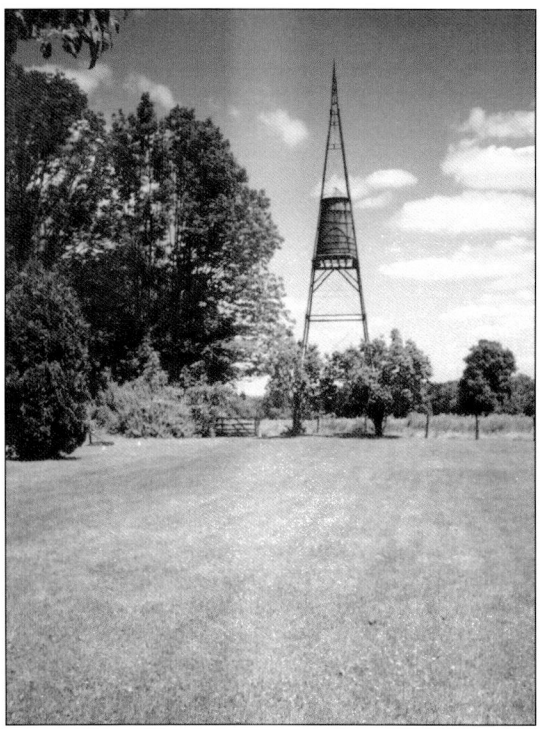

A WATER TOWER. Although the blades are missing, the tower of an old windmill water system still stands on the McCaw farm, on the east side of the town green. Many Lebanon farms, including five farms around the green, had windmills before electricity came into use. Water piped from a well was stored in a tank halfway up the tower. Gravity fed the water to the barns and the house when spigots were opened. (Courtesy LHS.)

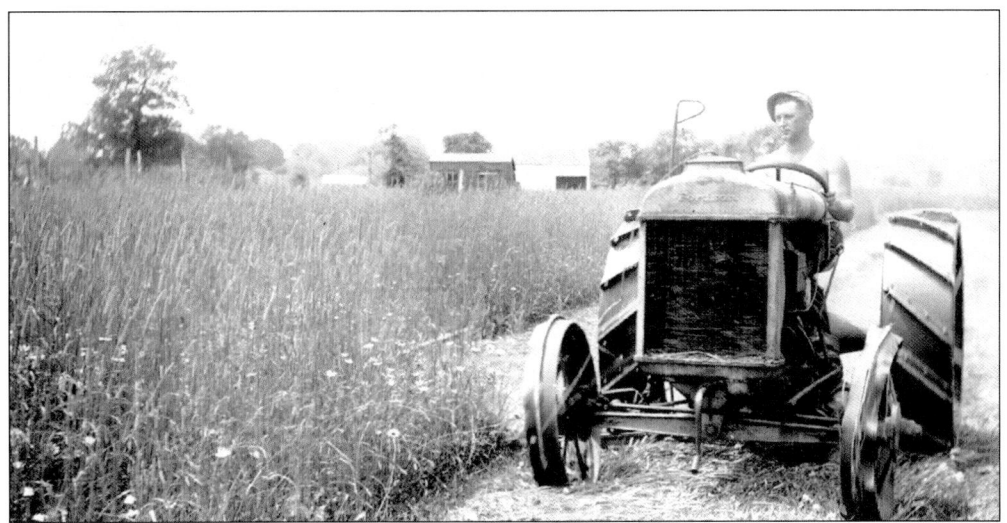

FARM EQUIPMENT. In this 1935 photograph, Pete Taylor drives a very early Fordson tractor, which did not have pneumatic tires. Tractors gradually replaced the horses, oxen, and mules that had served farmers for centuries. (Courtesy Robert Slate.)

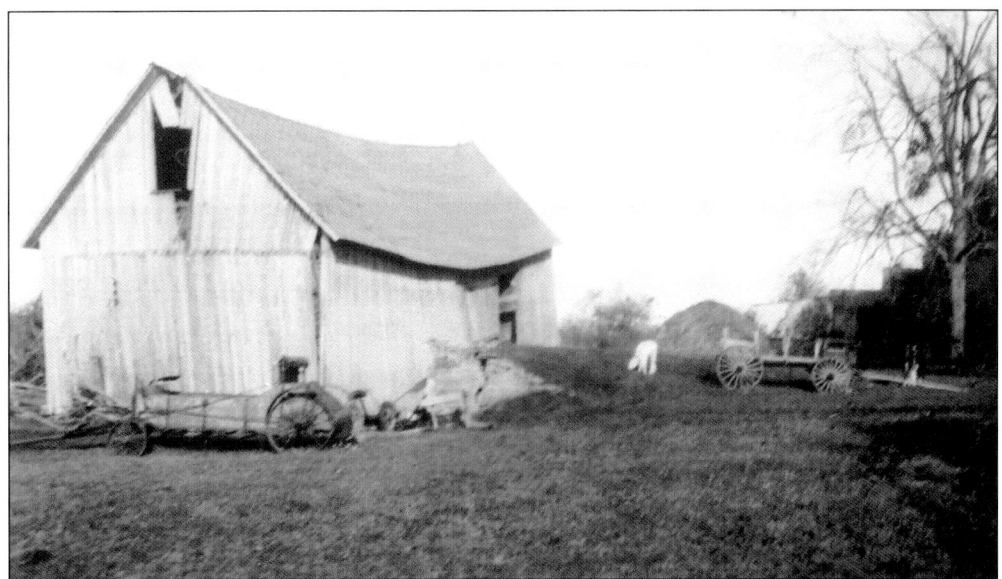

STORM DAMAGE. The destructive force of the 1938 hurricane laid waste to much of the town, which stood in the direct path of the storm. Farmers suffered the most, for many lost the barns, outbuildings, orchards, and animals that had provided them with their livelihood. This barn, owned by Leslie Clark Sr., had to be torn down and replaced with a new barn. That barn is now the antiques shop on Route 87. (Courtesy Ed Tollmann.)

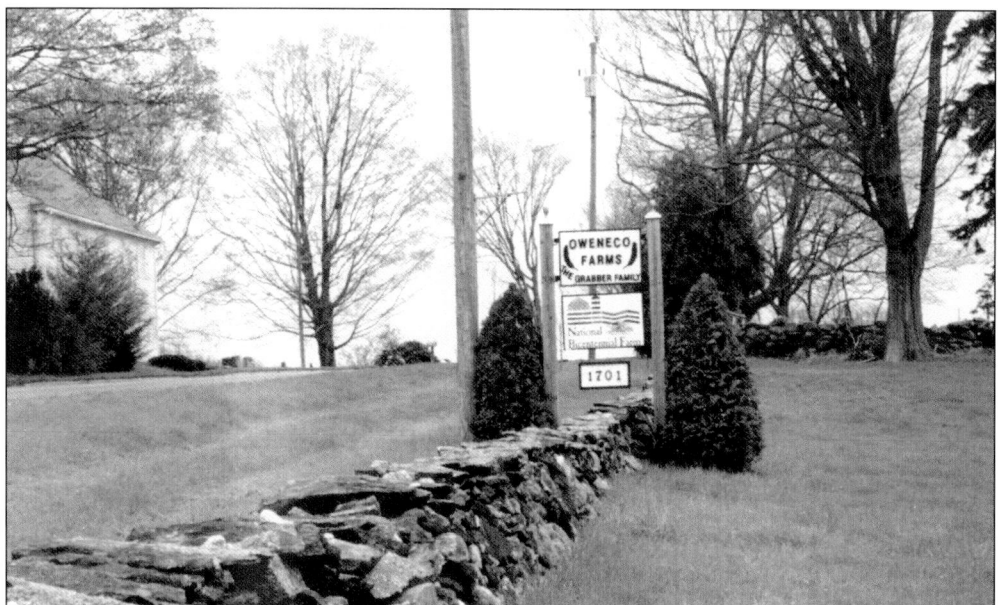

THE OWENECO FARM. The Oweneco Farm has been farmed by the same family for over 300 years. Brothers Henry and Spafford Grabber operate the farm their ancestor Thomas Spafford bought from the son of Uncas, the Mohegan chief, 10 generations ago in 1701. The original 120-acre parcel has expanded to over 300 acres through purchases of contiguous land. The Grabbers concentrate on raising corn and hay. (Courtesy LHS.)

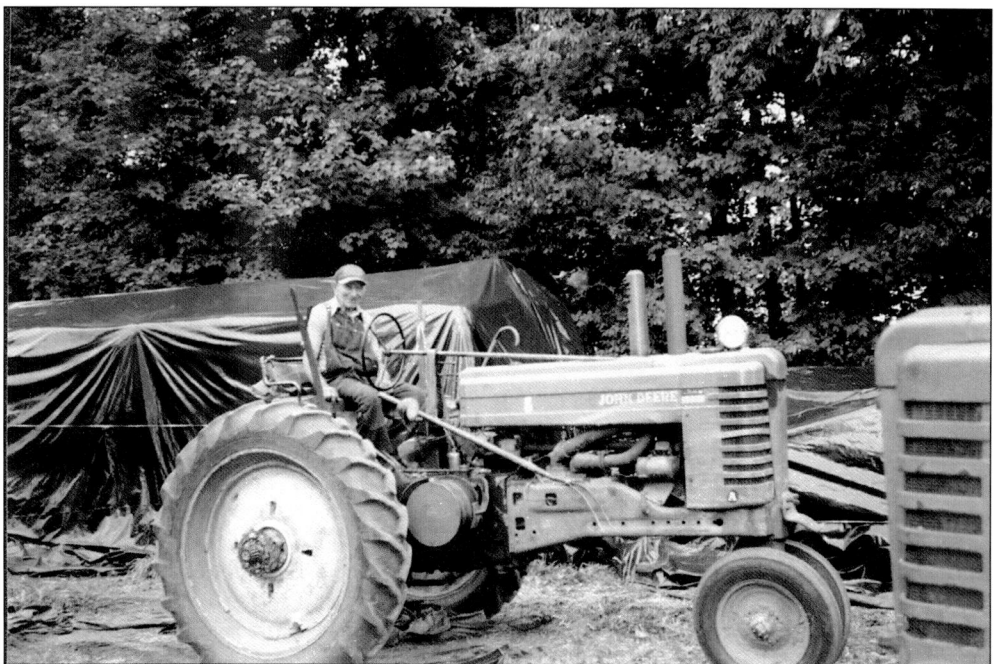

STILL WORKING. Meyer Himmelstein, born in 1919, bought a used John Deere tractor in 1948 to pull the hay baler he had bought the same year. The hay baler Meyer purchased was one of the first in Lebanon. Both machines, still in working condition, are used on the farm today. The Himmelstein farm is located on Exeter Road and North Street. (Courtesy Eva Himmelstein.)

Five
The Village Hill Neighborhood

The history of the Village Hill German population of Lebanon is a story of faith, family, and farming. Bonded by common culture and traditions, the Germans made their pilgrimage to America in the early 20th century in search of freedom and opportunity. Their ancestors before them had emigrated from Germany to Poland and Russia in their search for a better life, free of religious and ethnic persecution.

Karlswalde, their last home in Europe before their voyage to America, was a beautiful village in the western part of Ukraine, near the Polish border. Formerly a Mennonite village, it contained large homes and well-kept farms. The new German settlers who had migrated from Poland prospered there for 50 years. They built their own school and church and kept up their German language and traditions. Forced to flee because of the unrest and upheaval prior to World War I and the Russian Revolution, many of them came to the United States.

Upon their arrival, they were met by family members who provided shelter and job opportunities. They settled in Poughkeepsie, New York; Boston, Massachusetts; and Long Island. They found jobs as gardeners, railroad workers, factory laborers, domestics, and tradespeople. They learned English and became part of the American mainstream. But some of them never gave up the dream of owning land and farming again in the old tradition. Spurred on by Philip Krause, who had recently moved to Village Hill, relatives moved to Lebanon as land became available. The farms were run down and abandoned, a far cry from the fertile farmland of Ukraine. By 1928, 12 families, former residents of Karlswalde, had moved into the Village Hill area, in close proximity to each other. It reminded many of Karlswalde. Each farm had about 100 to 150 acres of land, as well as a house and barns.

The people survived because of their community spirit, or *Gemeinschaft*. Still mindful of the old traditions, they worked together during labor-intense seasons, sharing tools, horses, and machinery and cooperating during harvesting, ice-cutting, and animal-husbandry chores. They harvested corn and hay and raised cows, pigs, chickens, and other fowl. They sold milk, eggs, vegetables, and fruit directly into the marketplace. Women and children worked alongside the men as they became small farm-family entrepreneurs. They had to struggle to make ends meet, but the land provided them sustenance. Industrious and hardworking, they added to the Lebanon economy.

Of paramount concern to the new settlers were their spiritual needs. The first families to arrive in Connecticut found a German-speaking minister from the New London mission for the Lutheran church. The small congregation, consisting of German-speaking communicants from Lebanon, Coventry, and Willimantic, was founded in 1916 and held services at the Ebenezer Lutheran Church in Willimantic each Sunday afternoon. In 1937, the congregation purchased the Village Hill Schoolhouse for the purpose of conversion into a church for the Redeemer congregation. It took seven years to build and was completed in 1944. The simple charm of the church design is enhanced by original woodcarvings rendered by Gottlieb Laibrandt, a master craftsman, on the altar, pulpit, and windows. The church has been designated a historic site and has been placed on the Connecticut State Register of Historic Places. It has become a landmark of the Village Hill section of Lebanon.

The "Karlswalders" had finally found their home in a country where their way of life was not threatened. Many of the descendants of these immigrants still live in the area and are actively involved in community activities. The Village Hill area was often called the "other Karlswalde." This unique neighborhood is an excellent example of a transplanted European culture existing in a traditional New England town.

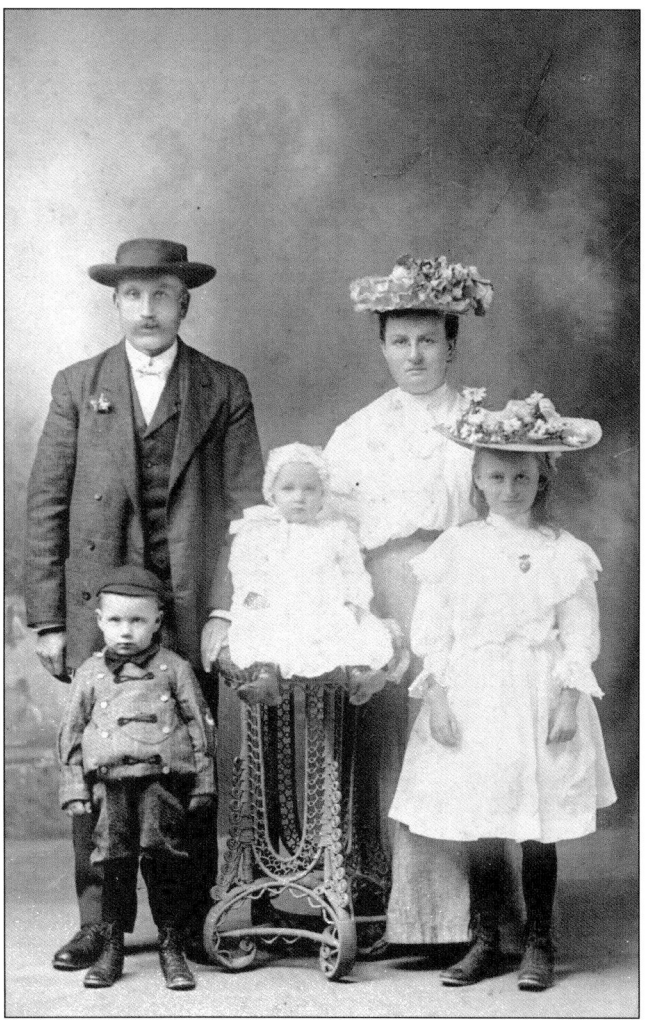

THE FRED KRAUSE FAMILY, c. 1906. Entering Ellis Island on February 22, 1905, the Krause family made its way to Poughkeepsie, New York, where Fred worked as a gardener for eight years before moving to Village Hill in Lebanon to join his brother Philip and purchase a nearby farm. This photograph shows Fred and Elizabeth Krause with their children, son Edmund (left) and daughters Frieda (center) and Caroline (right). (Courtesy Claire Krause.)

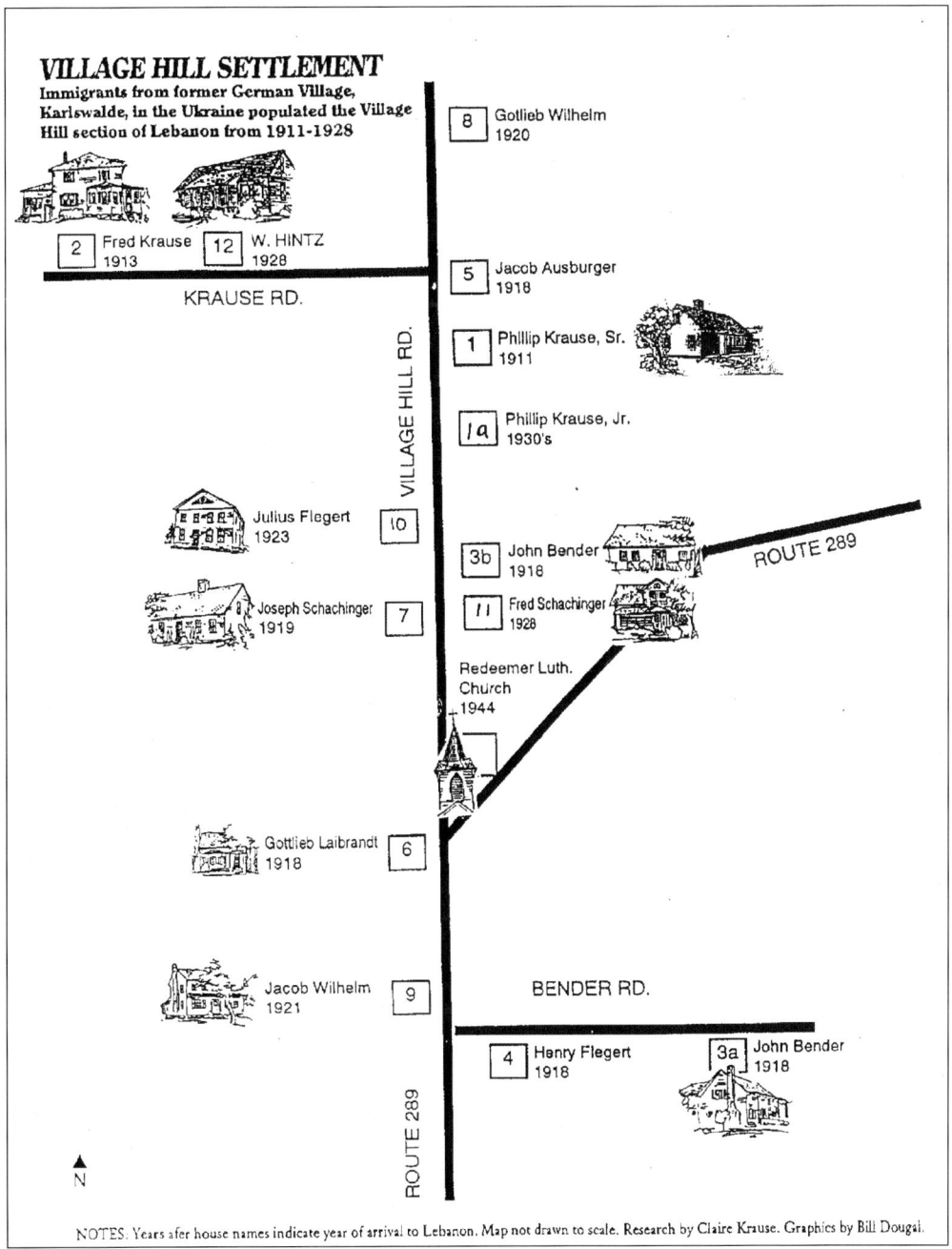

A VILLAGE HILL SETTLEMENT MAP, 1994. This map displays the homes of the first German Village Hill settlers (1914–1928) and includes the settlers' names, the years of their arrival, and the locations of their homes. (Research by Claire Krause, graphics by Bill Dougal; courtesy Claire Krause.)

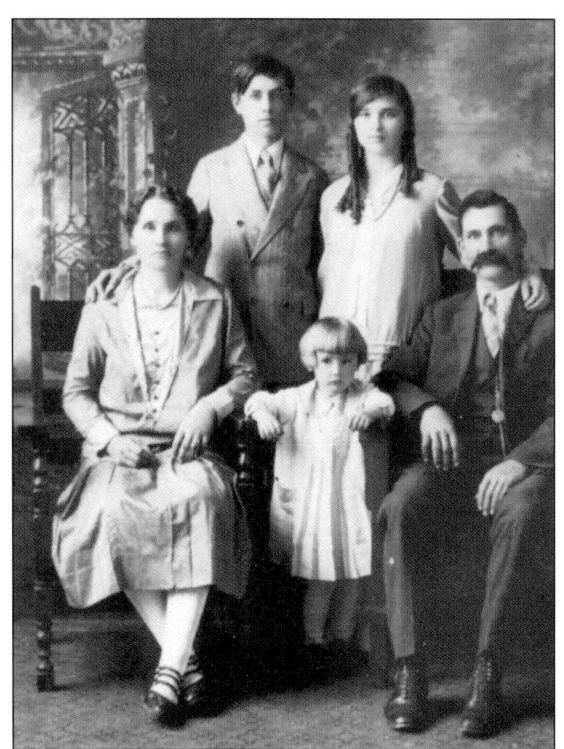

THE GOTTLIEB LAIBRANDT FAMILY, C. 1927. Gottlieb and Agatha Laibrandt emigrated from Ukraine in 1913. They first came to Boston, where Gottlieb worked as a cabinetmaker, building showcases for the F. W. Woolworth Company. They then moved to Village Hill in 1918 and purchased a farm near family and friends. Shown here, from left to right, are the following: (first row) Agatha, daughter Helen, and Gottlieb; (second row) son John and daughter Martha. (Courtesy Claire Krause.)

THE JOHN AND JUSTINA BENDER WEDDING, 1908. This wedding photograph of John and Justina (Schachinger) Bender was taken in Ostrog, Russia, near Karlswalde. The Benders came to the United States in 1909, settling in Jamaica, New York, where John worked for the Long Island Railroad. They arrived in Lebanon in 1918 and purchased a farm in Village Hill. (Courtesy Claire Krause.)

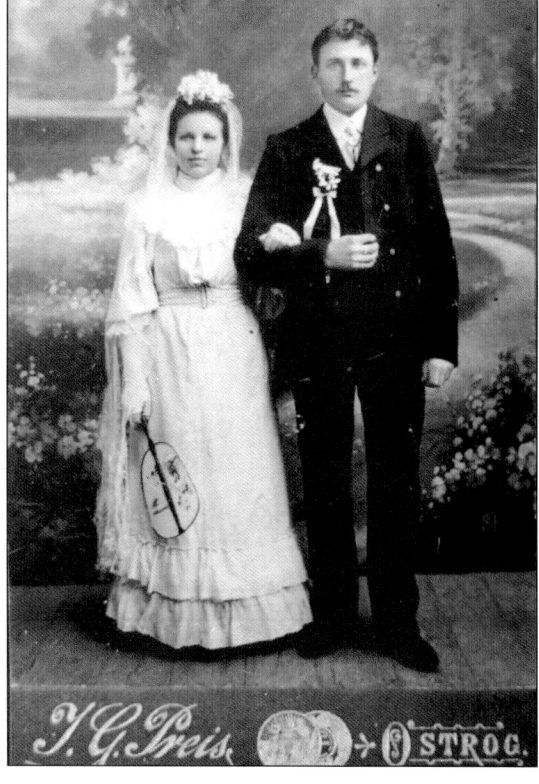

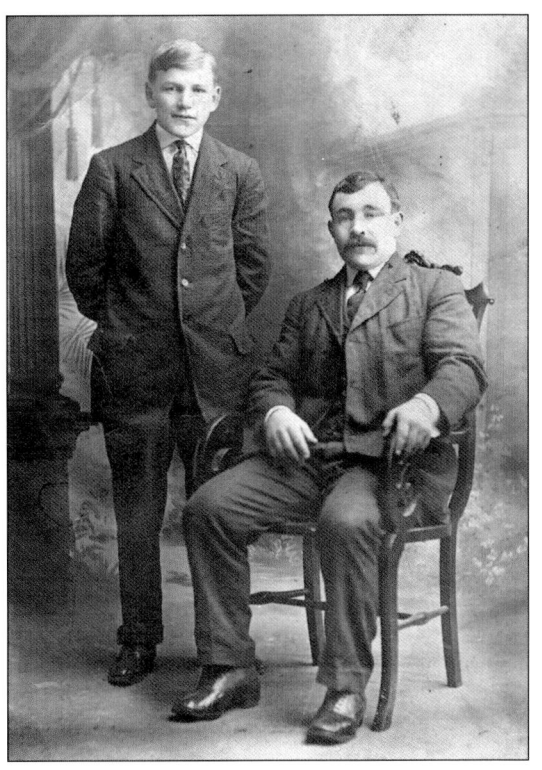

THE SCHACHINGER BROTHERS, c. 1908. Fred (left) and Joseph Schachinger sent this photograph to their family in Karlswalde shortly after arriving in the United States. Fred worked as a baker in Jamaica, New York, while Joseph worked for the Long Island Railroad. Their two sisters, Justina and Lydia, followed them, and they all moved to Village Hill and bought land on Village Hill Road. (Courtesy Claire Krause.)

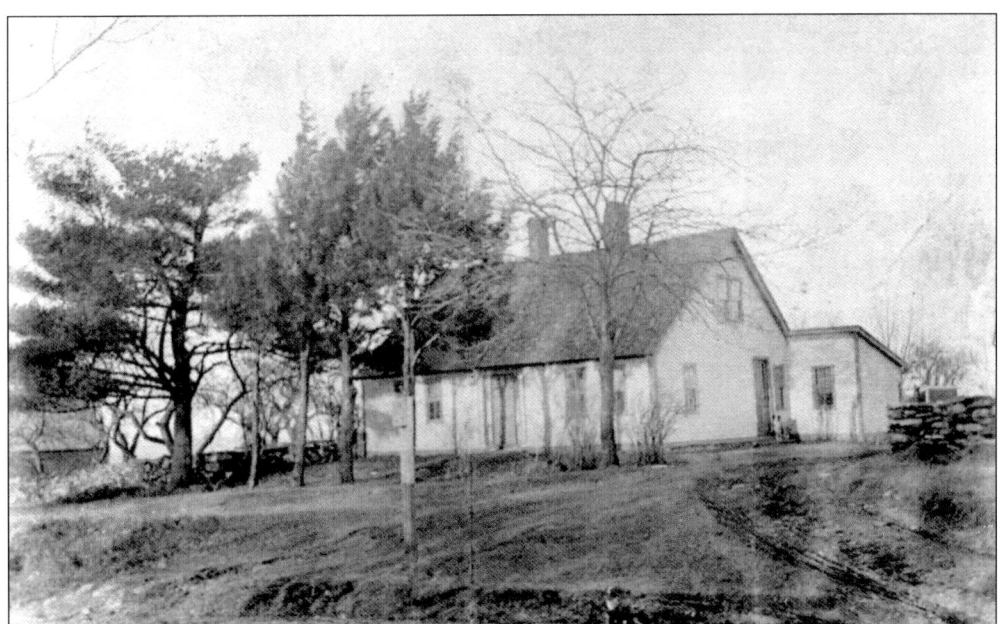

THE BEAUMONT HOMESTEAD, c. 1920. The first German settler to purchase land in Village Hill was Philip Krause in 1911. It was later discovered that his home on Village Hill Road was the birthplace of Dr. William Beaumont, the world-famous pioneer physiologist. After the house was moved to the Lebanon Green in 1976, the vacant lot was donated to the town for a park. (Courtesy Claire Krause.)

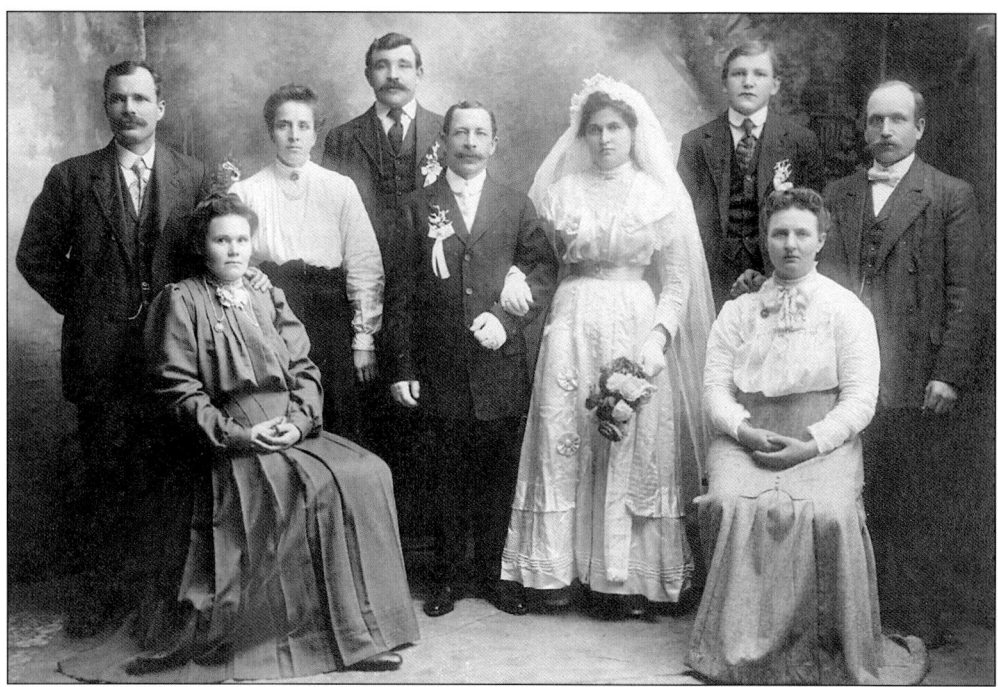

THE JACOB AND JUSTINA WILHELM WEDDING, C. 1908. One of the first weddings of the newly arrived Karlswalde immigrants took place in Jamaica, New York. Pictured, from left to right, are the following: Philip Wilhelm; his wife, Elizabeth (seated); Anna Bender; Joseph Schachinger; Jacob and Justina Wilhelm; Fred Schachinger; Fred Krause; and his wife, Elizabeth (seated). With the exception of Philip and Elizabeth Wilhelm, they all moved to Village Hill as land became available. (Courtesy Claire Krause.)

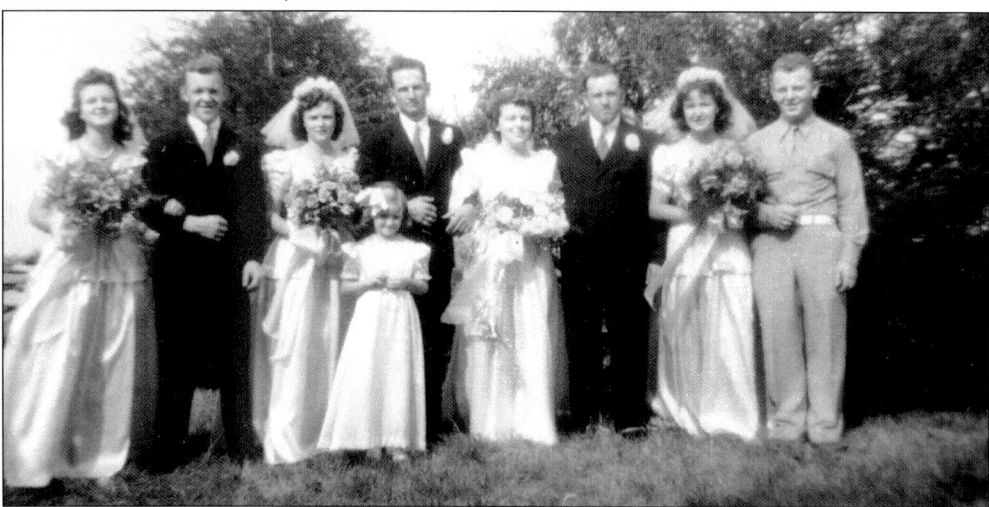

WEDDING BELLS, VILLAGE HILL, SEPTEMBER 1944. The first wedding held in the newly built Redeemer Lutheran Church on Village Hill Road in Lebanon was that of Arnold Krause and Helen Flegert. Seen here, from left to right, are Claire Schachinger, Harry Flegert, Helen Bender, Barbara Bender (flower girl), Harold Krause, Helen (Flegert) Krause, Arnold Krause, Mildred Schachinger, and Arthur Flegert, all first-generation descendants of the Karlswalde Germans. (Courtesy Claire Krause.)

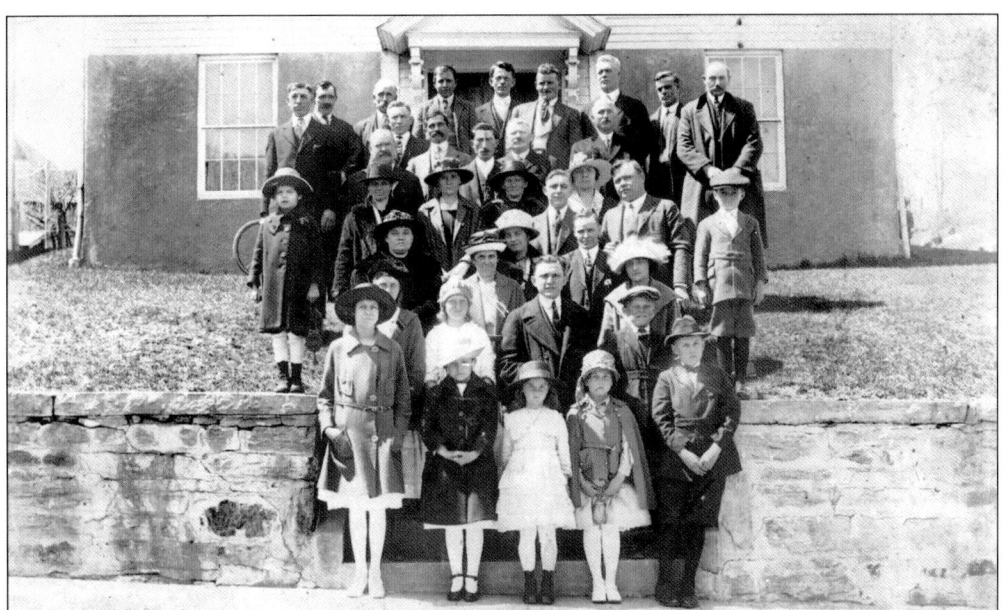

THE EBENEZER LUTHERAN CHURCH, WILLIMANTIC, C. 1919. Services for the Redeemer Lutheran Church, organized in 1916, were first held in the Ebenezer Church until the new Lebanon sanctuary was built. Here, the congregation appears on the steps of the Ebenezer Church; members of the Bender, Krause, Laibrandt, Schachinger, and Ausburger families can be seen. (Courtesy Claire Krause.)

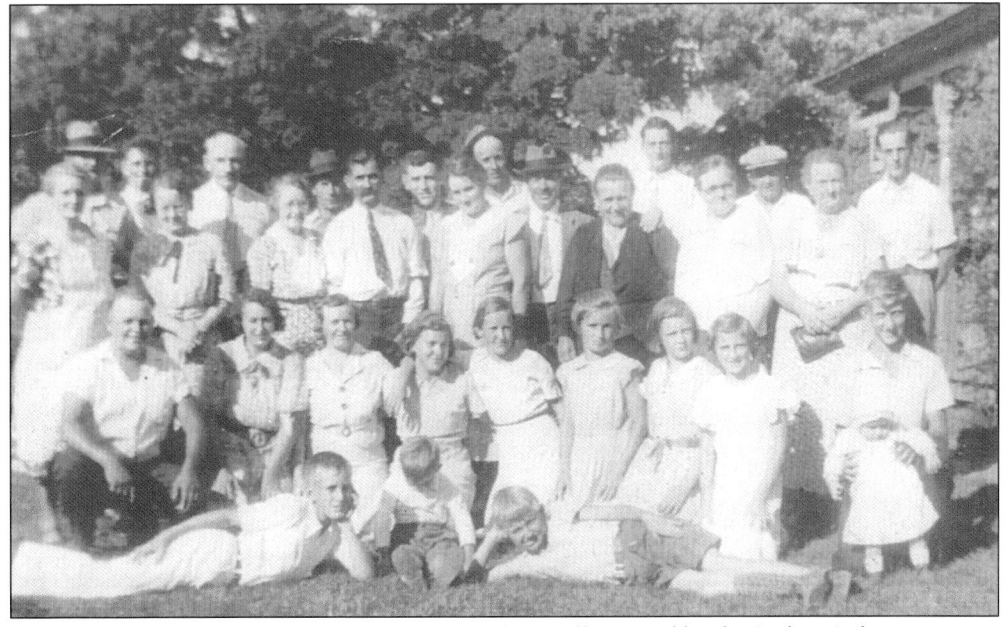

THE VILLAGE HILL KAFFEE KLATCH, C. 1936. Originally started by the Ladies Aid organization of the church, the Kaffee Klatch quickly became family oriented, as evidenced by this photograph taken at the John Bender farm. "Gossip over a cup of coffee" also included home-baked goods made by the hostess of the day, camaraderie, and games for the children. Held monthly, these get-togethers were a popular pastime. (Courtesy Claire Krause.)

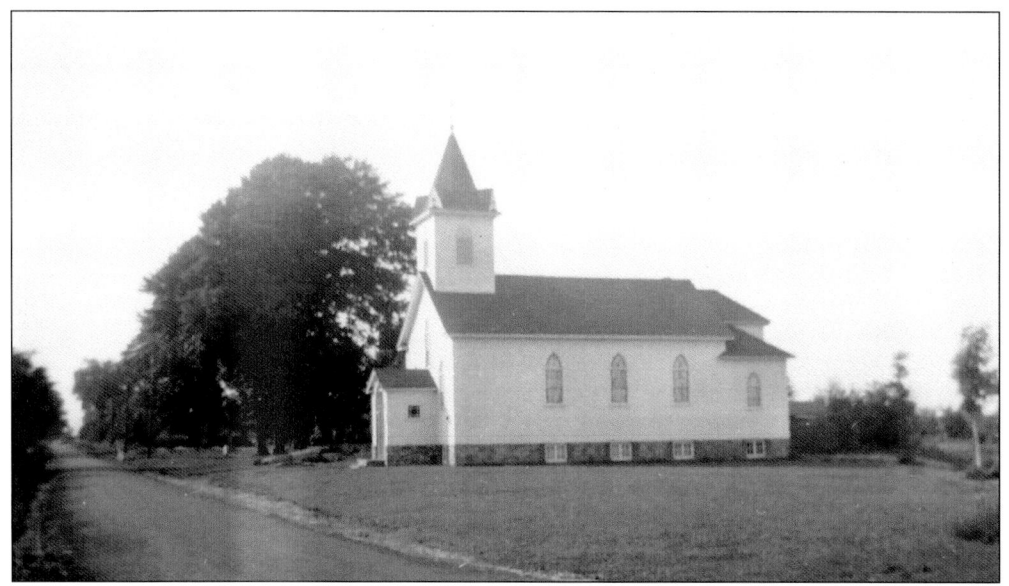

THE REDEEMER LUTHERAN CHURCH, 1944. The newly built church was situated on a rise at the junction of Village Hill Road and Beaumont Highway, about five miles north of Lebanon Center. The congregation was comprised of parishioners from Lebanon, Willimantic, and Coventry. Redeemer has become a landmark of Village Hill and is listed on the Connecticut State Register of Historic Places. (Courtesy Helen Bender.)

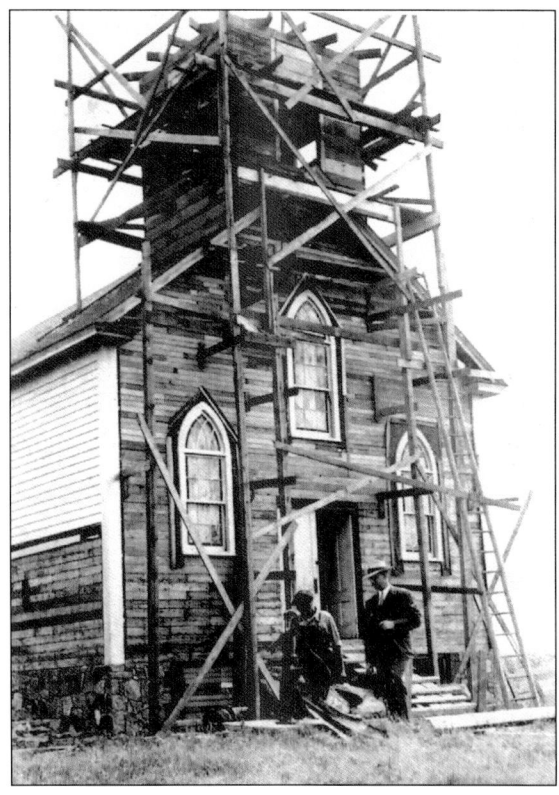

THE REDEEMER CHURCH STEEPLE, c. 1940. Entertaining a visitor from Detroit, Michigan, Gottlieb Laibrandt pauses in his work on the church steeple. Laibrandt, a master craftsman, received his early training in Karlswalde, Ukraine. The Lebanon church was designed after the Karlswalde Lutheran Church, which he helped to build there. The church took seven years to build and was completed entirely with the parishioners' volunteer labor. (Courtesy Helen Bender.)

THE REDEEMER CHURCH SACRISTY, c. 2002. The central point of the altar is a large canvas painting of Christ entitled Come Unto Me. It was set into the paneling of the altar and framed in native oak by Gottlieb Laibrandt. Intricate carvings rendered by Laibrandt are evident throughout the church—on the altar, in the oak chairs, on the baptismal font, and in the pulpit. (Courtesy Claire Krause.)

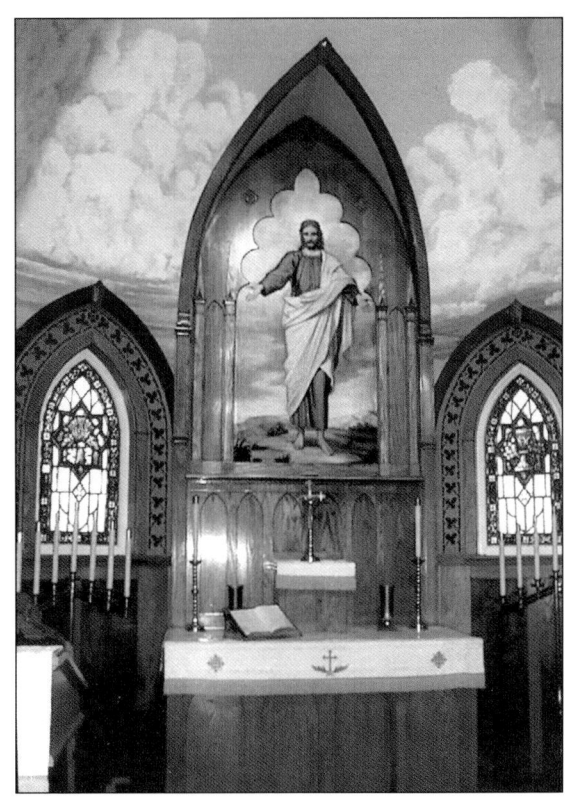

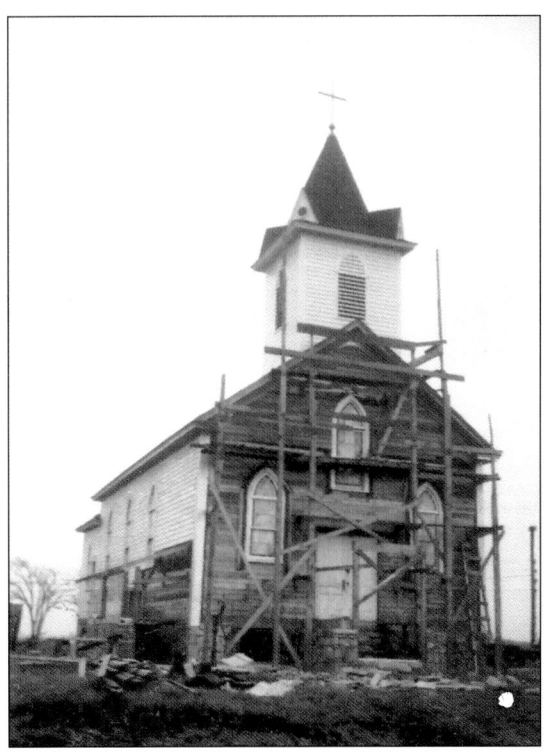

THE REDEEMER BELL TOWER, C. 1940. The church exterior nearly completed, work on the interior began, taking several years to finish. The church is located on the original foundation of a one-room schoolhouse—School District No. 1, dating back to 1850—that had been destroyed in the hurricane of 1938. The men in the congregation used as much lumber from the old schoolhouse as possible to build the church. (Courtesy Helen Bender.)

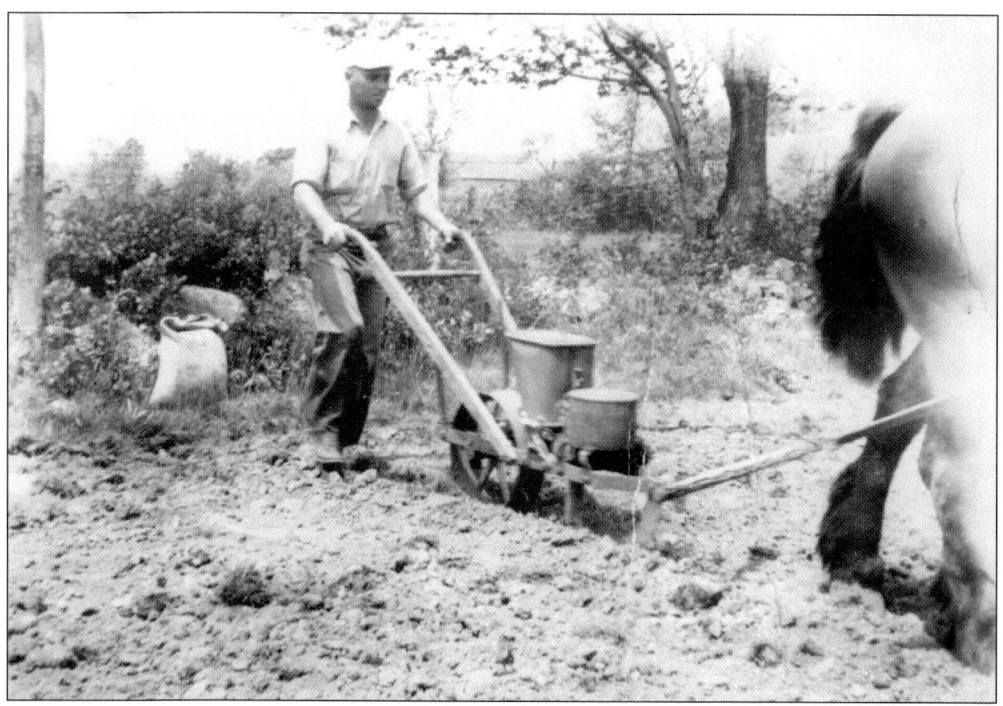

PLANTING CORN, THE LAIBRANDT FARM, C. 1939. Mid-May, when the weather was warm, the fields were marked and prepared for planting corn. Hand-planters were used in the smaller fields, and horse-drawn planters were used for the larger fields. Here, John Laibrandt guides the horse-drawn planter as a helper leads the horse up and down the rows. (Courtesy Helen Bender.)

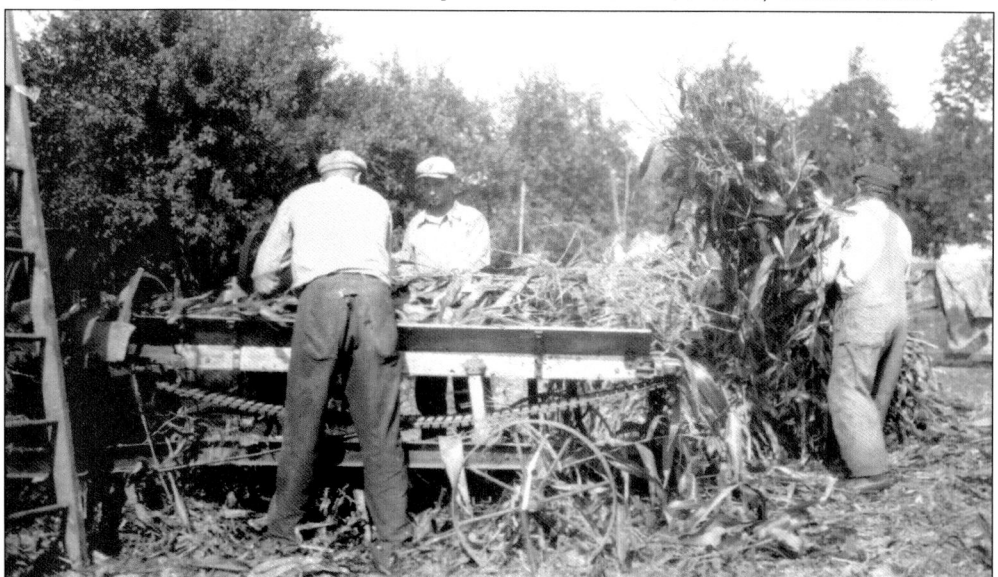

BRINGING IN THE SHEAVES, C. 1930. Corn was harvested in the fall, when it was ripe. Hand-cut in the fields, it was loaded onto a wagon, taken to the barn, and blown into the silo. In this photograph, from left to right, Village Hill farmers Edmund Krause, John Laibrandt, and Gottlieb Wilhelm load corn through the blower into the silo at the Fred Krause farm. (Courtesy Claire Krause.)

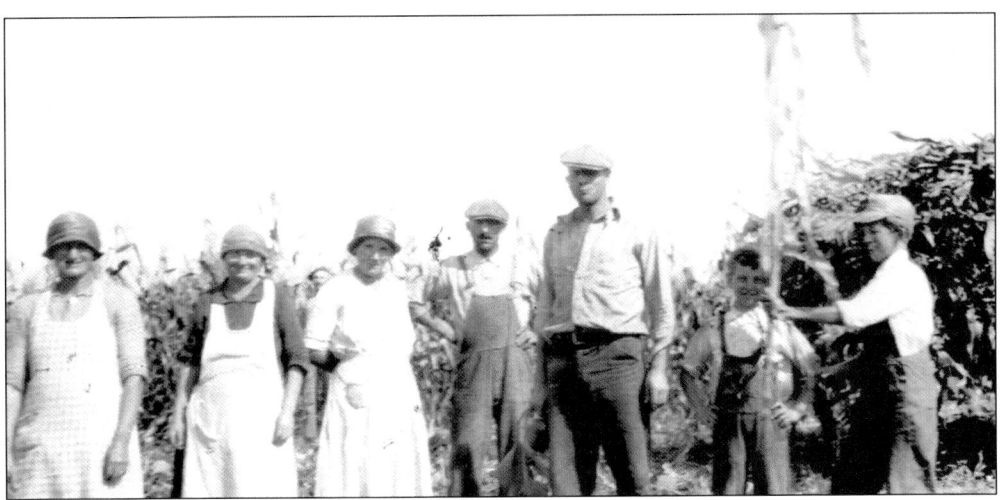

HARVESTING CORN, THE FRED KRAUSE FARM, C. 1930. Stopping only to have its photograph taken, this team of men, women, and children labored to harvest the corn before the fall frost. Families went from farm to farm, sharing machinery and labor. The women at each home prepared meals for the crew. This photograph shows, from left to right, Christine Wilhelm, Caroline Ausburger, Agatha Laibrandt, Jacob Ausburger, Edmund Krause, Harold Krause, and Ewald Wilhelm. (Courtesy Claire Krause.)

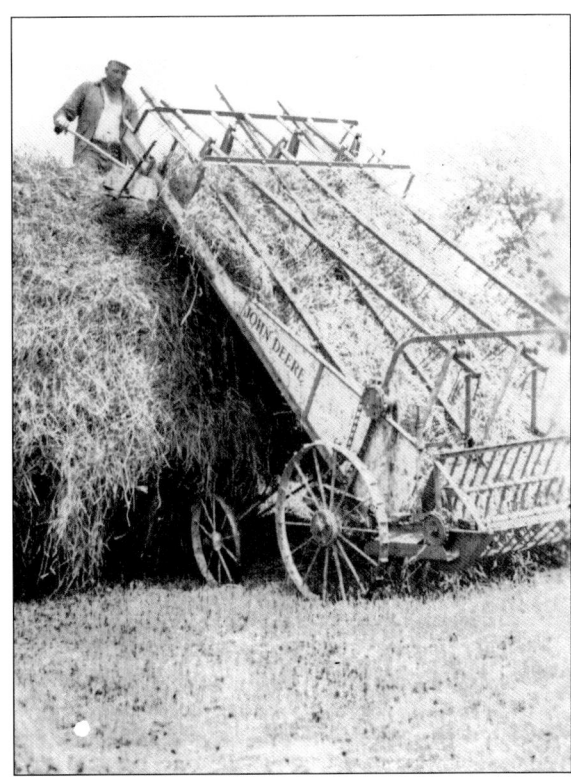

A HAY-LOADER, C. 1930. Finding an easier way to load hay on a wagon, the Krause farm purchased this John Deere hay loader for $175. Hay was mowed in the field, raked, and then put on the wagon using the loader. The wagon was taken to the barn, where it was unloaded using a large hayfork and horsepower, making the process less labor intensive. (Courtesy Claire Krause.)

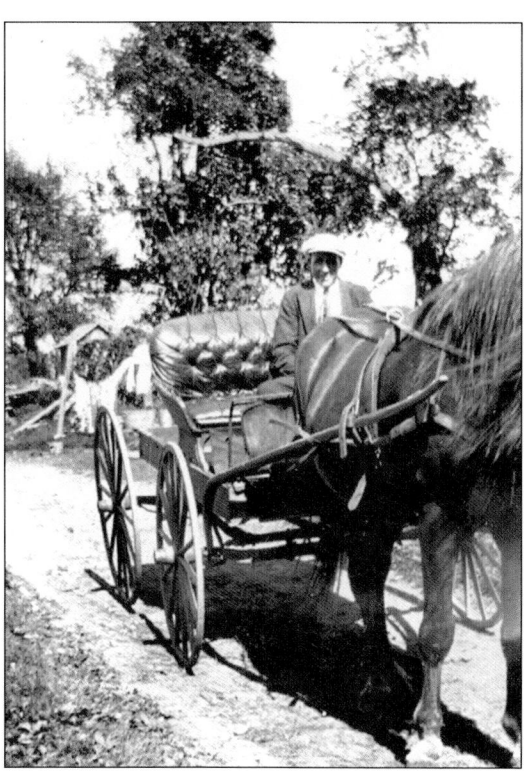

"PEAS, CORN, POTATOES!" C. 1920. During the summer, Village Hill farmers sold their produce in the streets of Willimantic. Going door-to-door, hawking or "peddling" their wares, they sold homegrown fruits and vegetables by the quart for "5 cents, 10 cents, 25 cents," until all the items were sold. Here, Fred Krause goes to market on his special wagon led by Pete, his trusted horse. (Courtesy Claire Krause.)

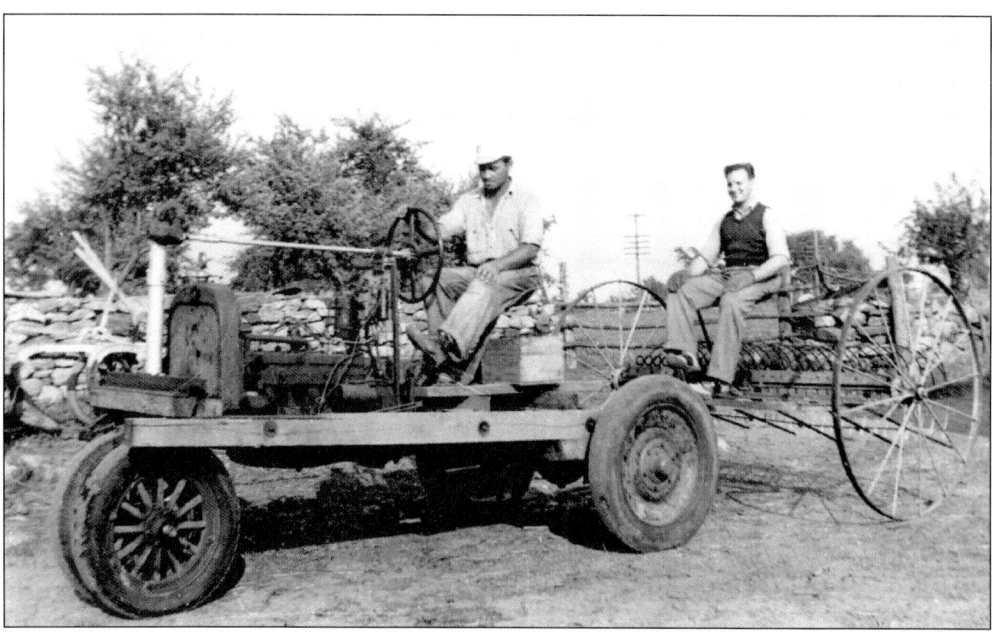

THE HORSELESS FARM MACHINE, C. 1941. This homemade tractor, made up of spare car and truck parts on a three- by six-foot wooden frame, was used for pulling farm equipment. John Laibrandt, the driver, and Edward McSweeney, the hay-rake operator, prepare to rake the hay fields on the Laibrandt farm. These machines, sometimes called "Doodle Bugs," provided much pleasure for the farm family. (Courtesy Helen Bender.)

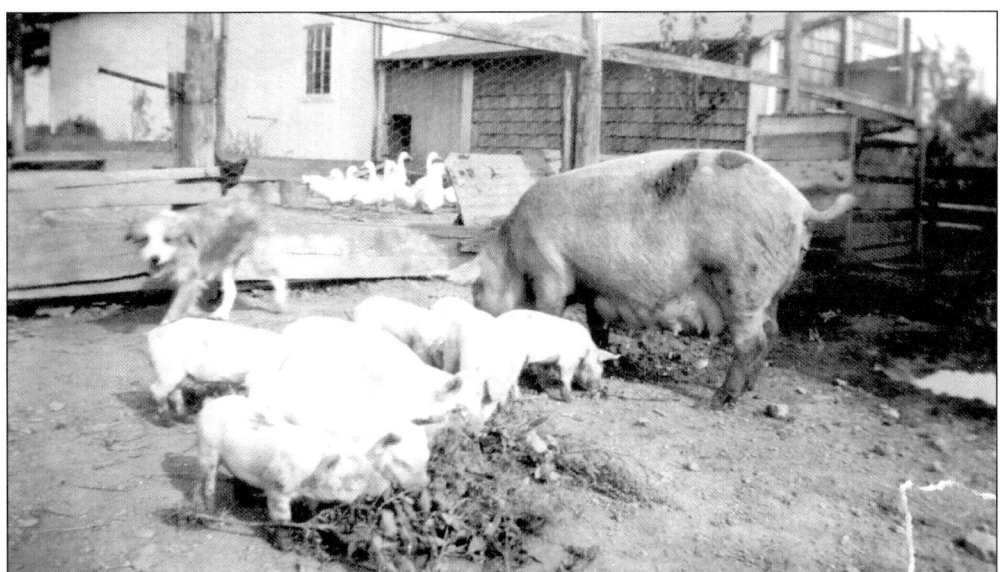

"And on This Farm There Was . . . " the Laibrandt Farm, c. 1940. A typical farm in Village Hill had cows, horses, pigs, ducks, chickens, and geese, which provided milk, eggs, meat, and fowl for the table. The farm dog helped to herd and guard the animals. Every household had a vegetable garden for personal consumption, and enterprising homemakers preserved enough food to last the family through the year. (Courtesy Helen Bender.)

A Pork Fest, the Laibrandt Farm, c. 1940. Every fall, when the weather turned cold, it was time to butcher the pigs for the family's winter food. In another cooperative effort with other "Village Hillers," the pigs were cut up into serving size (ham, bacon, and chops). Smaller pieces were ground up to make sausages, which were then smoked in the smokehouse; the fat was rendered to make lard. (Courtesy Helen Bender.)

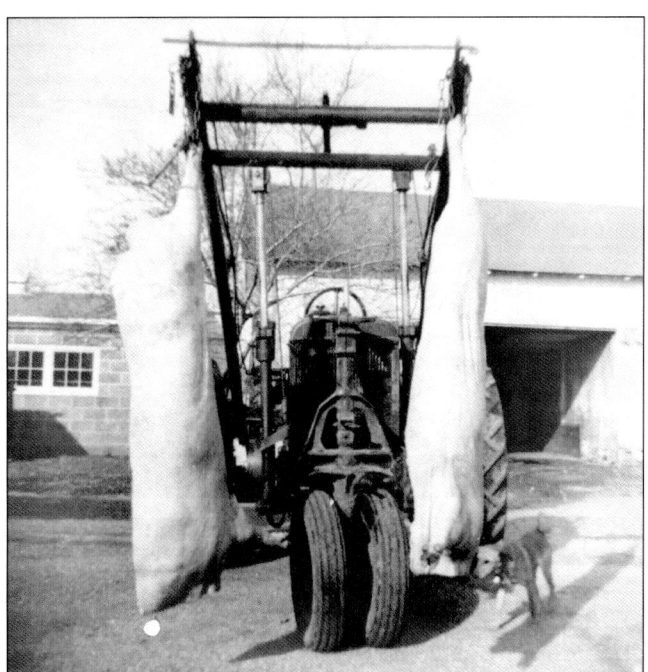

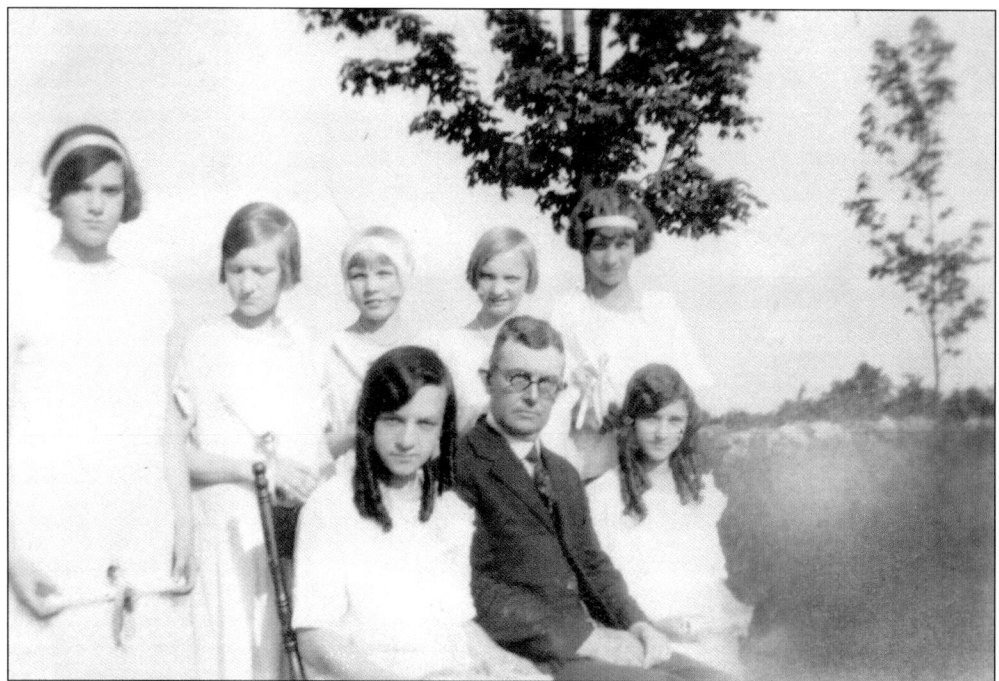

GRAMMAR SCHOOL GRADUATION, 1927. Graduations from the one-room schoolhouses were held at the Lyman Memorial High School in Lebanon. This photograph shows the eighth-grade girl graduates from the Village Hill School. Pictured, from left to right, are the following: (first row) Eleanor Schachinger, teacher George Briggs, and Martha Laibrandt; (second row) Lillian Fishbein, Florence Oden, Agnes Bergeson, Lillian Bergeson, and Wilma Krause. (Courtesy Claire Krause.)

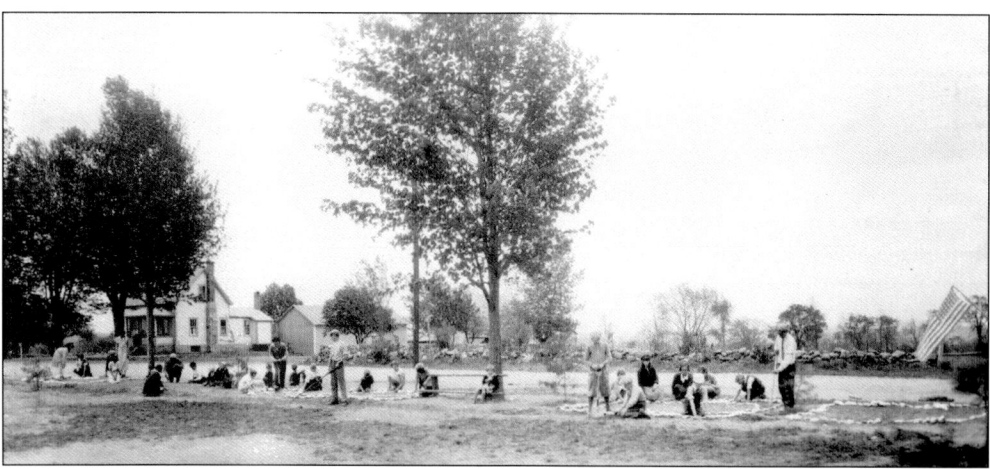

ARBOR DAY, THE VILLAGE HILL SCHOOL, 1935. Celebrating Arbor Day, students at the Village Hill School planted small flower gardens from seeds at the site of Village Hill Road. Seen here, from left to right, are Mildred Segal, Helen Wilhelm, Eleanor Wilhelm, Helen Bender, Lawrence Flegert, Eugene Brisson, Arthur Flegert, Helen Laibrandt, Arthur Ausburger, unidentified, Irene Carney, Edward Bender, Harry Flegert, Edward Bender, Edith Carney, Harriet Hinckley, Harold Wilhelm, and Armand Brisson. (Courtesy Helen Krause.)

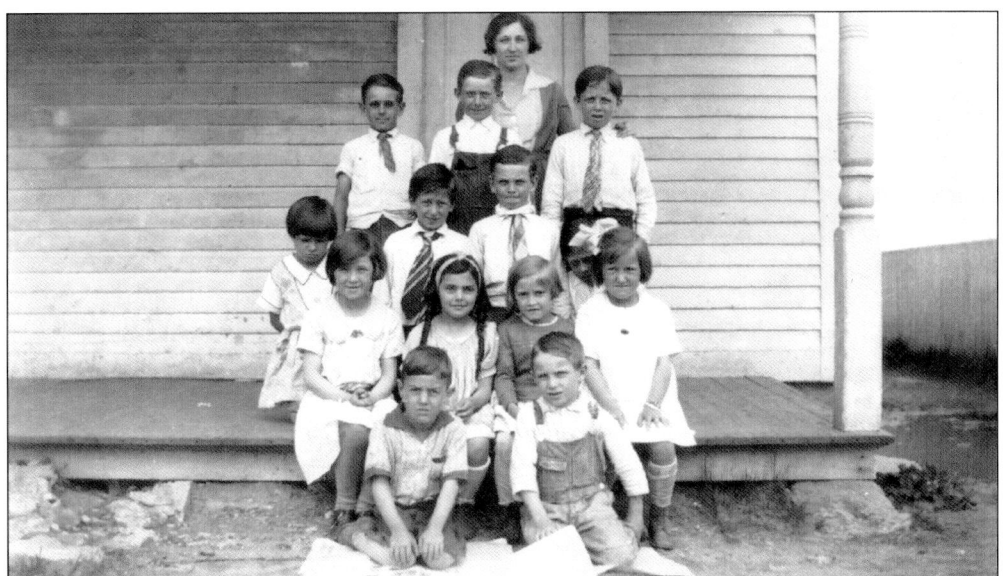

"SCHOOL DAYS, SCHOOL DAYS," 1931. Lower-grade students from Village Hill pose in front of the one-room schoolhouse with their teacher, Rose Gold (standing in the back row). Pictured, from left to right, are the following: (first row) Arthur Tanner and Otto Ausburger; (second row) Martha Stebner, Mildred Segal, Helen Laibrandt, and Mildred Schachinger; (third row) Pearl Wallace, Harold Wilhelm, Harold Krause, and George Wilhelm (behind Mildred); (fourth row) Ernest Brisson, Arthur Ausburger, and Philip Flegert. (Courtesy Helen Krause.)

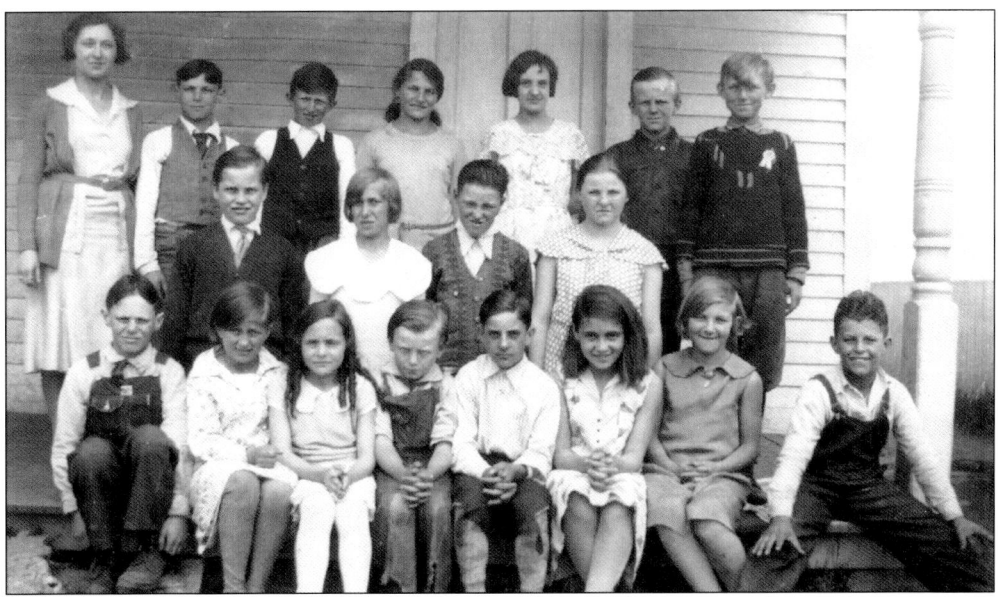

"THE THREE Rs," 1931. Upper-grade students from the Village Hill School appear with their teacher, Rose Gold. Shown, from left to right, are the following: (first row) Jacob Segal, Helen Wilhelm, Lena Segal, Arthur Flegert, Armand Brisson, Rose Kadupski, Helen Flegert, and Edward Wilhelm; (second row) Lawrence Flegert, Elsie Wilhelm, Arthur Stebner, and Edna Flegert; (third row) teacher Rose Gold, Philip Segal, Ewald Wilhelm, Jeanette Segal, Anna Brisson, Julius Flegert, and Arthur Bender. (Courtesy Helen Krause.)

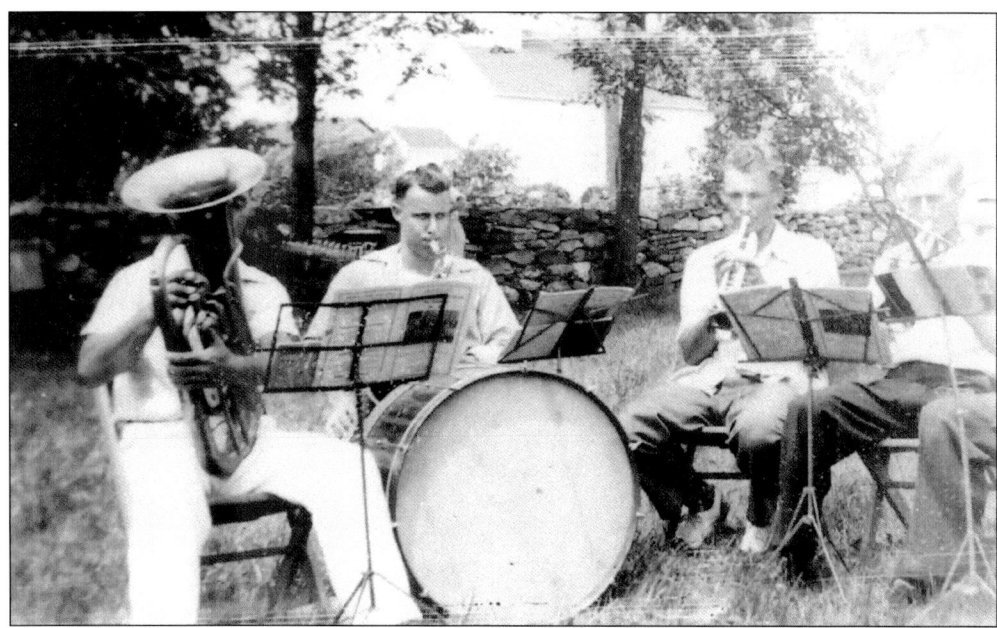

THE VILLAGE HILL BAND, C. 1945. The Village Hill Band played lively music for special occasions. Here, the band plays for the Fourth of July musical chairs game. Band members seen here are, from left to right, John Laibrandt (tuba and drums), R. Clinton Card (saxophone), Harry Cadow (trumpet), and Arthur Ausburger (trumpet). Absent is Arthur Bender (clarinet). (Courtesy Helen Bender.)

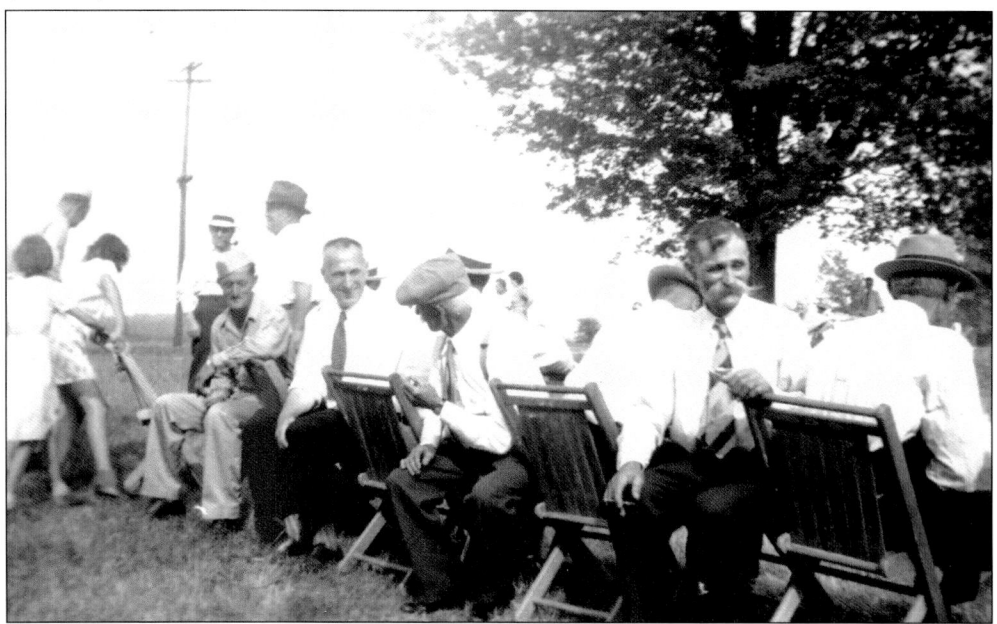

MUSIC, MUSIC, MUSIC, C. 1945. The church picnic, initiated by the Ladies Aid Society, attracted many church members with delicious food offerings, including the all-time favorites—grinders and strawberry shortcake. Activities included children's games and races, musical chairs, an adult shoe-kick, and an afternoon softball game for all ages. This photograph shows the men of the church testing their skill in a game of musical chairs. (Courtesy Helen Bender.)

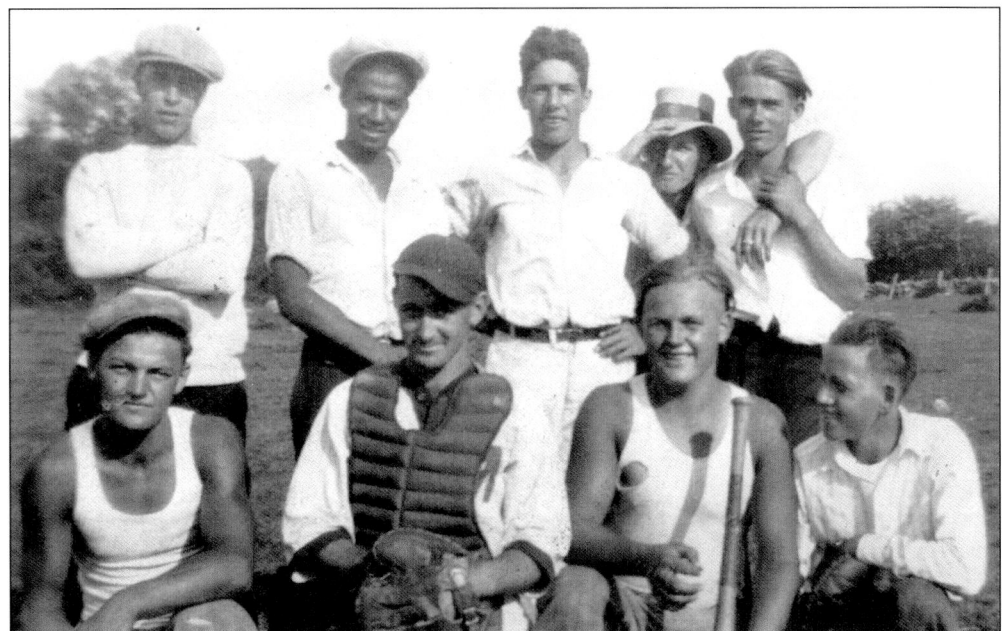

PLAY BALL, C. 1930. The Village Hill baseball team played teams from Eagleville, South Windham, Chestnut Hill, Columbia, and Lebanon. Playing each summer for about seven years, the team won many games and had a loyal following. Members pictured here, from left to right, are the following: (first row) Walter Bender, Frank Kadupski, Arnold Bender, and Arnold Krause; (second row) Leo Dubriel, Oscar Flippen, Ruby Segal, Edmund Krause, and John Kadupski. (Courtesy Marion Russo.)

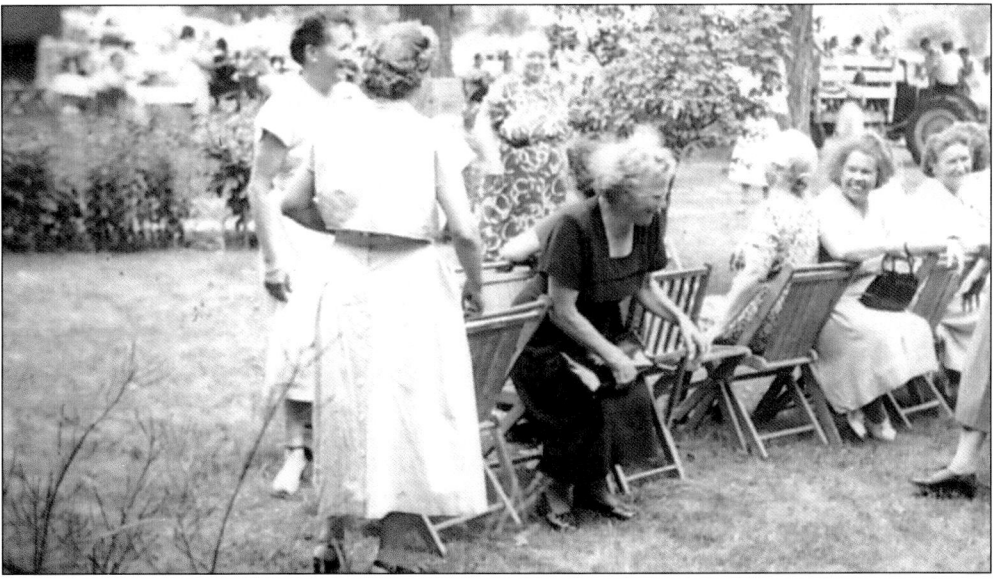

FUN ON THE FOURTH, C. 1940. The Fourth of July picnic was held on the Redeemer Lutheran Church lawn each year. Visitors and guests came annually from Boston and New York and occasionally from Michigan, Kansas, and Canada to enjoy the reunion of families and friends. Here, women enjoy a game of musical chairs. The tractor-driven hayride is visible in the background. (Courtesy Claire Krause.)

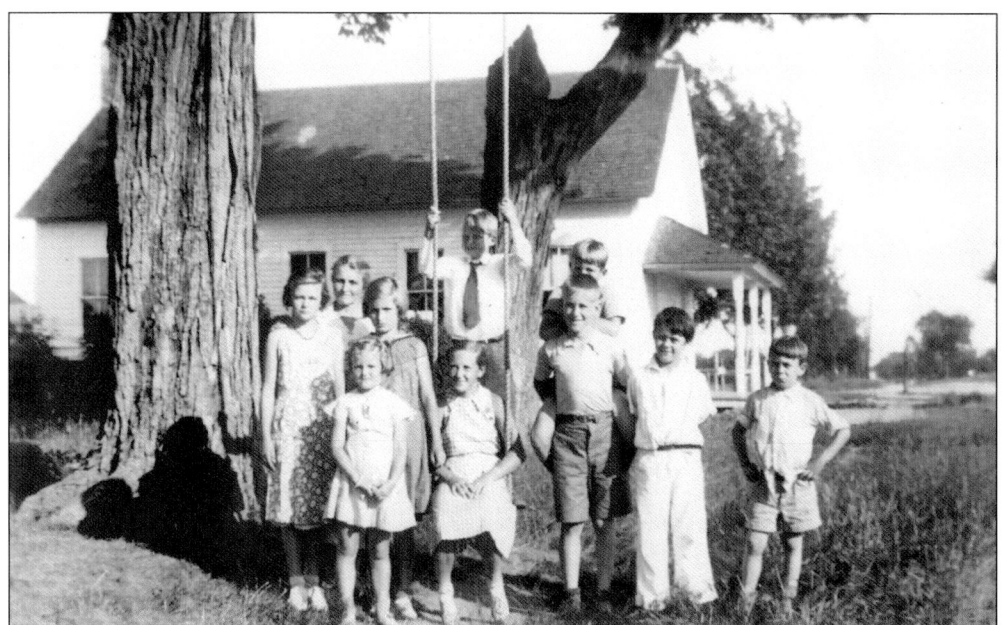

IN THE GOOD OLD SUMMERTIME, C. 1935. The hanging of the rope swing on the maple tree near the school coincided with the New York City and Boston relatives' annual visit to Village Hill. Standing on the left of the swing are, from left to right, Helen Bender, Justina Bender, Irma Engelbrecht, and Claire Schachinger. On the swing are Edward Bender and Mildred Schachinger. To the right of the swing are Fred Schachinger, Arthur Engelbrecht, Harold Wilhelm, and Albert Wilhelm. (Courtesy Claire Krause.)

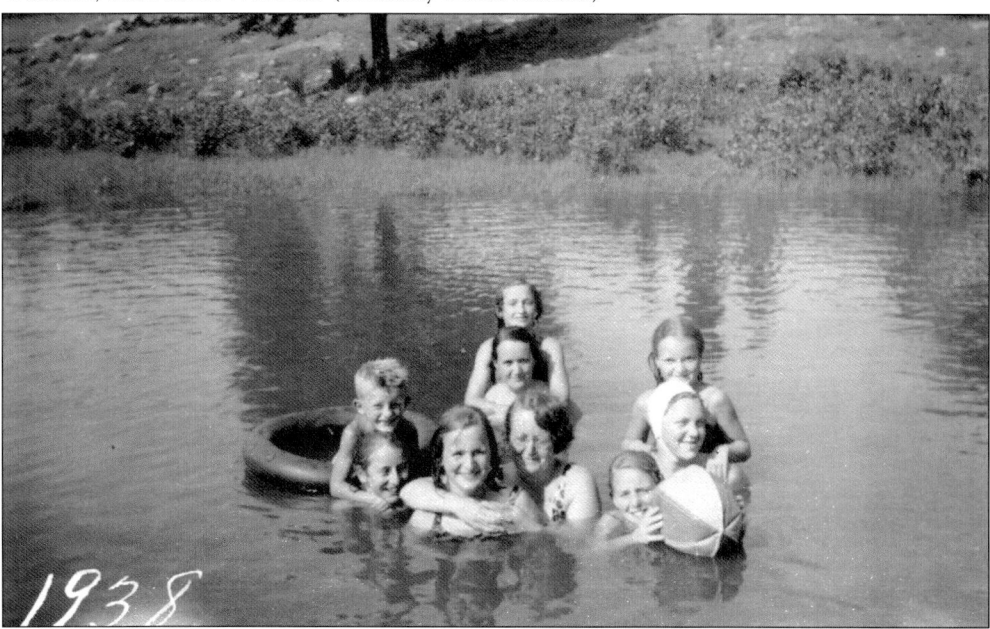

THE OL' SWIMMING HOLE, FLEGERT'S POND, C. 1938. Every summer afternoon after chores, Village Hill children and their friends would have a refreshing swim in the pond. The younger swimmers used tire inner tubes to keep afloat. There was a diving board for the more adventurous. No summer day was complete without this dip in the water. (Courtesy Helen Krause.)

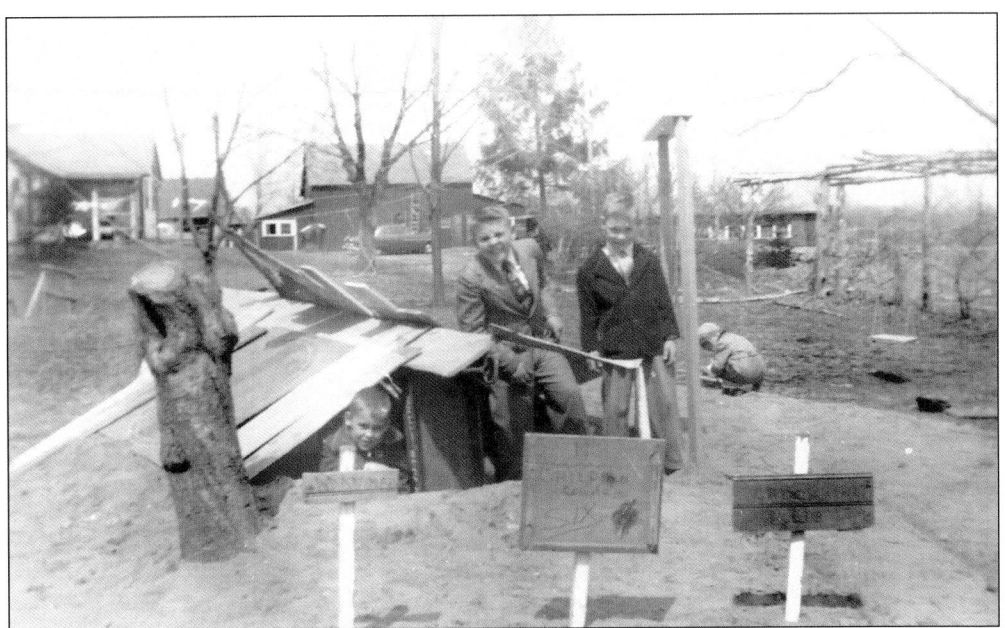

FARM FUN, C. 1950. Charles Bender, Billy Scar, Ronald Bender, and James Bender, seen here from left to right, play in a sand pile in Arthur Bender's backyard. In the background is the John Bender farm with its variety of buildings: barn, milk house, chicken house, smokehouse, pig house, icehouse, tool shed, and woodshed. (Courtesy Helen Bender.)

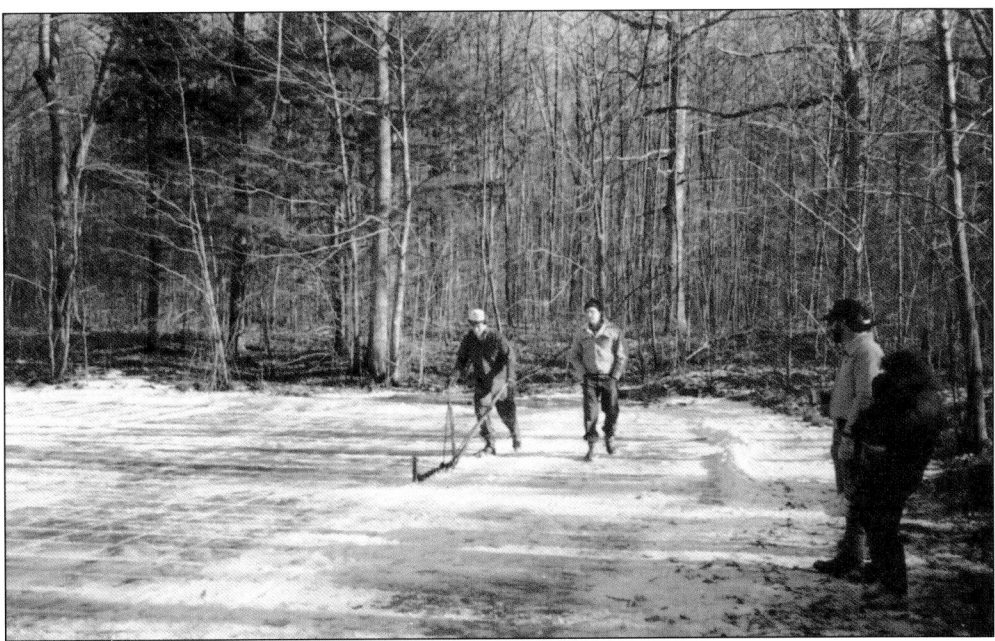

MARKING ICE, THE LAIBRANDT FARM, 1978. Ice cutting, a necessity for farms before the advent of refrigeration, was usually scheduled at the end of January, when the ice was thickest (about 8–10 inches). The ice had to be squared off using a special marker that scraped lines across the ice, as shown in this photograph. The Bender family organized this ice-cutting reenactment. (Courtesy Helen Bender.)

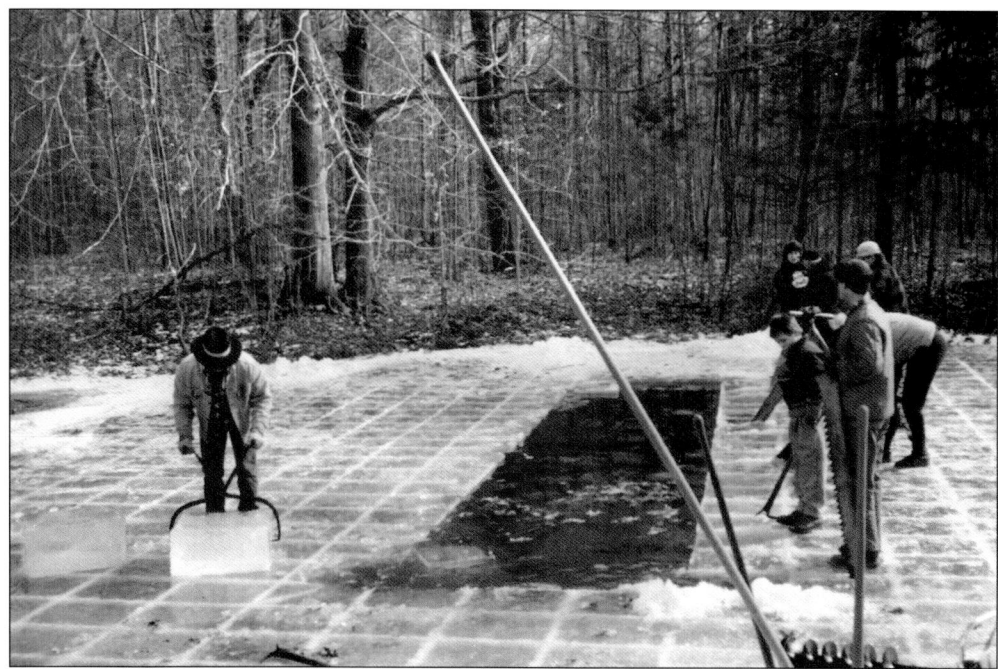

CUTTING ICE, THE LAIBRANDT FARM, 1978. Ice was cut about 6 to 12 inches deep and sawed into square blocks. Ice tongs and ice picks were used to pick up the blocks and load them onto a wagon. The blocks were then unloaded in the ice house, where they were covered with sawdust and stacked carefully in order to last through the summer months. (Courtesy Helen Bender.)

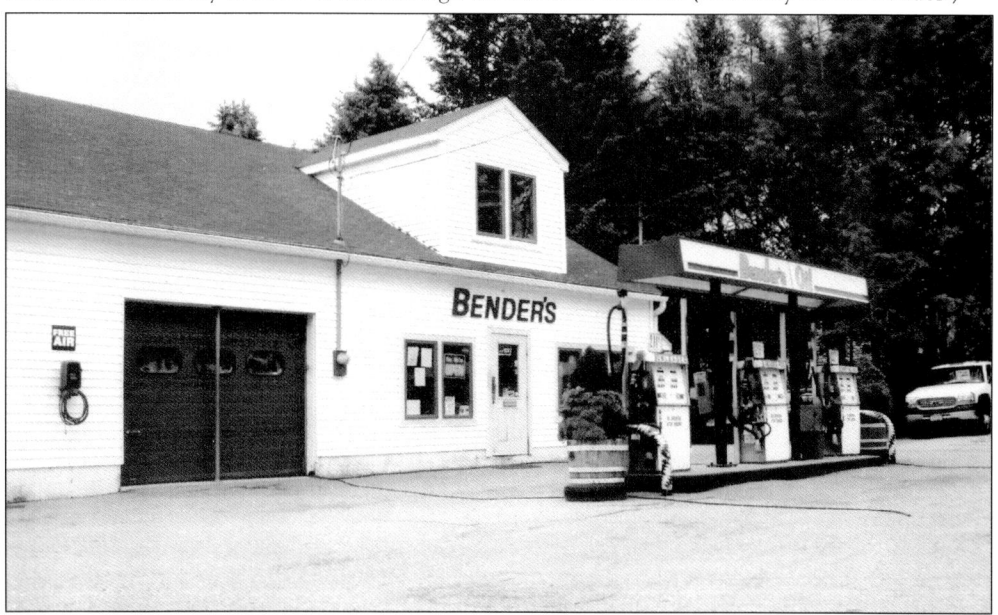

BENDER'S OIL SERVICE, 2004. In 1947, Arnold Bender opened the first locally owned and operated fuel-oil business. Starting with one truck, he gradually built up the business. At first, the gas station included a small convenience store. Later, it was a used-car business as well as an automobile parts and repair shop. In 1959, Arnold's brother Arthur joined him, and the partnership became mainly a fuel-oil business, as it is now. (Courtesy Helen Bender.)

Six

School Bells

The Puritan ethic of early town settlers placed a strong emphasis on education and learning. Children were taught at home and then at local primary schools. Ministers usually tutored the boys who wanted to go on to higher education.

The earliest record found of a school dates from 1717, when the town voted to set up two schools. The following year, the town approved several more schools in outlying districts. There is no record of where these schools were located, but they would have been primary schools. Jeremiah Mason, born in 1768, grew up in the Goshen neighborhood and recalled in his memoirs that there was no school building in his district when he was a child. School was held in a room in a private home in the winter months.

The "country money," the contribution the Colonial legislature made to operate the schools, supplied most of the money for their operation. Local school taxes were negligible for much of the 18th century. The ecclesiastical societies were in charge of the schools from 1712 to 1795.

The Tisdale School, founded by Jonathan Trumbull and several townspeople, was built on the site of the present town hall in 1743. It provided a quality education for tuition-paying students. The school became known by the name of its master, Nathan Tisdale, who started teaching at the school in 1749. Tisdale taught the standard classical curriculum and added courses in surveying and navigation. Most of the students were boys.

In the North Society, Eleazar Wheelock conducted a school for college-bound boys in his home. In 1754, he opened a school for American Indian children, whom he hoped to train as missionaries. It was called Moor's Indian Charity School, named after the benefactor who donated land and a building. Joseph Brant, the celebrated Mohawk Indian chief, attended the school as a youth.

Towns were allowed to establish local school districts within the societies beginning in the late 1790s. Neighboring families could join together, agree to build a school, hire a teacher, and tax themselves to pay the cost. District committees were set up to oversee the schools, prompting the beginning of the 16 school districts in Lebanon during the early 19th century.

The one-room schools each had a wood stove and an outdoor privy. There was no standard curriculum and no standard term calendar. Students ranged in age from 4 to 20 years old. Teachers boarded with families in the district and displayed wide variations in teaching quality. There was never enough money, either from district taxes or the state school fund, to properly fund teacher salaries and provide adequate supplies. In spite of these deficiencies, the one-room schools provided basic skills in reading, writing, and arithmetic, which served their students well.

It was not until 1909 that the state abolished the independent school districts and set them under a town school committee. In 1910, the local districts deeded their properties to the town. A few schools were closed for economy. In 1919, the number of schools was reduced from 14 to 9. Final consolidation of the one-room schools had to wait until 1936, when a federal grant enabled the town to build the central elementary school on Route 207.

In the meantime, Lebanon finally opened its first high school in 1922. Prior to that time, students wanting a high-school education had to travel to Colchester, Norwich, or Willimantic.

In 1920, the town received a large bequest to build a high school from the estate of George W. Lyman, who had no children. The construction fund was augmented by town appropriations, and the first high school was opened in 1922. In accordance with a clause in Lyman's will, the school was named after him. Now at its third location, the Lyman Memorial High School still carries the name of the man who left his fortune to benefit the town's children.

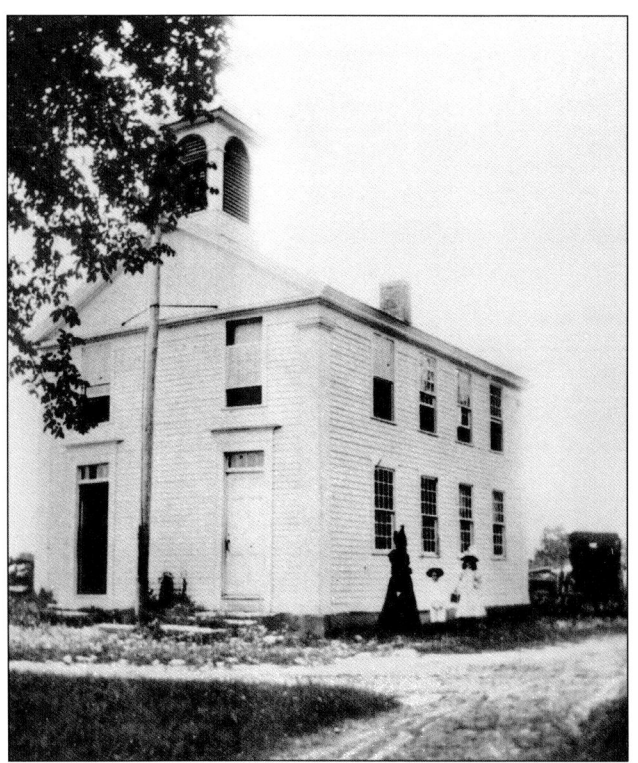

THE OLD GOSHEN SCHOOL. The Goshen Hill Schoolhouse, shown here in 1898, at one time housed a "select school" called the Goshen Academy in an upper room. Students paid private tuition to attend and took coursework beyond the elementary-school level, but it was not a true high school. The Goshen School was torn down after years of abandonment. (Courtesy LHS.)

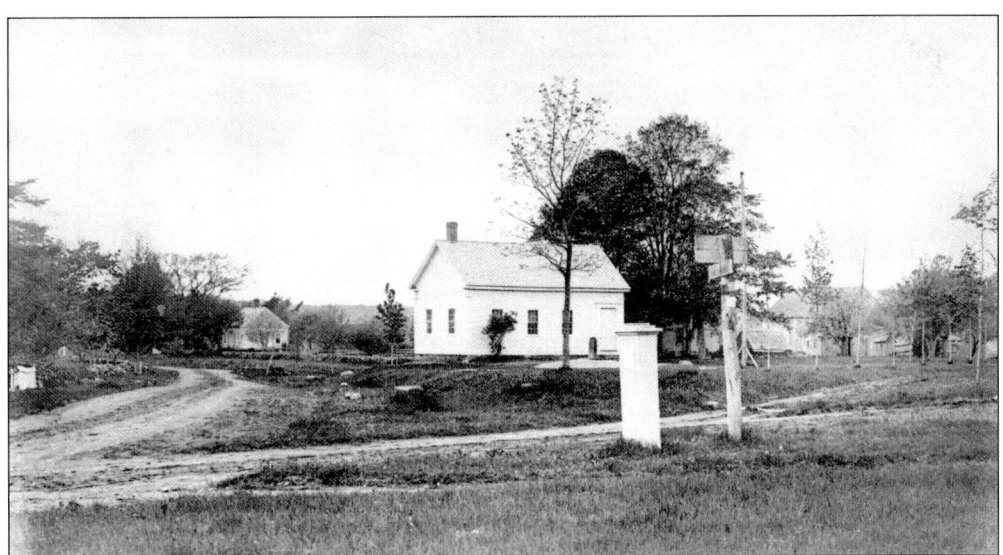

SCHOOL NO. 5. This school was located at the junction of Routes 87 and 289, on a small triangle of land with dirt roads around all sides. In the 1930s, the state rebuilt the corner, closing the road behind the school and reducing the frontage. The school has been moved, but the town still owns the small parcel in front of the house. This photograph was taken c. 1904. (Courtesy Robert Slate.)

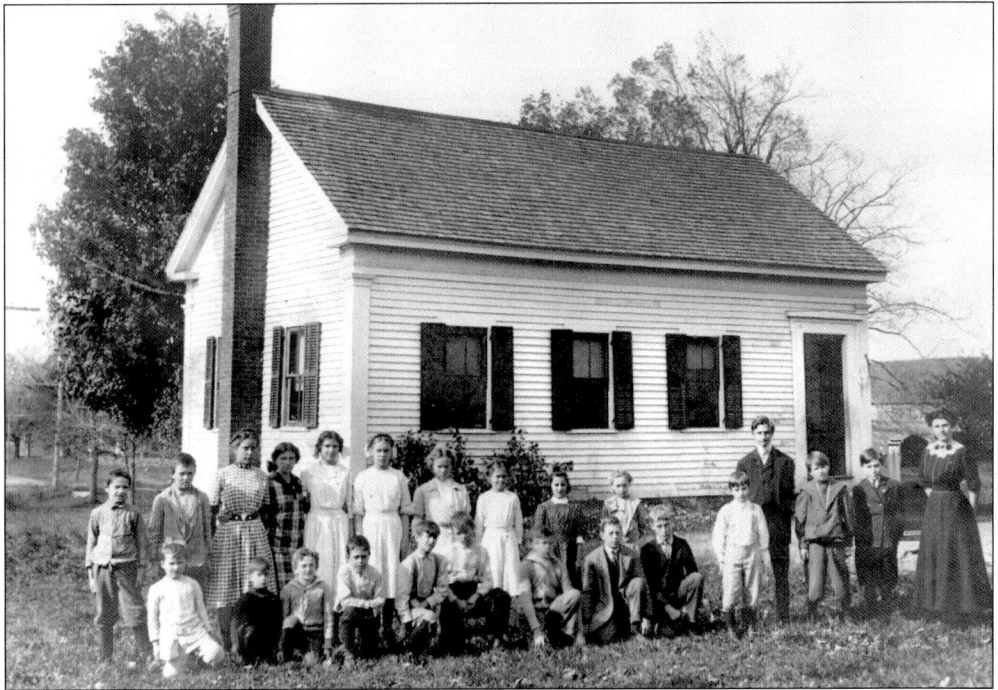

THE CHILDREN OF SCHOOL NO. 5. This photograph, taken after 1904, displays how the chimney was moved to the side of the building. When the one-room schools were consolidated in 1936, the building was sold to the adjacent landowner. The land under the school, however, was owned by the town, and no improvements could be made. The building was eventually moved to Chappell Road, where it is now a residence. (Courtesy LHS.)

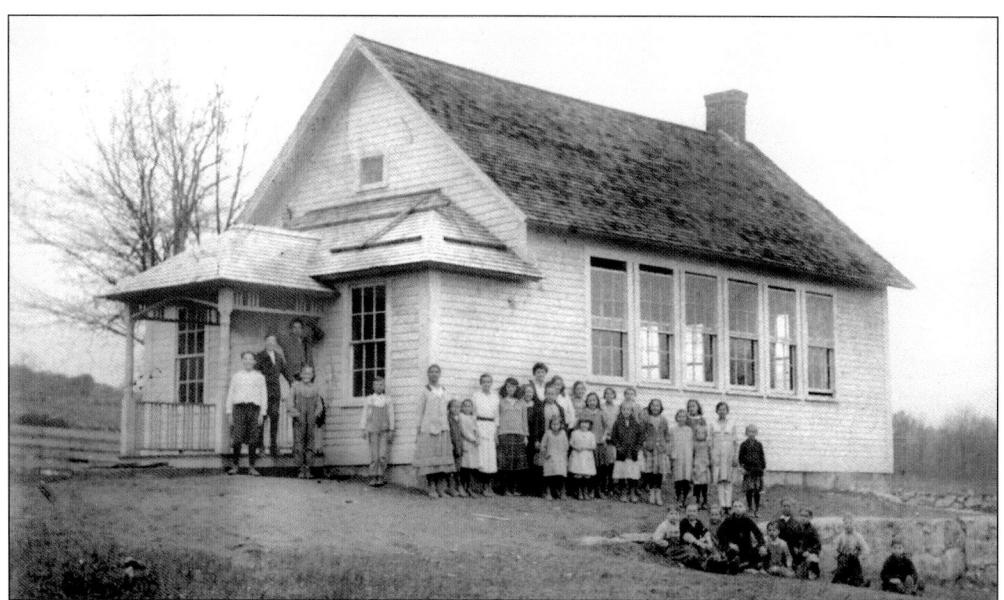

SCHOOL NO. 9. Located along a curve on Waterman Road, this school was near the Hayward Rubber Company's mill on the Yantic River. Many of the children of the Irish immigrants who worked in the mill attended this school. When the state reconstructed Route 2, a new section of Waterman Road was built to form a straighter intersection at the highway bridge approach. The old street is now an extension of McGrath Lane, where the school was converted to a residence. (Courtesy LHS.)

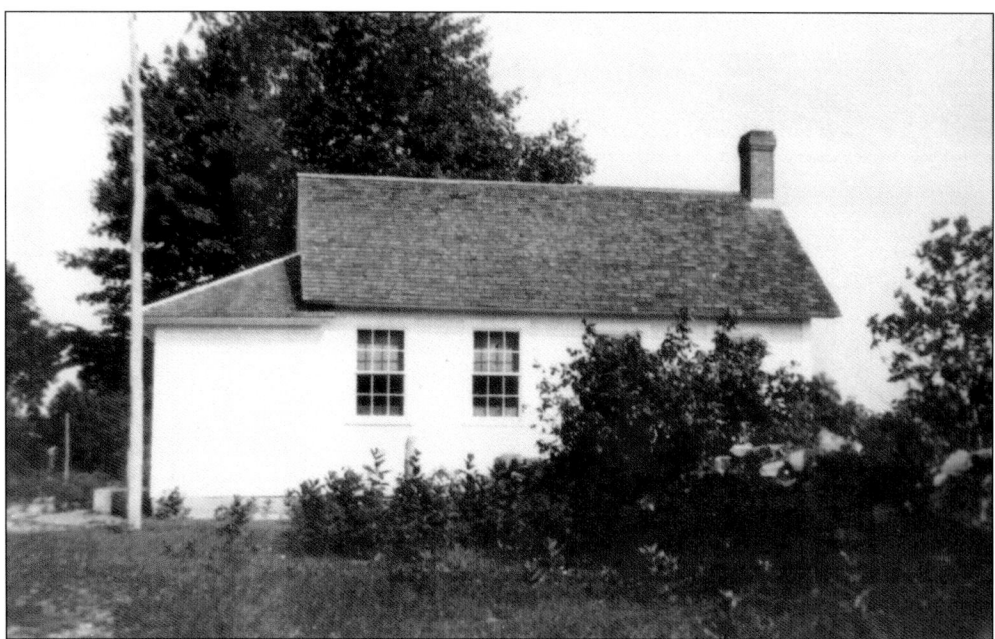

SCHOOL NO. 16. This school was located on Tobacco Street at the corner of Clarke Road. This 1914 photograph, taken by teacher Georgia Robinson, shows a side view of the building and includes the flagpole. (Courtesy LHS.)

THE CENTER SCHOOL. School No. 6 was in the town center, between the First Congregational Church and the corner store. In 1937, after the new elementary school had opened, it became the town library. The town purchased the parcel in 1966 and demolished the store to build a new library. When the new library was completed, the old school was torn down and the brick walkway and the Trumbull monument were installed. (Courtesy Ed Tollmann.)

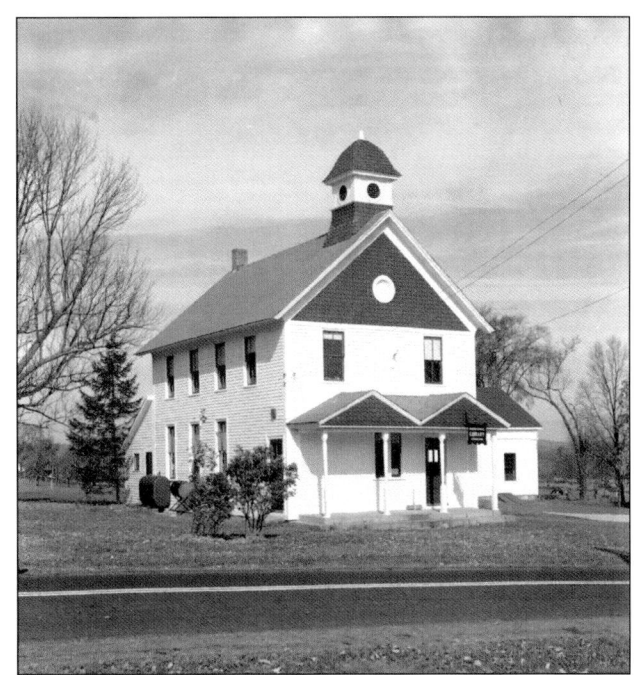

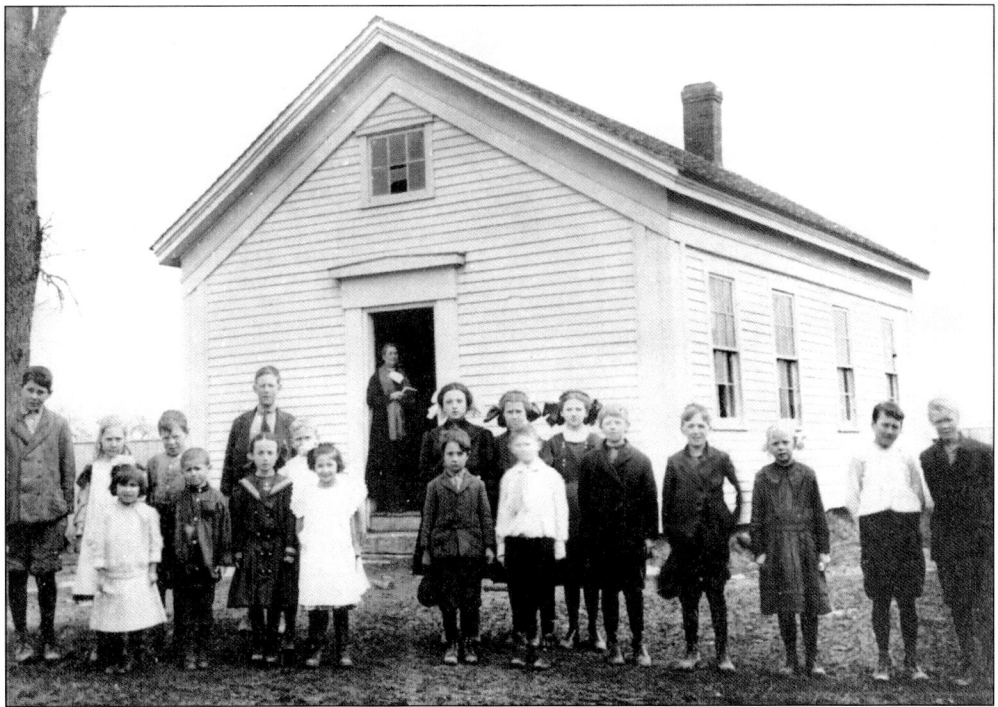

THE OLD VILLAGE HILL SCHOOL. This photograph of School No. 1 was taken c. 1900. Nineteen students appear in front of the school; the teacher is in the doorway. The school burned in 1918 and was replaced in 1919. That building, later sold to the Lutheran Church, was severely damaged in the 1938 hurricane. The scrap wood was saved and used in constructing the church. (Courtesy Helen Krause.)

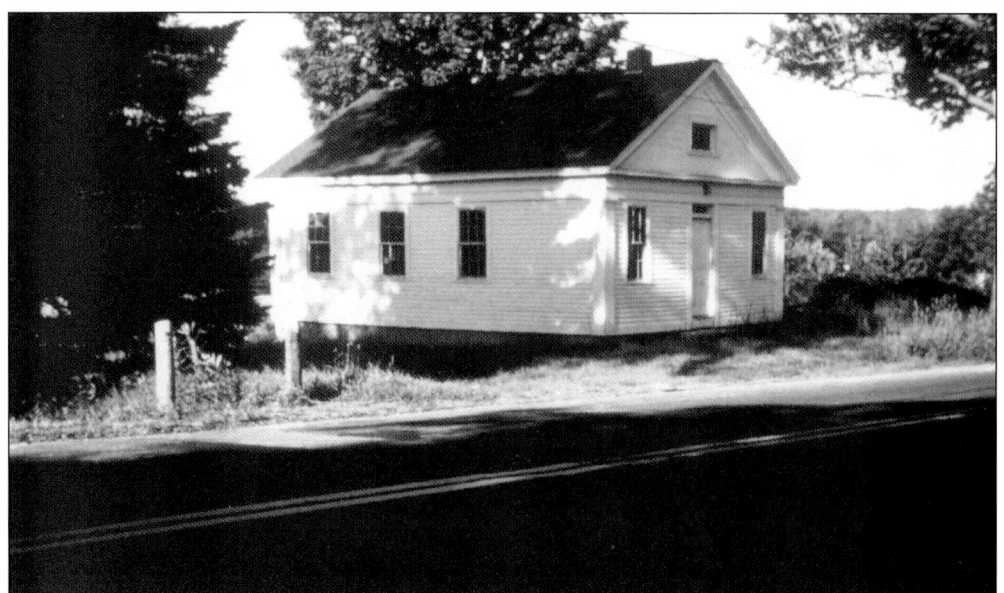

SCHOOL NO. 13. Located on Route 207 across from the intersection with Clubhouse Road, this building is now a private residence. When the schools were consolidated in 1936, a number of the old schoolhouses were sold and converted into dwellings. (Courtesy LHS.)

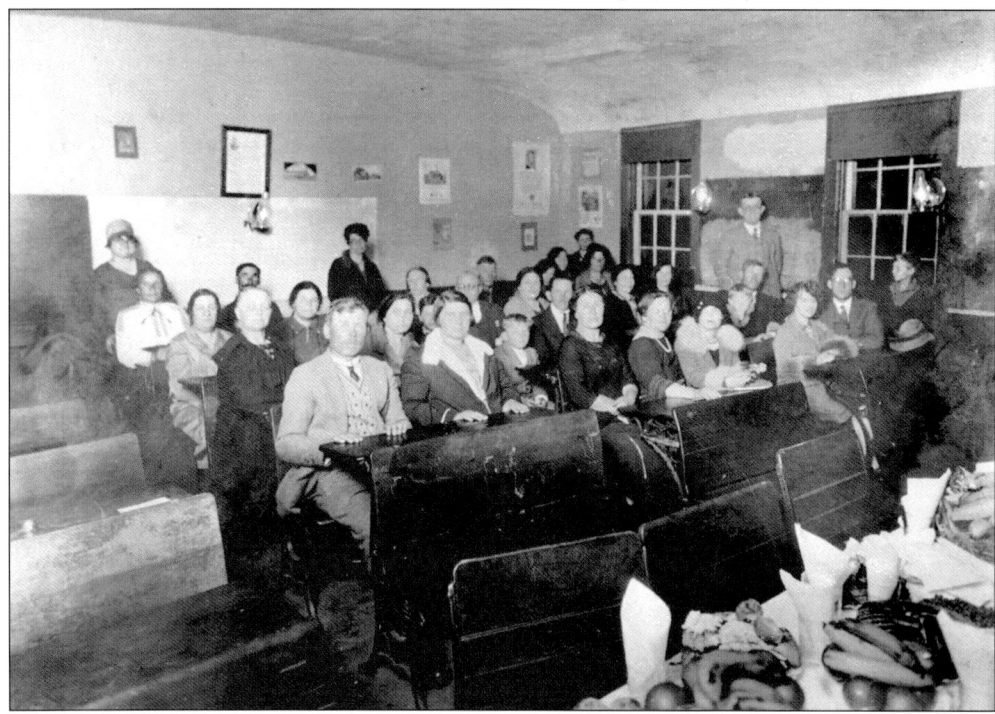

AN ADULT CLASS. In 1928, 22 immigrants who had moved to Lebanon to farm petitioned for a night school, where they could learn more about farming and where those who were foreign-born could study the English language. Many had heavy mortgages and needed to learn modern farming techniques in order to prosper. The adult school was set up in School No. 13 and proved very successful. Here, a night school class graduates, probably in 1929. (Courtesy LHS.)

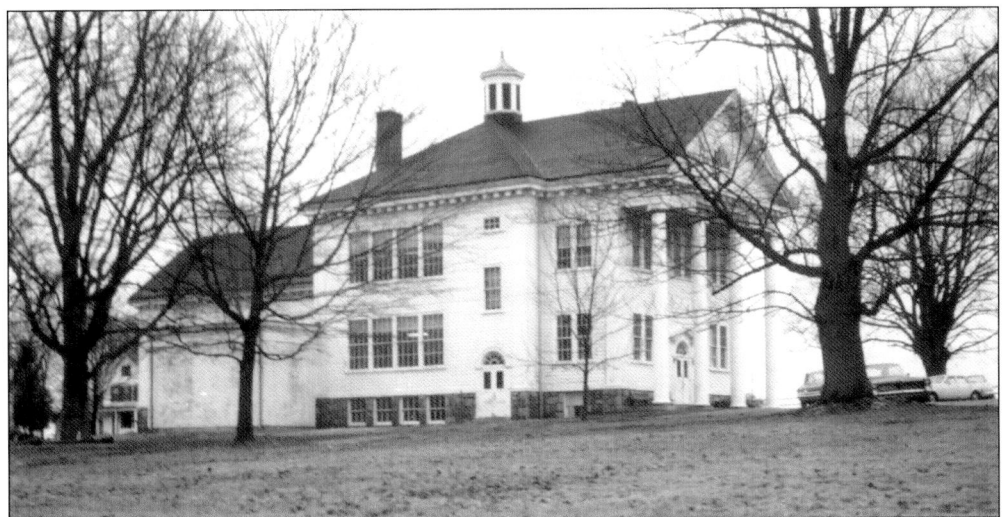

THE FIRST LYMAN MEMORIAL HIGH SCHOOL. In 1920, George W. Lyman left the town a generous bequest toward a high school; town appropriations supplemented those funds. To make room for the school, the old town hall was moved across Route 207 to a site north of the present library. The school opened in September 1922. After a combined junior-senior high school was built in 1958–1959, town offices were eventually moved into this building. (Courtesy LHS.)

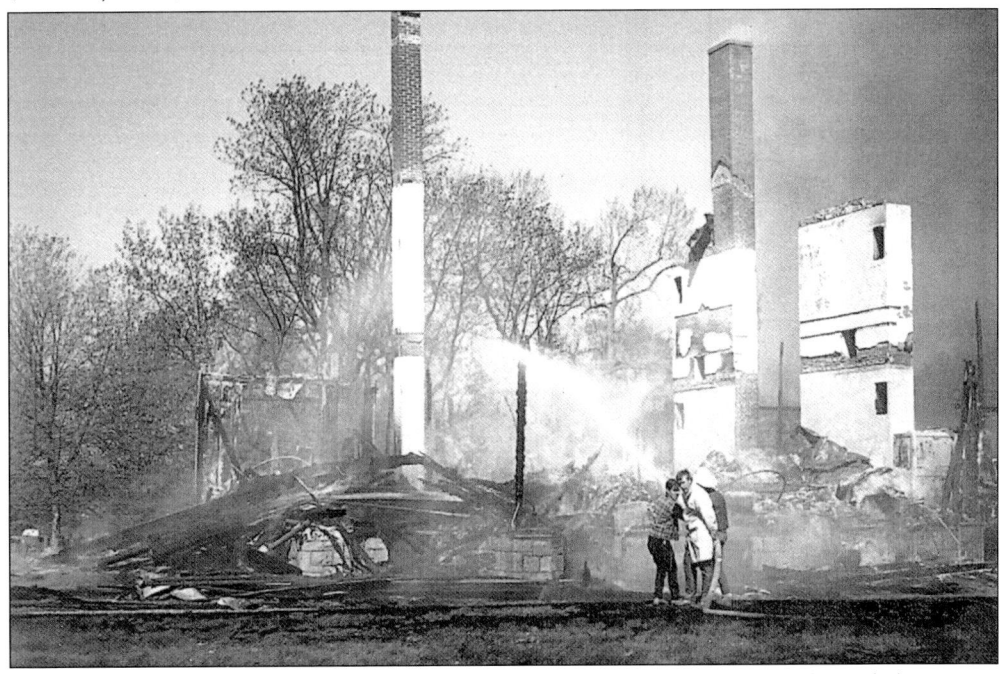

TOWN HALL DESTROYED. For a time, the old high school housed an overflow of elementary school children until a new addition to the elementary school was built. A fire-proof vault was then installed in the high school, and town offices were moved from officials' homes to the high school building. On May 7, 1968, a spectacular fire leveled the structure. Many records were lost, but the town's land records and the town clerk's records were saved, as they were in the vault. (Courtesy LHS.)

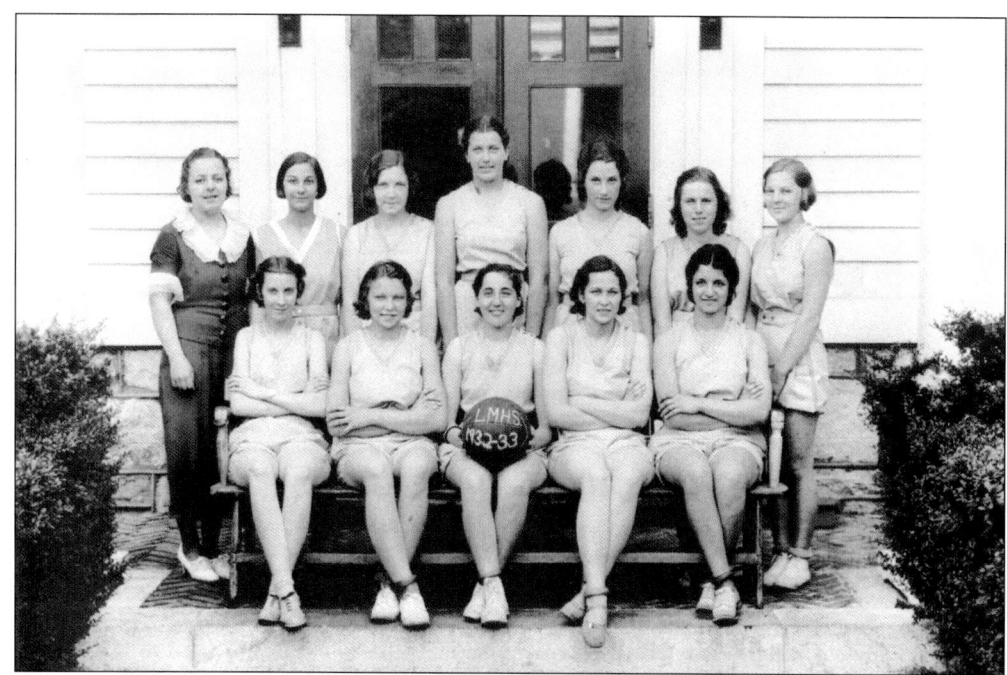

THE FIRST GIRLS' BASKETBALL TEAM. Girls were able to participate in a formerly all-male sport when they organized a basketball team in 1931. Teacher Rima Campo was their coach. Pictured, from left to right, are the following: (first row) Edith (Jones) Burgess, Elsie (Lamonte) Ferry, Hazel (Cummings) Sweet, Fannie Weronik, and Mary (Marasculo) Brewster; (second row) Coach Rima Campo, Delphine Ladd, Phyllis (Hoxie) Bartizek, Olive (Cox) Brown, Rose Cohen, Olga Schweitzer, and Sophia (Horiska) Dziadul. (Courtesy LHS.)

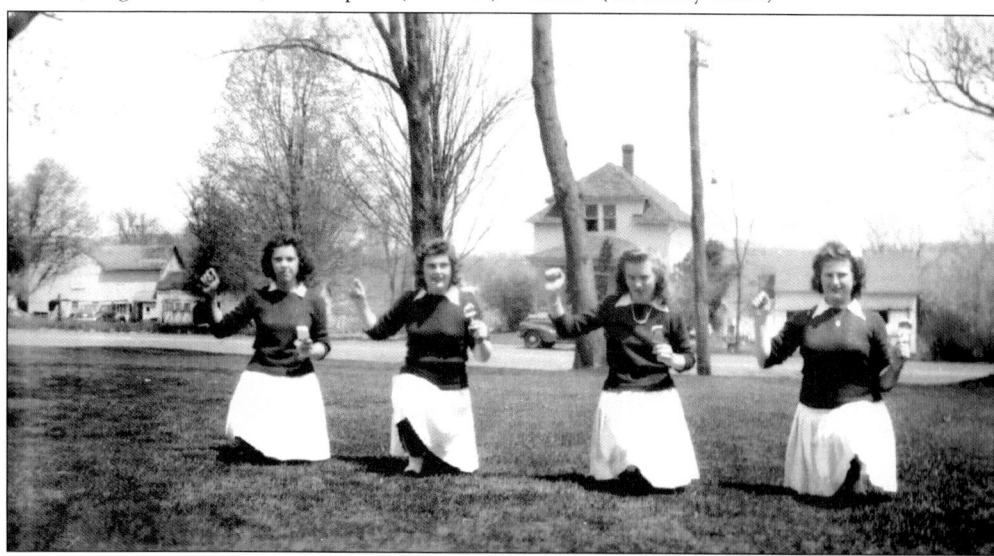

THE FIRST CHEERLEADERS. These four young women were the first cheerleaders at the Lyman Memorial High School. Organized in 1946, the cheerleaders were, from left to right, Burtis Blakeslee, Jonica Grabber, Cynthia Clarke, and Gloria Petrofsky. They wore red sweaters and white skirts. This photograph was taken on the lawn on the east side of the old high school. (Courtesy Gloria Bigenski.)

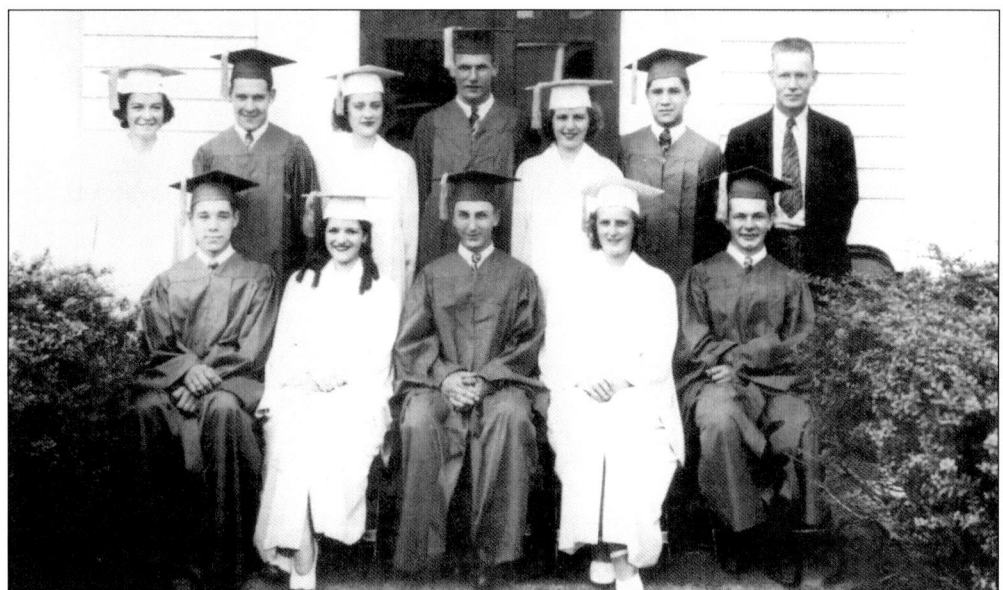

THE SMALLEST GRADUATING CLASS. With only 11 members, the Lyman Memorial High School Class of 1944 was the school's smallest. Pictured, from left to right, are the following: (first row) Wallace Blakeslee Jr., Ethel (Chalifoux) Fontaine, Walter Dziadul, Michaeline Watras, and Lyndon Briggs; (second row) Gladys (Kneeland) Wright, Oliver Manning, Katherine (Kelley) Malone, William Wasylishyn, Helen (Plonowsky) Walsh, Joseph Sanzone, and Principal E. Fenn Nourse. (Courtesy LHS.)

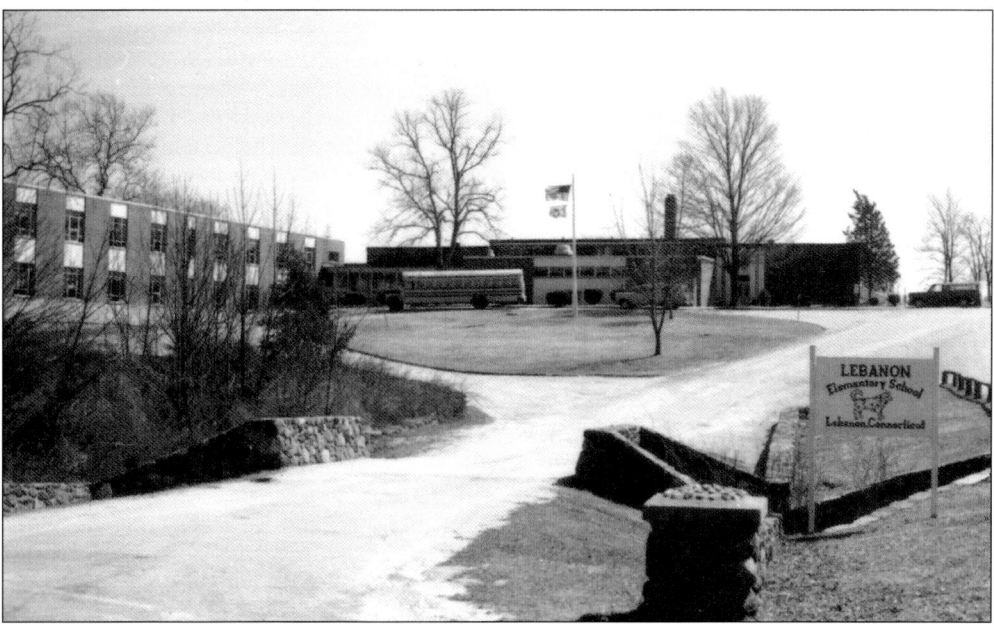

THE LEBANON ELEMENTARY SCHOOL. In 1936, the one-room schools were consolidated into a central elementary school on Route 207 with the aid of a federal grant. A 1937 report noted that the children no longer had to go outside to use toilet facilities or to get water from wells! This 1980s photograph shows some of the additions necessitated by the growing population. Voters approved yet another expansion in February 2004. (Courtesy LHS.)

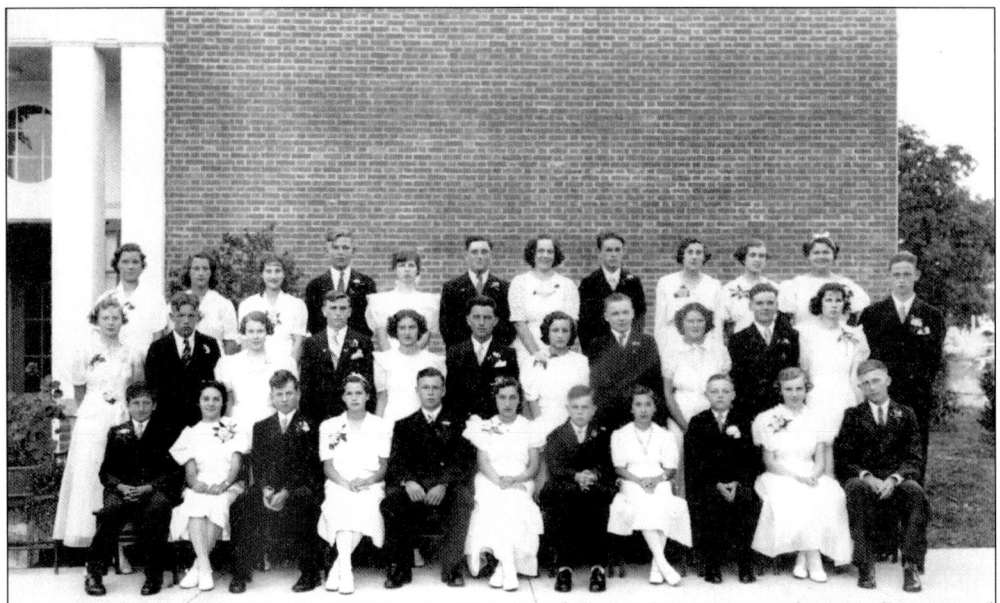

THE FIRST GRADUATES. In June 1937, 34 children graduated from the eighth grade in the new Lebanon Elementary School. The graduates ranged in age from 12 to 16 years—remember, they were coming from the one-room school system, which had a wide variation in grade levels. On the list of occupations for their fathers, all but two are recorded as farmers, an indication of how rural Lebanon was at that time. (Courtesy Harold Krause.)

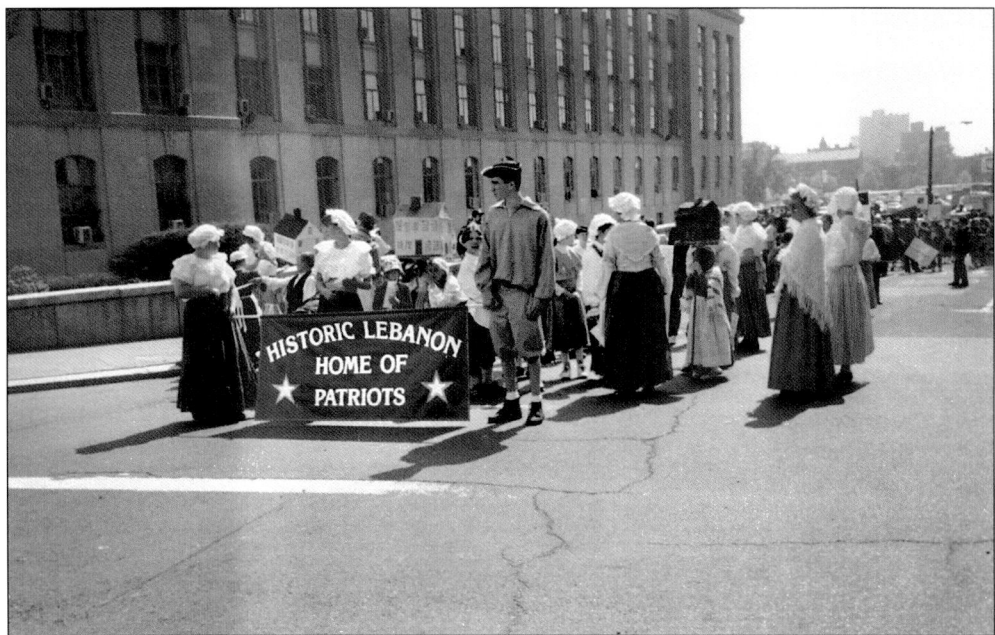

A HARTFORD PARADE. Teachers and students from Lebanon public schools marched in the state parade celebrating the New Old State House on May 11, 1996. The theme was "Historic Lebanon, Home of Patriots." Fourth-graders designed models of five historic buildings to carry. They were backed up by high school band and chorus members as they marched to the song *We're Proud to Come from Lebanon*. (Courtesy LHS.)

Seven

LEBANON IN WORLD WAR II

On December 7, 1941, the Japanese bombed Pearl Harbor. Germany and Italy declared war on the United States on December 11. Our country was at war and quickly mobilized. In Lebanon, a farming town of only 1,467 residents, at least 146 young men and women served in the armed forces. They served on land and sea and in the air, from Europe to Africa to the Pacific Islands and China. Seven lost their lives. Many were wounded or missing in action until located in prisoner-of-war camps.

Those who remained at home served the war effort in other ways. Many residents held defense jobs, labored to increase farm output without extra hands, and volunteered as air-raid wardens and aircraft spotters.

To tell their story, Ed Tollmann planned a small exhibit of his World War II memorabilia with the Lebanon Historical Society. The idea grew, as families and veterans added enough material to fill an entire exhibition room.

The exhibit, From Home Front to Battlefield: Lebanon in World War II, opened after the town's annual Memorial Day parade in 2001. Originally scheduled to be open for a year, the exhibit was not closed until December 7, 2003. It touched the hearts of all who saw it. The walls were covered with photographs of young Lebanon soldiers, fresh-faced in their uniforms. Their going-away parties, wartime weddings, and visits home were all chronicled. Their medals, Purple Hearts, Bronze Stars—even their old uniforms—were there. The flag presented to the family of Anthony Musial, who lost his life, was there. So was the bullet-holed helmet worn by Ewald Wilhelm when he was wounded in Italy

The home-front story was told, too. Ration books, civil defense identification cards, photographs, faded newspaper clippings, and artifacts such as a "victory" bike were found. Most touching were the letters from loved ones in the service.

All these things had been put away and saved for over 50 years. The story of how the war affected all of Lebanon was there.

This chapter provides an overview of the World War II exhibit. It also highlights how Lebanon has remembered and paid tribute to all her veterans over the years.

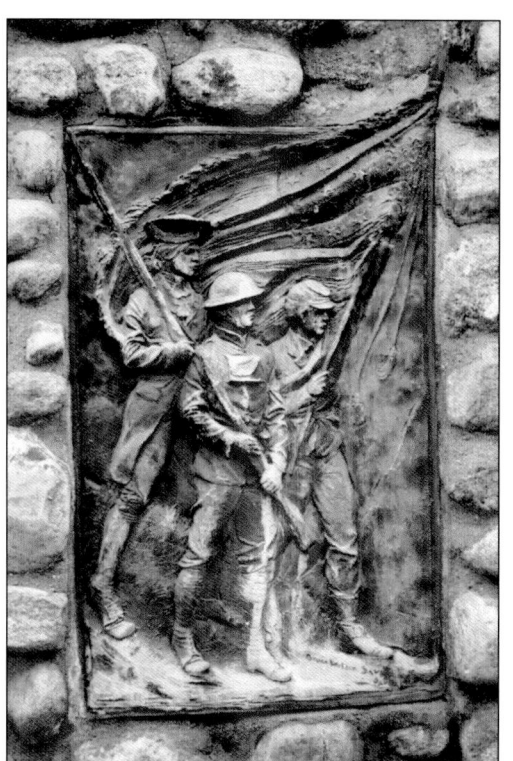

THE FLAGPOLE MONUMENT. The flagpole in front of town hall was erected in 1923 and was the first war memorial in town. On a bronze plaque is a composite of three soldiers, each one representing a different war: the American Revolution, the Civil War, and World War I. The plaque was created by Bruce Wilder Saville, a famous sculptor of that period. The monument symbolizes Lebanon's honor and respect for those who had served up to that time. (Courtesy LHS.)

THE EXHIBITION OPENS. All Lebanon veterans and their families were invited to a special reception and preview before the public opening of the exhibition From Home Front to Battlefield: Lebanon in World War II. Members of American Legion Post 180 of Lebanon were the color guard. The cover of the program featured a photograph of Arthur Stebner during World War II. Stebner was a past commander of the post. (Courtesy LHS.)

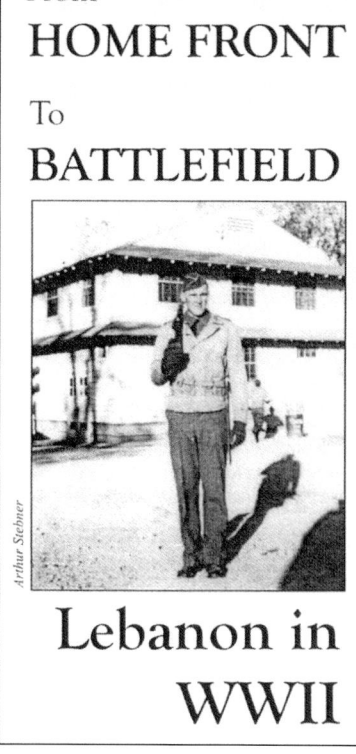

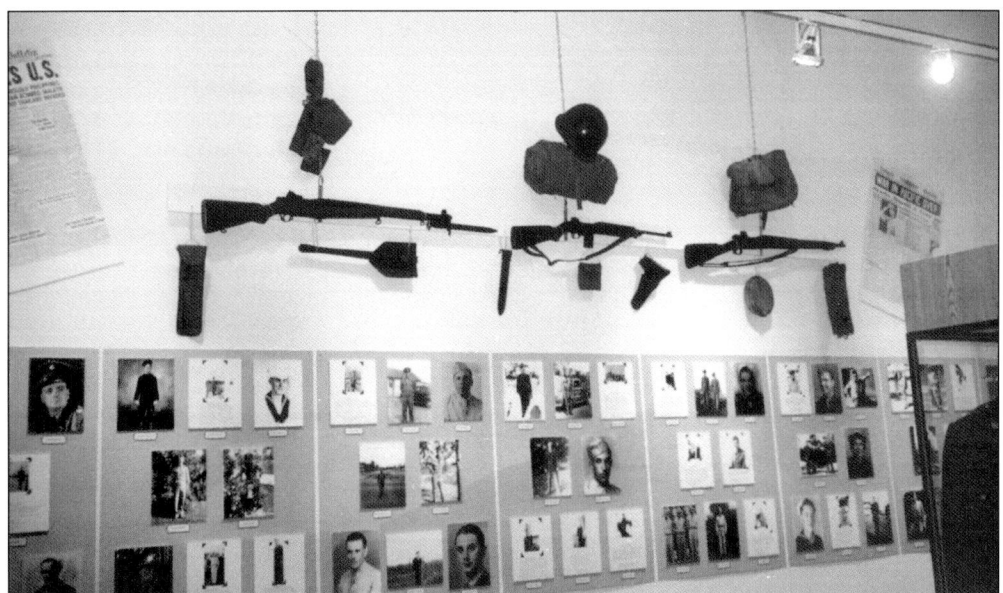

THE WALL OF HONOR. Photographs of young Lebanon servicemen and servicewomen in uniform lined one wall of the exhibition. Of the more than 146 people who served, 77 left wartime photographs that were located. Above the photographs were some of the many artifacts collected. The front pages of local newspapers featuring war news were enlarged and added to the wall display. (Courtesy LHS.)

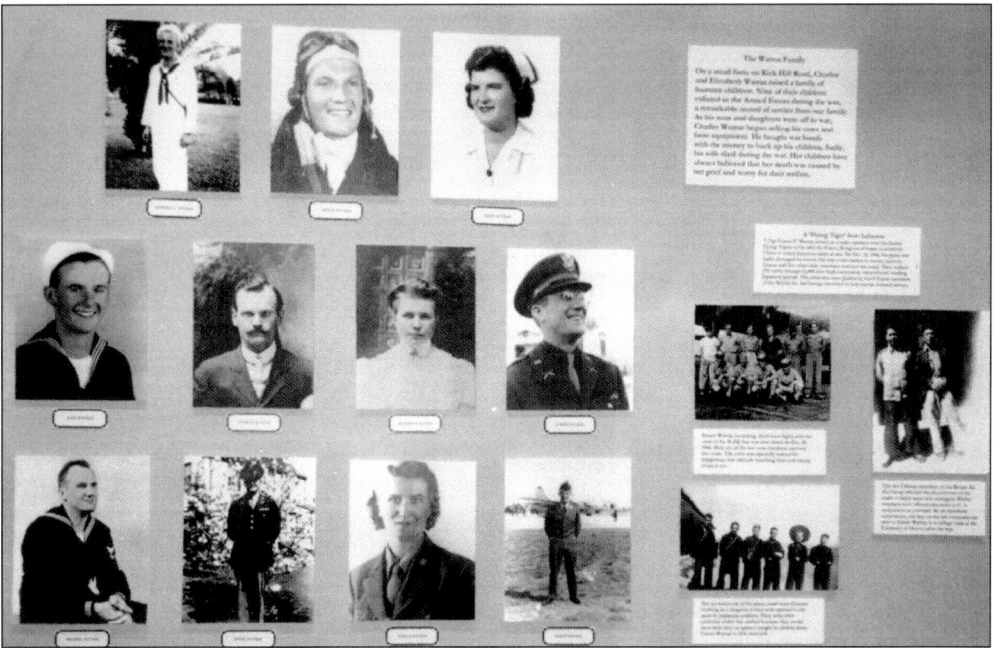

THE WATRAS FAMILY. On a small farm on Kick Hill Road, Charles and Elizabeth Watras raised a family of 14 children. Nine of their children—Edward, Ernest, Helen, John, Joseph, Michael, Peter, Stella, and Henry—enlisted in the armed forces during World War II, a remarkable record of service from one family. Photographs of Charles and Elizabeth, in the center, are surrounded by those of their uniformed children. (Courtesy LHS,)

101

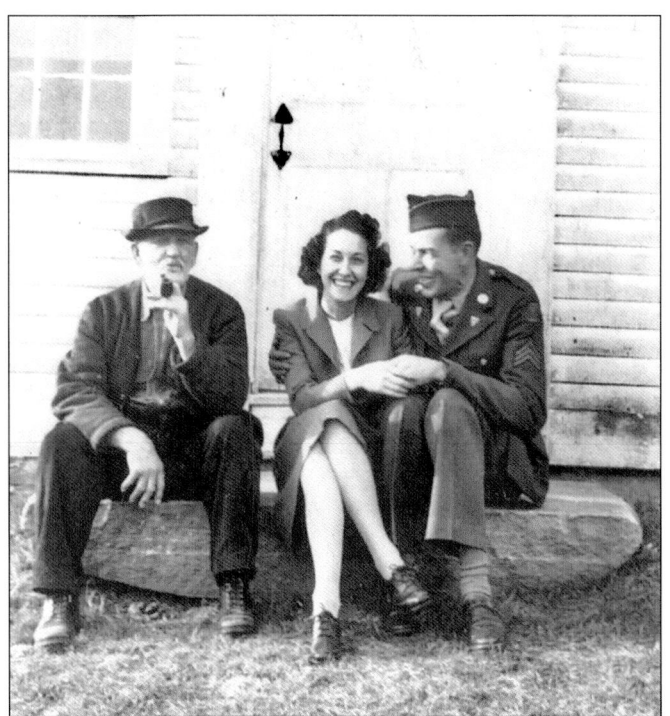

HOME ON LEAVE. Alton and Susie Slate pose for a picture with Alton's grandfather Albert Kingsley while Alton is home on leave. The photographs on this page and the following page are only four of dozens in the exhibit that reveal touching reunions of families and their soldier sons and daughters. (Courtesy Robert Slate.)

A WARTIME WEDDING. Edmund Szczurek married his sweetheart, Claire Lacouture, in one of several wartime weddings of Lebanon soldiers. Claire's mother, Rose, stands beside the bride. (Courtesy Edmund Szczurek.)

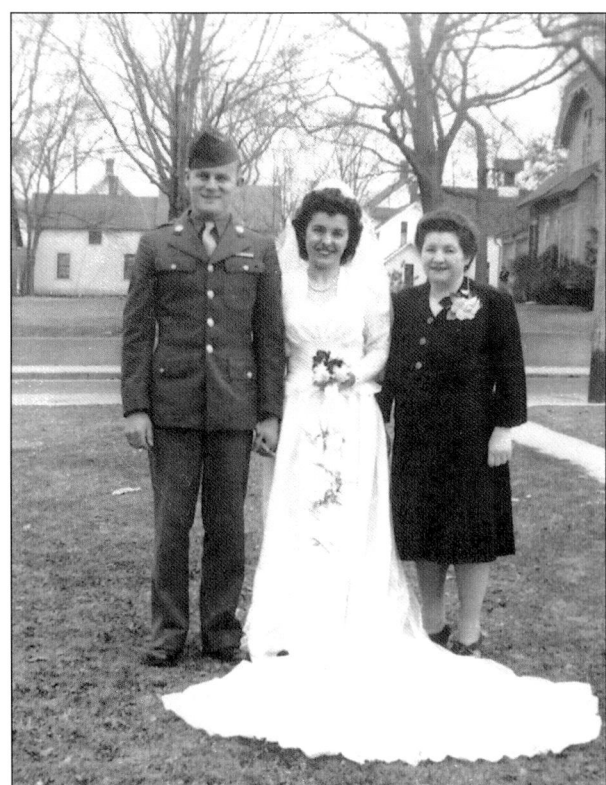

102

A Family Portrait. Albert and Phyllis (Hoxie) Bartizek had this portrait taken with their infant son Brian because Albert knew he would be shipped out to the Pacific when he returned to his base. (Courtesy Phyllis Bartizek.)

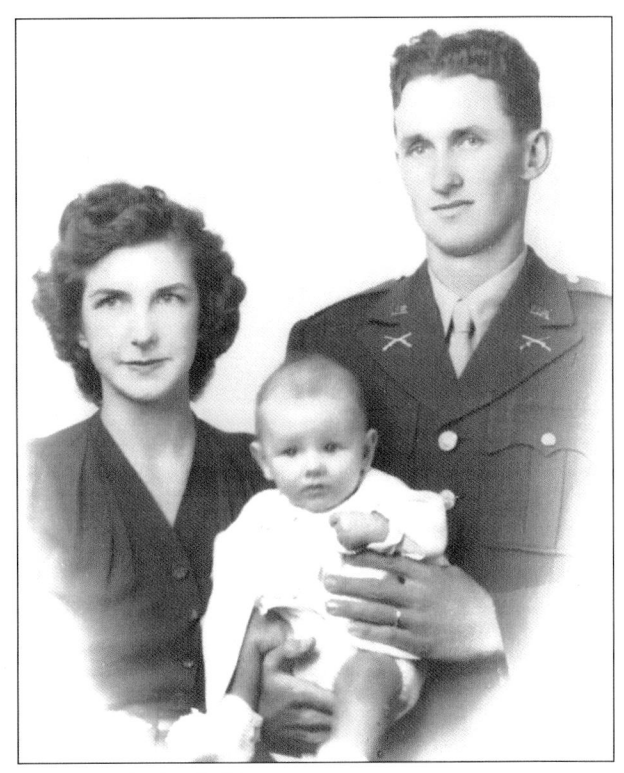

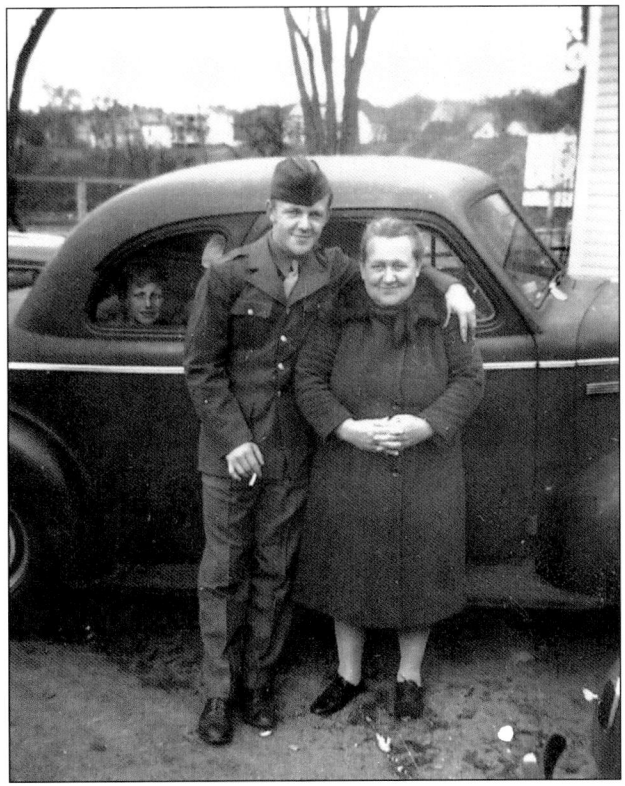

A Tender Goodbye. In this photograph, Harry Flegert hugs his mother, Lydia Flegert Ausburger, as he prepares to return to his base. (Courtesy Helen Krause.)

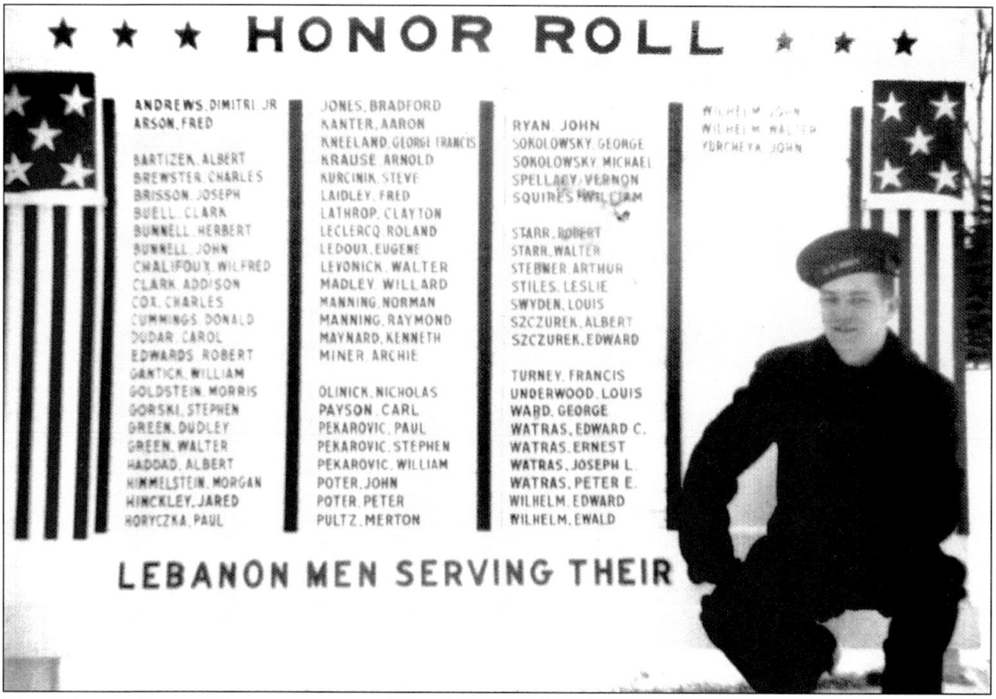

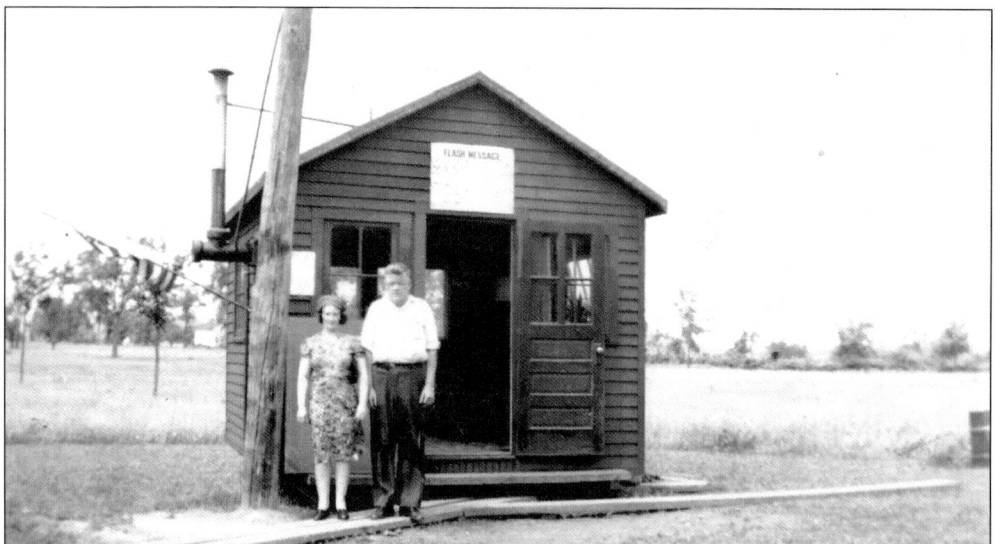

THE HONOR ROLL. The town erected this honor roll in front of the old town hall on the upper green in September 1942. Only the names of the soldiers from the first draft are listed. The names of all the soldiers who served are listed on the monument erected after the war, at the east end of the driveway into town hall. The young sailor is Wilfred Chalifoux. (Courtesy Helen Krause.)

A PLANE SPOTTER'S CABIN. A civilian plane-spotting post was set up on the town green opposite the War Office. The post was built by volunteers from timber salvaged from an old mill in Willimantic. The chimney pipe vented a small stove used in cold weather. Civilian defense volunteers manned the post 24 hours a day. Mr. and Mrs. William Congdon manned the post on Sundays from 12 noon to 2 p.m. (Courtesy LHS.)

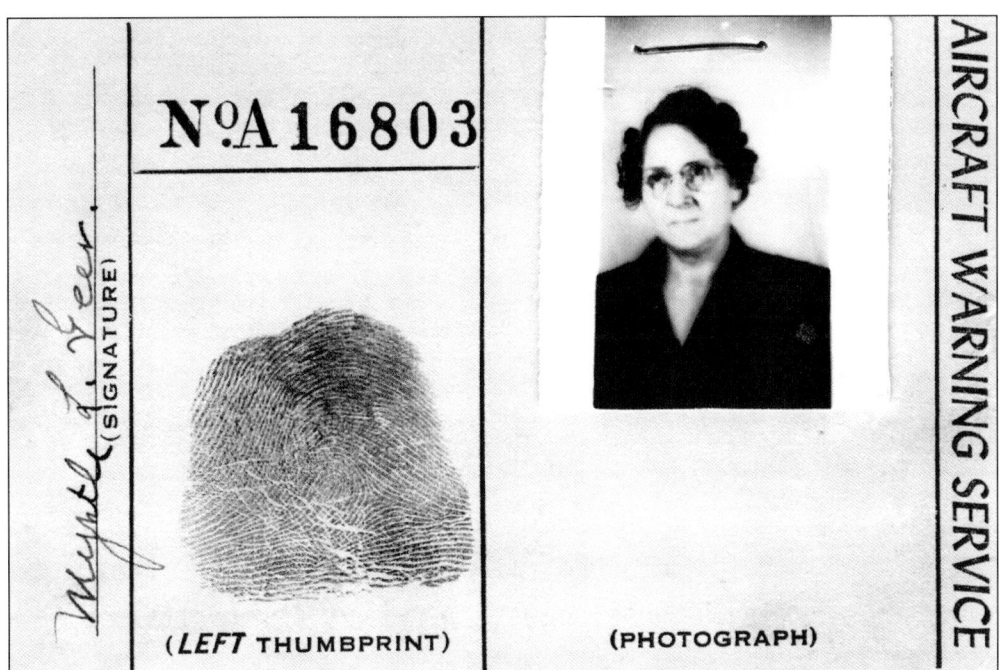

AN IDENTIFICATION CARD. The Lebanon post was one of an elaborate system of civilian plane-spotting stations organized along the Atlantic seaboard. Nearly 300 Lebanon residents volunteered to be spotters. They were issued official identification cards by the Aircraft Warning Service, which was part of the Army Air Forces. The photographs were taken by members of a high school camera club. The pictured card was issued to Myrtle L. Geer. (Courtesy Harold Geer.)

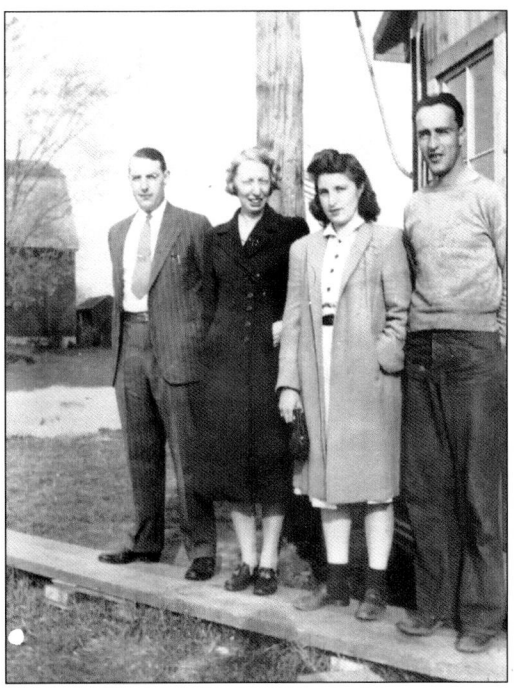

WORKING IN SHIFTS. The aircraft spotter's post had to be manned 24 hours a day, seven days a week. The town was divided into seven sections. Each section was assigned one day of the week to cover. Shifts were limited to two hours so as not to be a burden. On Mondays, Mr. and Mrs. Jared Hinckley (left) served from 6 to 8 a.m., followed by Mr. and Mrs. Karl Phillips (right) from 8 to 10 a.m. (Courtesy LHS.)

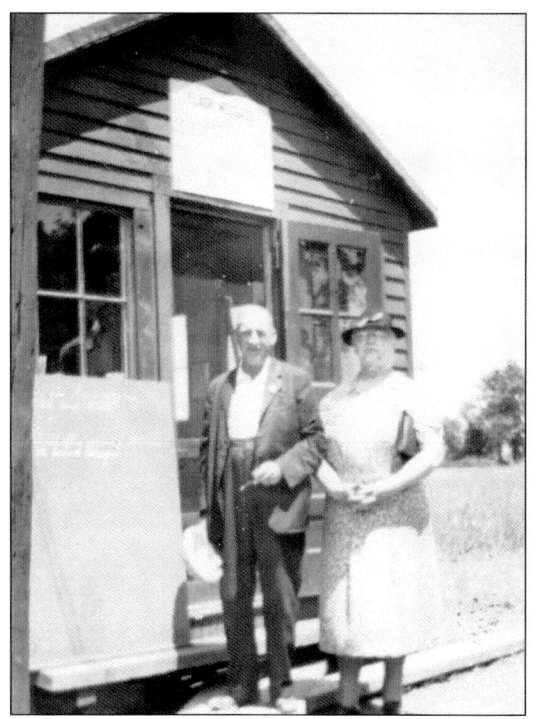

THE SATURDAY SHIFT. On Saturdays, William Connor and Sarah Abell showed up early at 6 a.m. Sarah Abell, Lebanon's town clerk at the time, was first elected in 1930 and served 35 years in that post until her retirement in 1965. Her father, Charles J. Abell, held the office from 1892 until his death in 1930. Sarah Abell had served as his assistant from 1918 until her own election in 1930. (Courtesy LHS.)

CHANGING SHIFTS. Mr. and Mrs. Vernon Boothby (left) change shifts with John and Helen Musial (right). Spotters were trained to identify the different types of aircraft. They listened for the sounds of planes, and when one flew near, they identified it and called in its location. In October 1943, as the threat of attacks decreased, plane spotting was reduced to an alert status. The service was officially terminated in May 1944. (Courtesy LHS.)

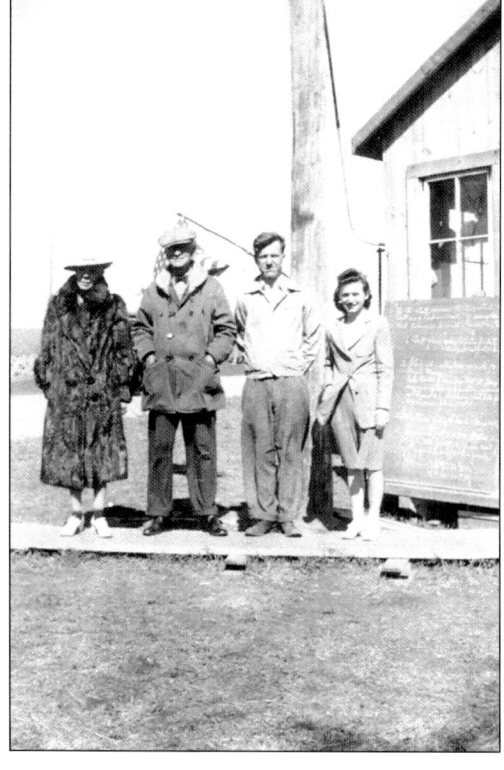

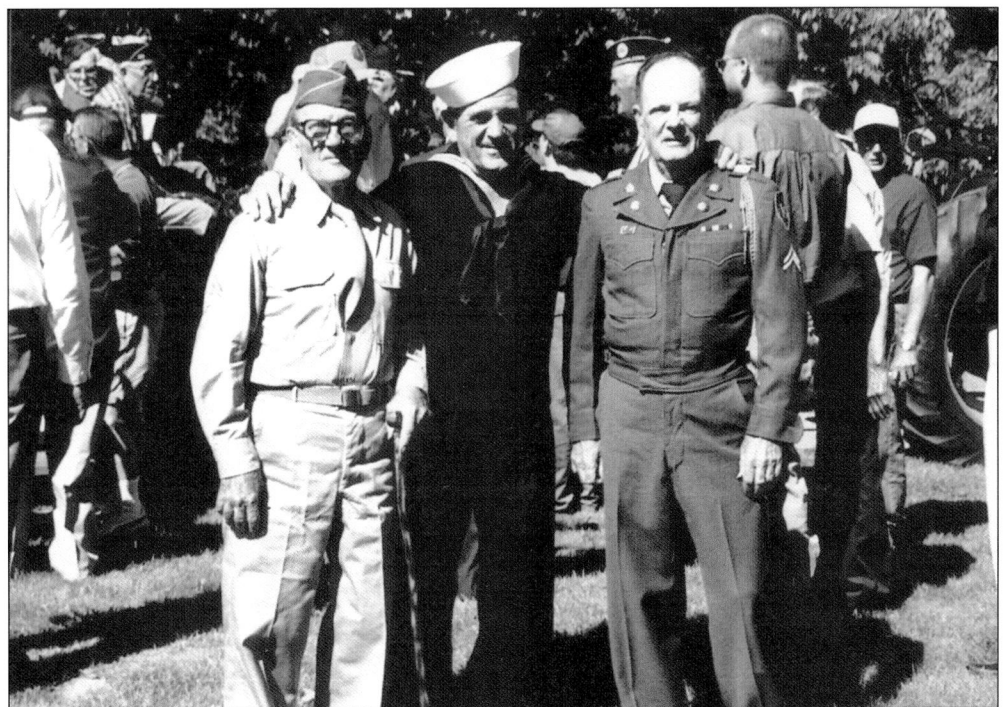

AT THE PARADE. Veterans attending the 2000 Memorial Day parade included, from left to right, brothers Joseph, Ernest, and Eugene Brisson. Many Lebanon families had two or three sons and daughters in the service at the same time during World War II. (Courtesy LHS.)

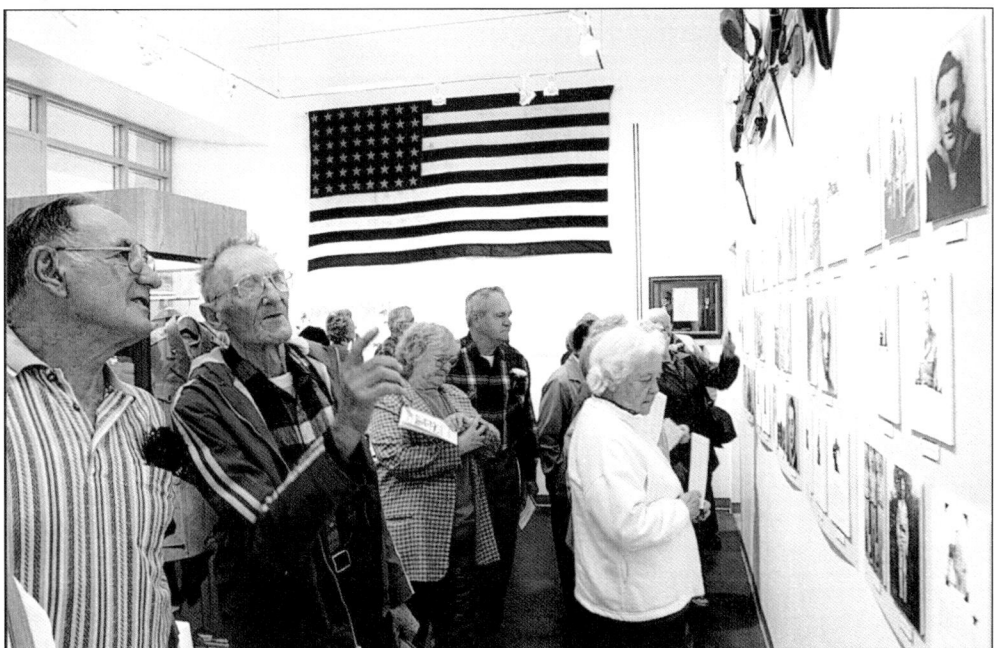

AT THE EXHIBITION. The World War II exhibit opened May 25, 2001, at the Lebanon Historical Society Museum. Locating their photographs on the Wall of Honor are brothers Stephen (left) and Nicholas Olenick. (Courtesy of the *Chronicle*, Willimantic, CT.)

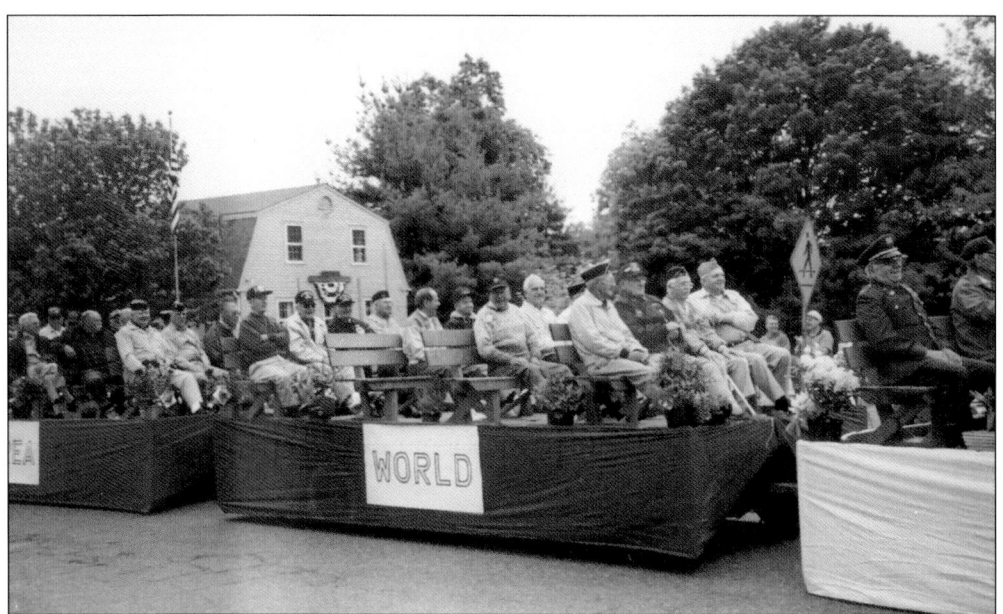

HONORING VETERANS. Charles Bender, remembering how veterans of World War I were honored when he was a boy, was determined to do something for veterans of World War II and other conflicts. Since older veterans were not able to march the length of the parade route, he provided decorated wagons for the 2000 Memorial Day parade. The wagons are now provided each year. (Courtesy LHS.)

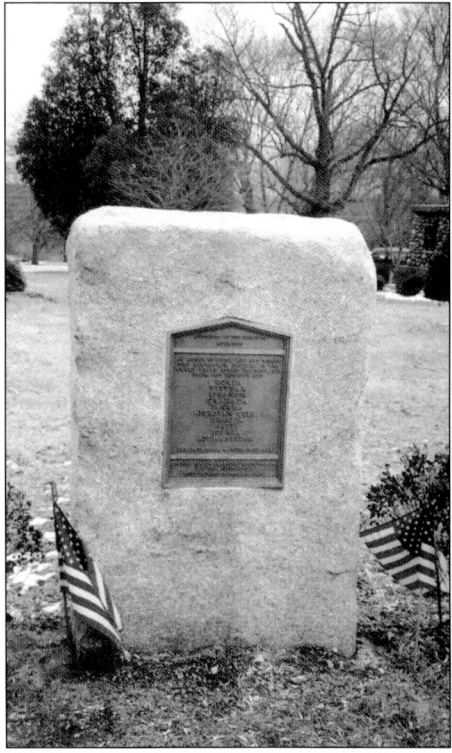

LEBANON REMEMBERS. On November 11, 2002, American Legion Post 180 dedicated a new war memorial at its headquarters to honor veterans of other conflicts since World War II, from 1946 through 2002: Korea, Vietnam, Lebanon, Granada, Panama, the Persian Gulf, Somalia, Haiti, Bosnia, and Afghanistan. It was moved to the town green in May 2003. The monument is made from the same stone as the base of the Statue of Liberty. (Courtesy LHS.)

Eight

LEBANON THEN AND NOW

Throughout more than 300 years of town history, thousands of families have lived in Lebanon. Some were here for a brief period; others stayed for many generations. Descendants of several families who settled the town in the 1690s still call Lebanon their home. No matter how recent or long ago their arrival, all of these families had an effect on the town. Their stories are the main fabric of our community.

In a sense, all of them were immigrants. The Clarke, Lyman, and Dewey families came to the frontier town of Lebanon from Massachusetts towns, primarily in the Northampton area; the Brewsters and Huntingtons arrived from Norwich, the Trumbulls from Simsbury. These are just a few of the more familiar names of those arriving in the early settlement period.

Over the years, other immigrant groups have arrived. Many took up the farms abandoned by Yankee settlers who were moving on to farmland in the upper New England states and the Midwest or to the cities to take urban jobs. Lebanon's population declined significantly in the 19th century. The first United States census, in 1790, showed a high of 4,166 people. It would not reach this figure again until 1980! In the early 20th century, the population averaged about 1,400 people. Only the arrival of new immigrants helped to sustain the town.

An influx of Rhode Islanders, leaving the poorer, sandy soils of that state, helped stem the population loss in the 19th century. These Rhode Island families—the Chappell, Tucker, Peckham, Browning, Briggs, Champlin, Nye, Larkin, and Sherman families, and many others—still have descendants in town.

Lebanon's closest brush with the Industrial Revolution came from the Hayward Rubber Company and two paper mills on the Yantic River. The rubber company, established in Colchester in 1847, opened a satellite mill in Lebanon in 1850 to process raw rubber. Large numbers of Irish immigrants, escaping the famine in their homeland, came to Colchester and Lebanon to work at the Hayward plants. There were about 200 Irish families in Lebanon alone by 1860. Some of the Irish worked on farms, but most worked at the rubber company.

When the rubber company closed in 1886, many of the Irish stayed on to work in the two paper mills on the Yantic. Both paper mills burned—the Browning Mill in 1893 and the Yantic River Paper Mill in 1913. Large numbers of Irish settlers left to find jobs in the cities. But the legacy of these immigrants remains in the first Catholic mission church established in Lebanon and in the family names—such as Lynch, Murphy, Dixon, Clifford, Duffy, McGrath, and O'Sullivan (now Sullivan)— that are an important part of town history.

The first Jewish immigrant arrived in 1890. As the 20th century dawned, many Jewish immigrants from Eastern Europe settled in the Goshen and Exeter areas, turning their poor land into thriving dairy and poultry farms.

A group of German immigrants from the Ukrainian village of Karlswalde settled as a close-knit community in the Village Hill area beginning in 1911. They built up the old farms into highly productive dairy farms.

Many Slavic people also found their way to Lebanon from 1900 to World War I. Coming from Czechoslovakia, Austria-Hungary, Poland, and part of Ukraine, they, too, bought old farms, but theirs were in scattered locations around town. After World War II, they were joined by a second group of Slavic immigrants.

During the 1950s, improved roads and the growth of jobs in surrounding towns made Lebanon attractive to different immigrants: city dwellers attracted by the rural landscape. The last interim census showed the population approaching 7,000.

Once everyone farmed. Now 90 percent of the population commutes out of town to work. In response to this shift, the town has developed a diversity of volunteer organizations to meet the needs and interests of both children and adults. Hundreds of residents give countless hours to the town commissions and boards and to numerous community and religious organizations. They provide the same connection to their community that the Grange and the Farm Bureau still nourish in their members.

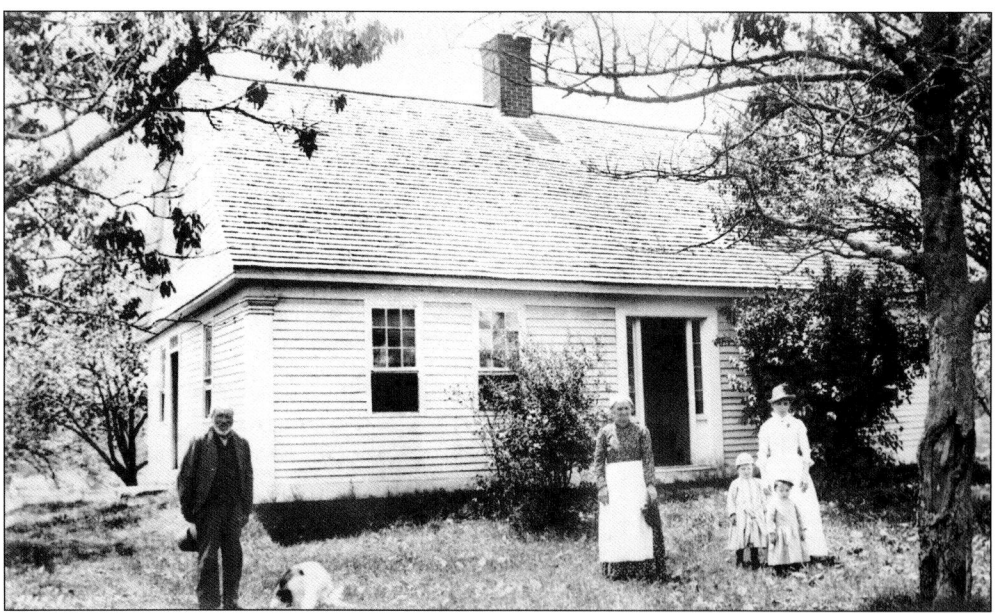

THE LYMAN HOUSE. Built in the very early 1700s, this house at 595 Trumbull Highway belonged to the Lyman family. Richard Lyman was a proprietor of the Five Mile Purchase. Shown c. 1890 are Thomas Lyman (left), his wife Harriet (center), and their daughter Mary Jane Lyman Kingsley (right). Mary Jane's daughters, Mary Matilda Kingsley (left) and Minnie Morgan Kingsley, stand in front of her. Mary Matilda Kingsley was Alton Slate's mother. The Jon Slate family now lives in the house, continuing the family tradition. (Courtesy Robert Slate.)

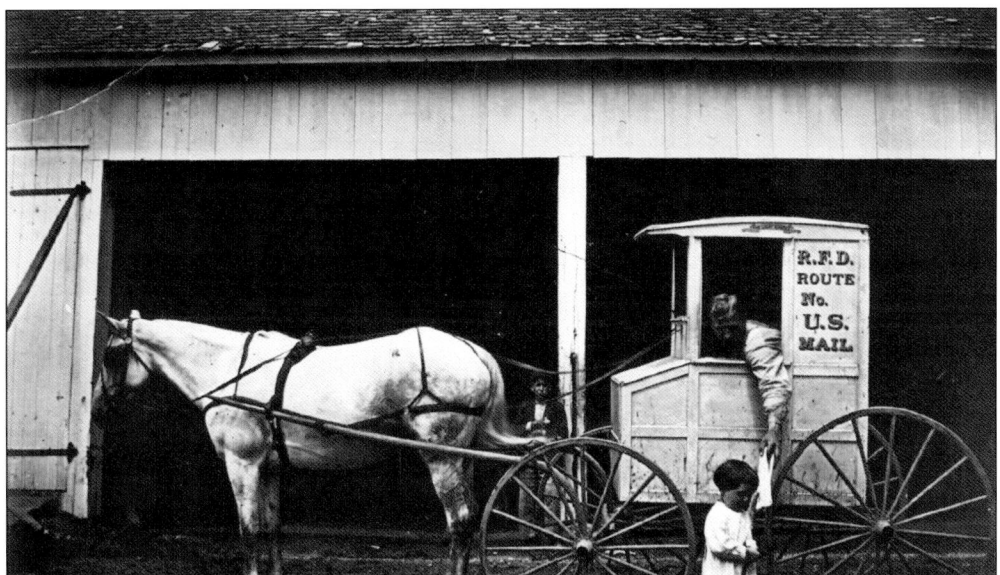

THE MAIL SERVICE. Rural free delivery was established in Lebanon in 1901, bringing mail service to outlying farms and homes. Burnette Cummings, one of the first carriers, is pictured here in the early 1900s. Even after automobiles became available, carriers had to use horses when the dirt roads turned to mud in the spring. (Courtesy Arlene McCaw.)

GOING FOR A RIDE. Three of the Cummings brothers—Leo, Carlton, and Rexford, shown from left to right—sit in a carriage at an unidentified farm sometime in the 1880s. They were three of nine children, only one of whom was a girl. Of the eight brothers, Carlton, known as "Chappie," and Rexford also became mail carriers like their brother Burnette. Rexford was a carrier for more than 30 years. (Courtesy LHS.)

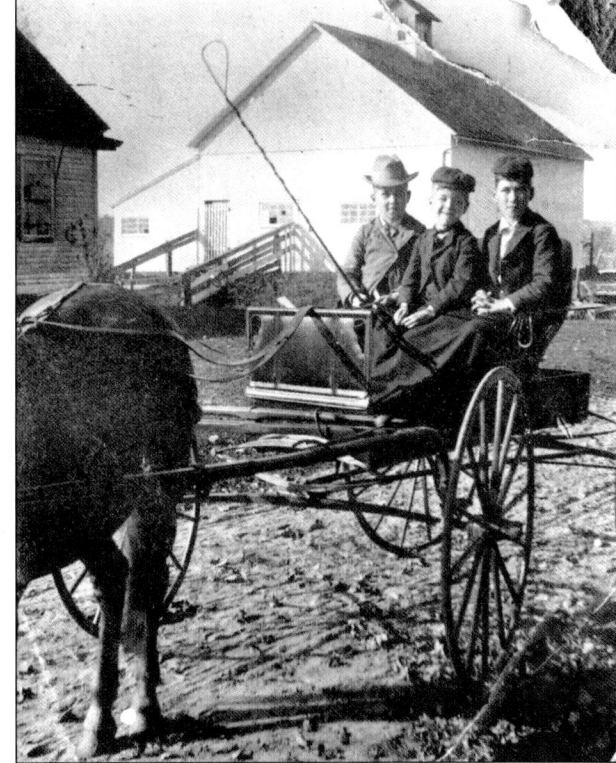

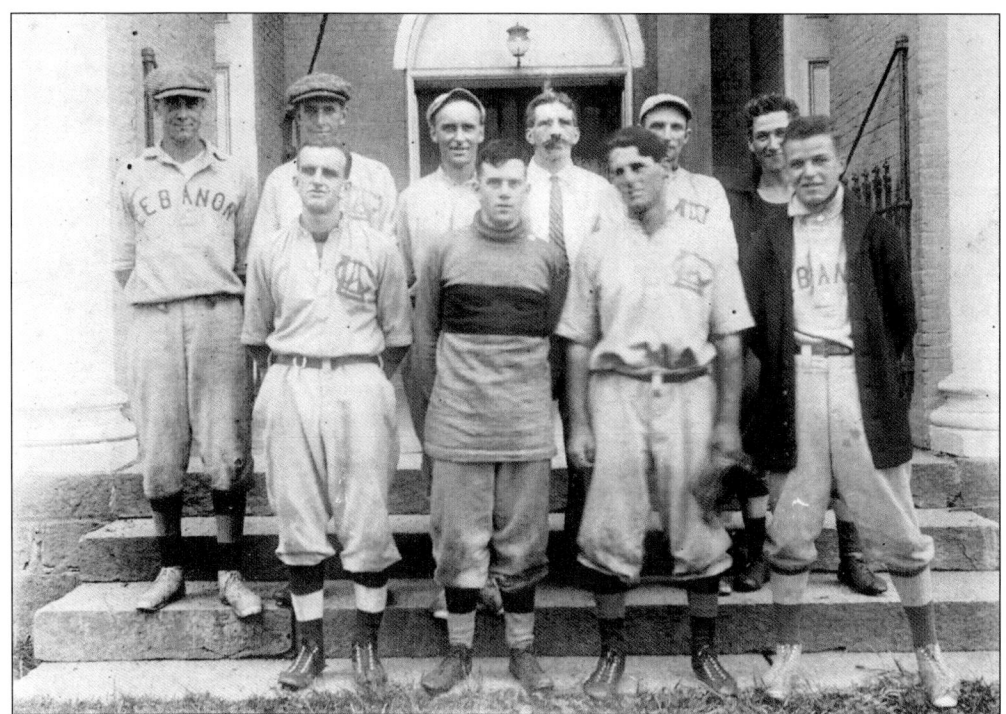

TEAMMATES. Baseball was a popular sport in Lebanon in the early 20th century. These young men, several of whom wear "Lebanon" shirts, were part of an inter-town league with intense rivalries. Appearing in this 1915 photograph, from left to right, are the following: (first row) Monroe Pultz, Harold Mason, Chauncey Williams, and Dick Brown; (second row) Elmer Geer, Myron Hoxie, Norman Pultz, Otto Pultz, Ed Jones, and Rex Cummings. (Courtesy Harold Geer.)

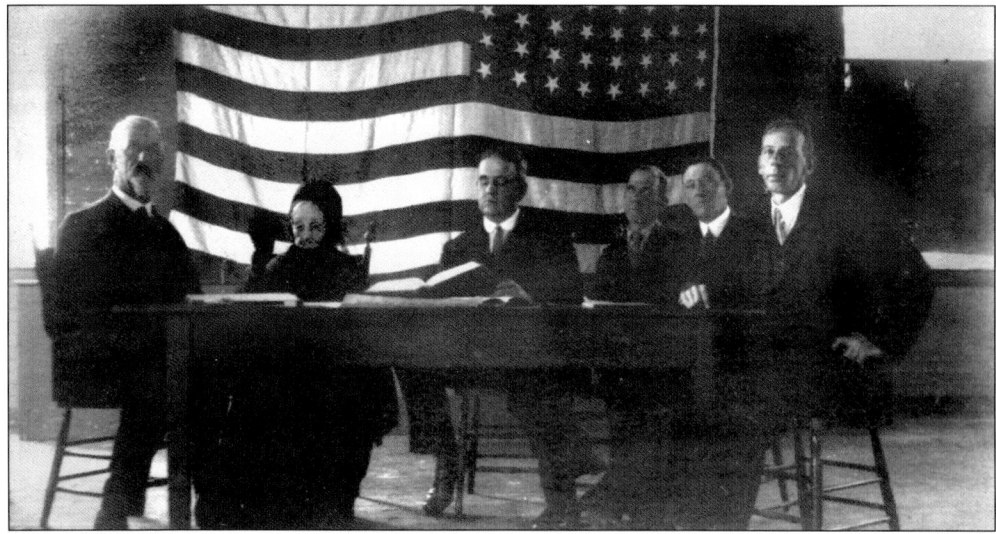

WOMEN GET THE VOTE. Elizabeth Clark Perry Lillie, aged 99 and three-quarters, was one of the first Lebanon women to register to vote in 1920. With her are, from left to right, Charles J. Abell, town clerk; Karl F. Bishop, first selectman; James Randall and Fred N. Taylor, registrars; and William B. Clark, selectman. Sadly, Lillie died just before she was to cast her first ballot. (Courtesy LHS.)

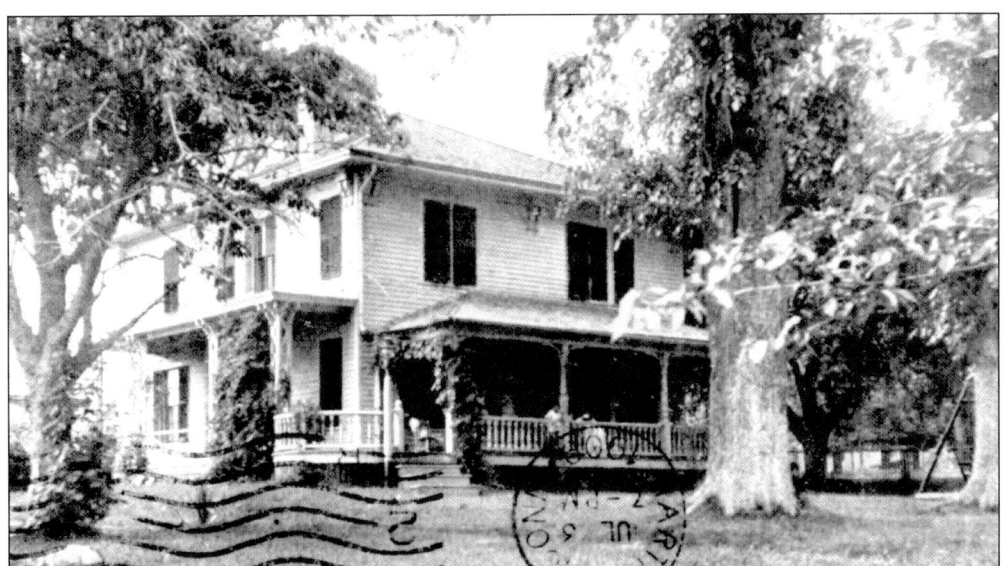

THE DR. DANIELSON HOUSE. Jesse Wright built this house at 927 Trumbull Highway c. 1860. His son Arthur Wright earned the first Ph.D. in science awarded in America. He was a pioneer researcher in physics and astronomy at Yale University. The Wright Nuclear Structure Laboratory at Yale is named for him. Dr. Edwin L. Danielson opened a medical office in the house in 1887 and practiced here until his death in 1918. (Courtesy LHS.)

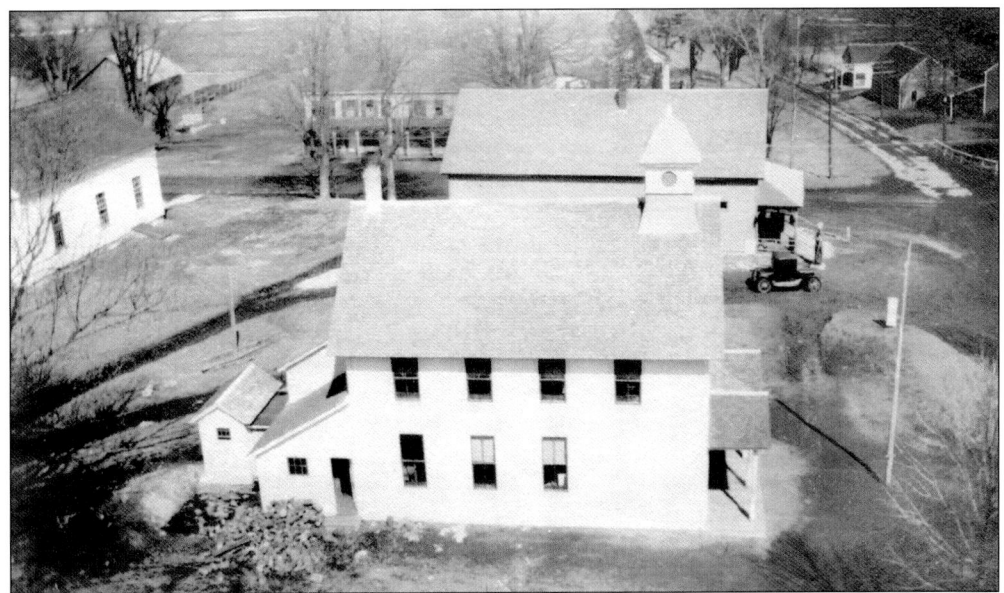

A BIRD'S-EYE VIEW OF THE TOWN CENTER. This photograph was taken from the steeple of the First Congregational Church in the 1920s. The Center School and the general store are in front. The library is now located on this corner. To the left is the old town hall. Across the street is the old boardinghouse, now the community center. The site of the present American Legion hall was occupied by a restaurant. (Courtesy Russell Blakeslee.)

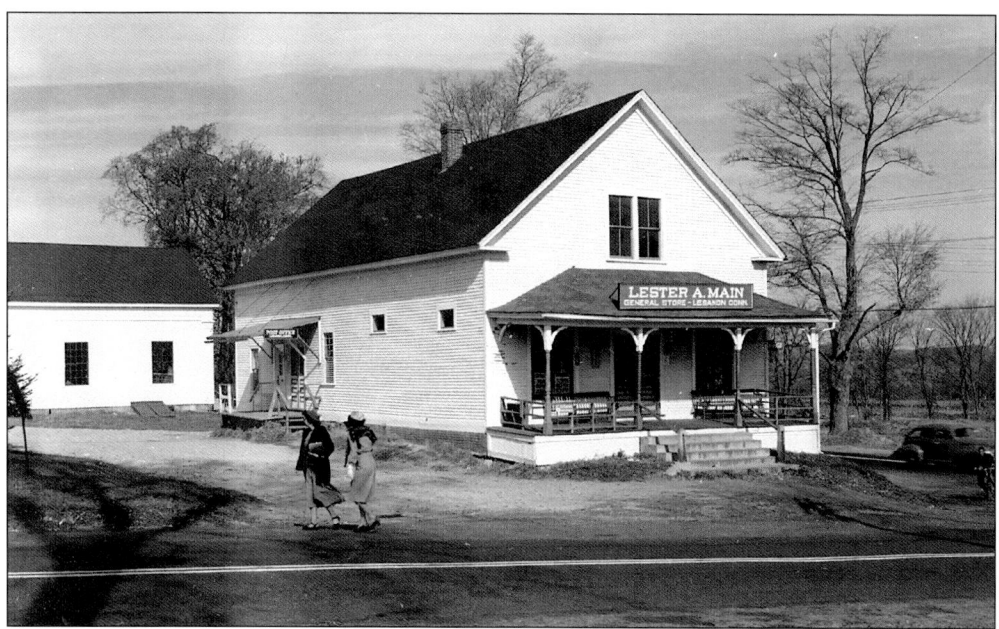

MAIN'S STORE IN THE 1950s. Lester A. Main operated this general store from 1929 until he retired in the 1960s. The town purchased the store and lot from the next owner in 1966 and razed the building to construct the new library building. Main sold everything from meat to work boots, and there were gasoline pumps on the highway side. The post office operated from the back of the store. (Courtesy Ed Tollmann.)

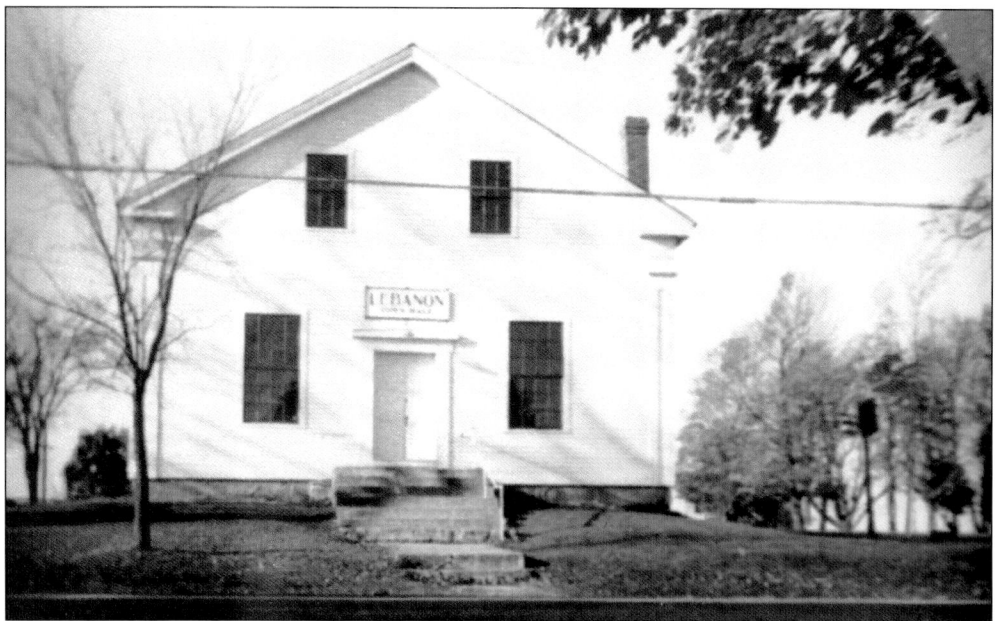

THE OLD TOWN HALL IN THE 1950s. Lebanon's first town hall was built in 1848 on the green, where the present town hall stands. In 1921, when the town decided to build its first high school on the site, the town hall was moved to the northern green, behind the store. The building was dismantled in 1968, and some of the lumber was used to panel a room in the community center. (Courtesy Ed Tollmann.)

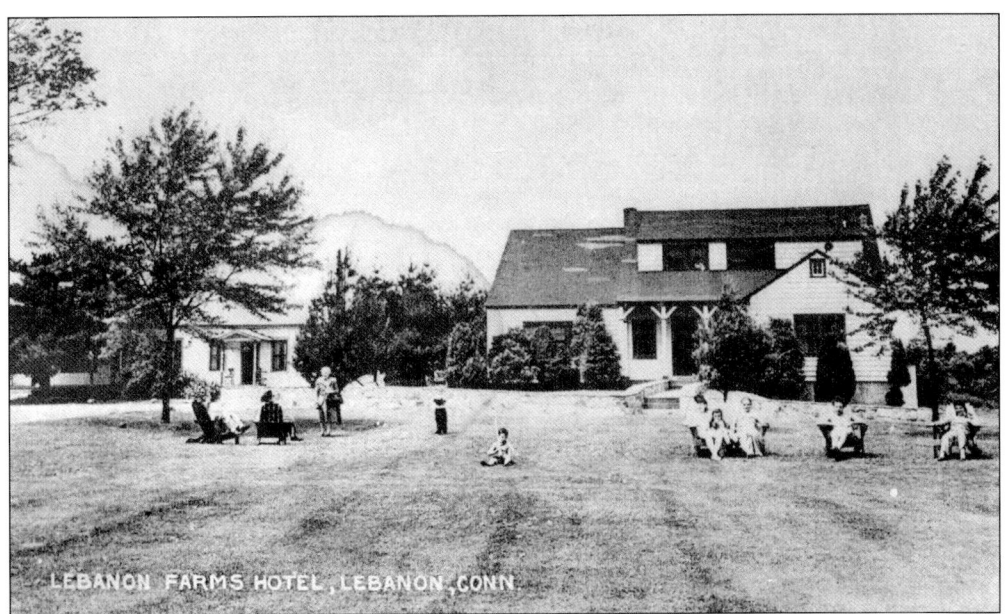

A SUMMER RESORT. The Lebanon Farms Hotel, on Camp Mooween Road on the Yantic River, was a popular place for city people to vacation. The big attraction was a beautiful nine-hole golf course. In the 1960s, the state acquired the golf course land in order to relocate Route 2, and the hotel went out of business. The site is now occupied by the Southeastern Council on Alcoholism and Drug Dependence facility. (Courtesy LHS.)

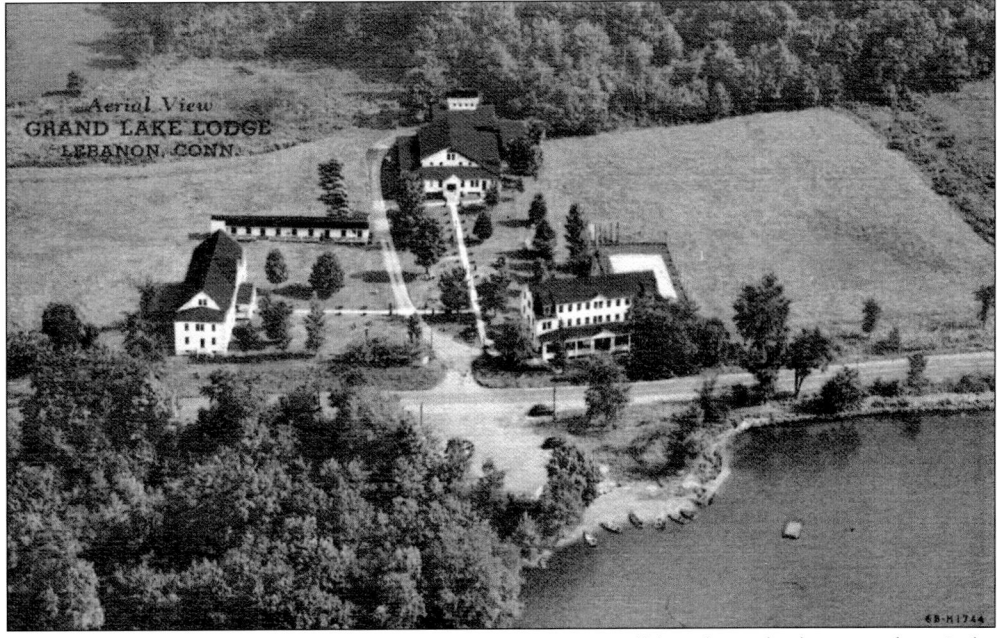

THE RESORT ON LAKE WILLIAMS. In the early 1900s, a small hotel was built across from Lake Williams. The hotel was greatly expanded in the late 1920s, when the Liebman family owned it. Called Grand Lake Lodge, the complex could serve 250 people a day. It was sold in 1957, then closed after a fire in 1976. In the 1990s, it was renovated and reopened as the Spa at Grand Lake. (Courtesy LHS.)

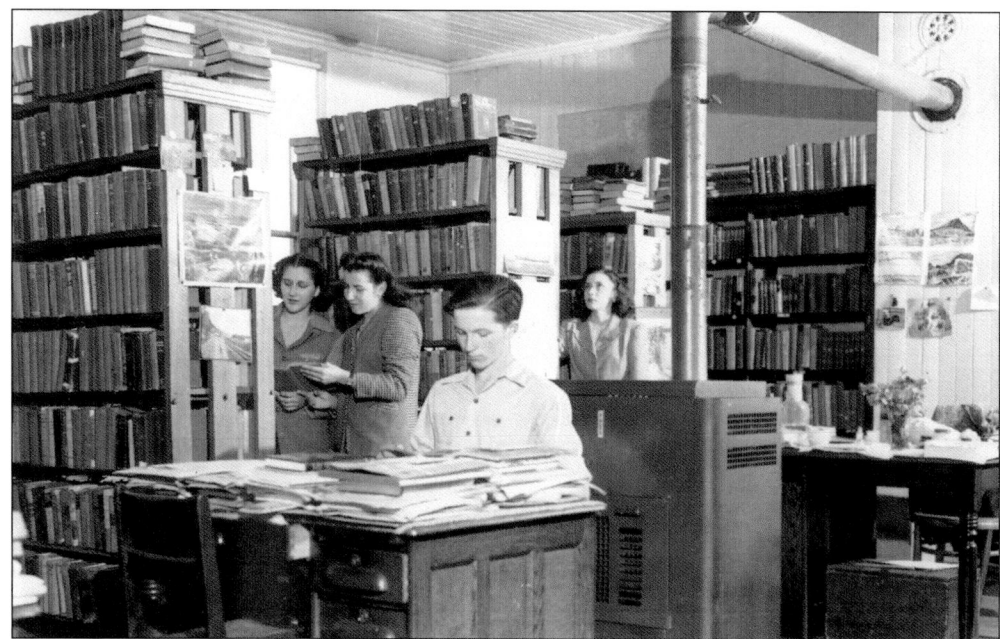

THE TOWN LIBRARY IN CENTER SCHOOL. The Jonathan Trumbull Library has had four different locations since it was established as the town's first public library in 1896. It was first located in the War Office, and it was then moved to the new high school on the lower green in 1922. In 1937, it was moved to the Center School, which had been vacated by the consolidation of elementary schools. The fourth location is the present library building. (Courtesy LHS.)

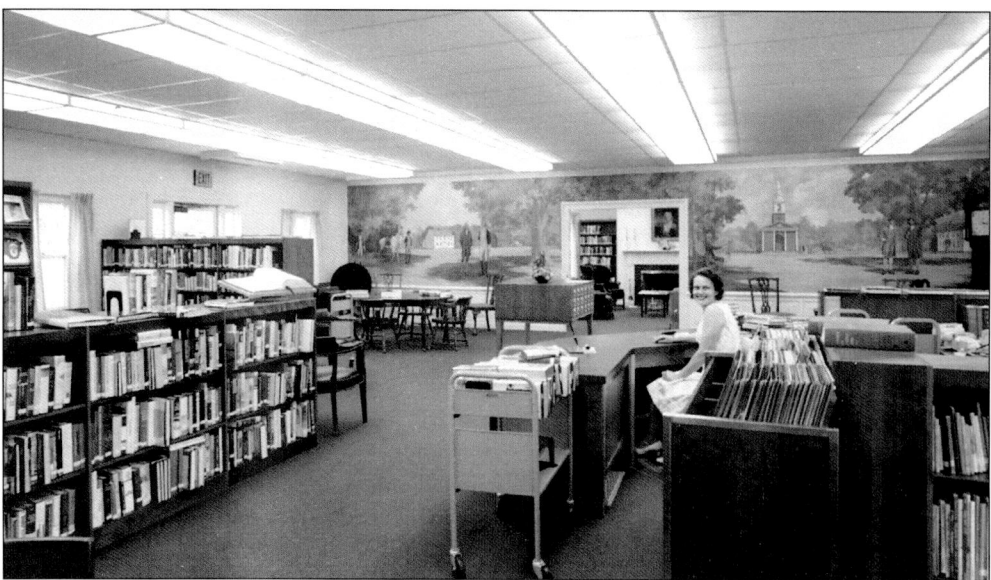

THE NEW JONATHAN TRUMBULL LIBRARY. Dolly Randall, library director, is all smiles as she surveys her beautiful surroundings in the new library building at the opening in 1968. The library was built next to the Center School, on the site of the former Main's store. The library and 1974 addition are gifts of the town's benefactor. The Center School was demolished after the new library opened. (Courtesy Barbara Wengloski.)

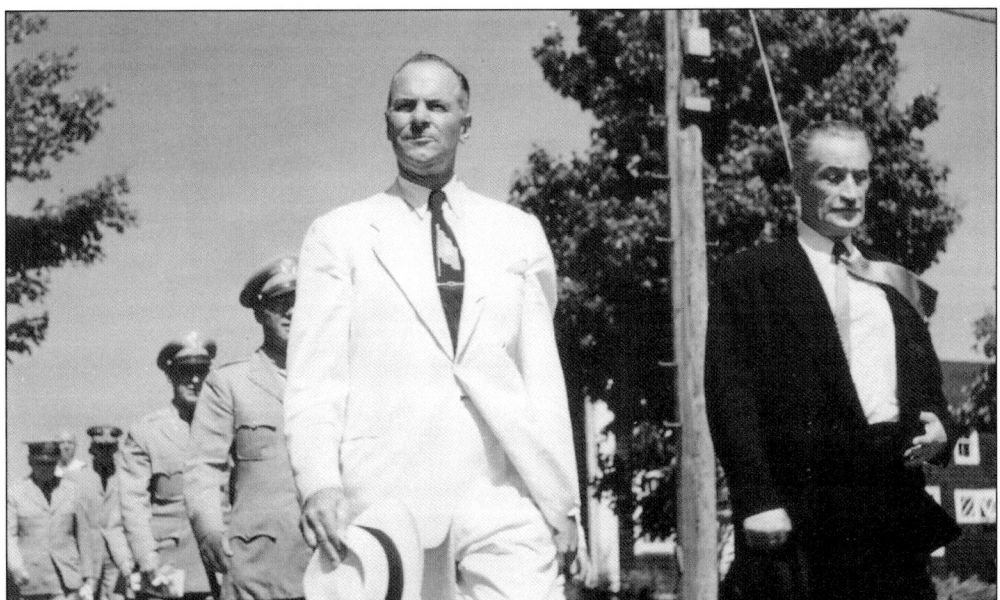

THE PAGEANTS. A series of historical pageants on the town green, beginning in 1949, enlisted hundreds of town residents in their production. Dramatic productions of Colonial and Revolutionary War events, they drew huge audiences. They were enlivened by periodic Boy Scout camporees on the green on the same weekends. Gov. John Lodge, left, marched in the 1952 pageant parade, and his wife performed in a skit. (Courtesy LHS.)

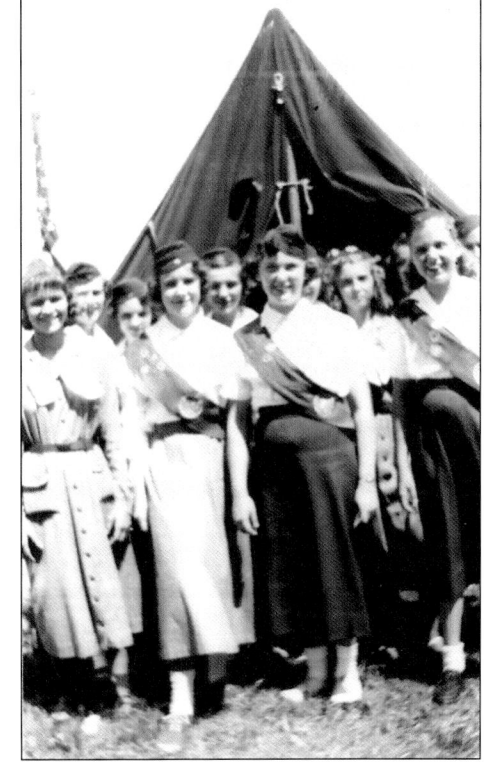

CAMPING AT THE PAGEANT. Posing in the front row are, from left to right, Jeanie Bender, Claire Kelley, Roberta Greenberg, and Jean (King) Reichard. They were among the Lebanon Girl Scouts camping on the town green during an early 1950s pageant. There are now 162 Lebanon girls registered in the 15 Lebanon troops. Both the Girl Scouts and Boy Scouts are active programs for Lebanon youth. (Courtesy Barbara Wengloski.)

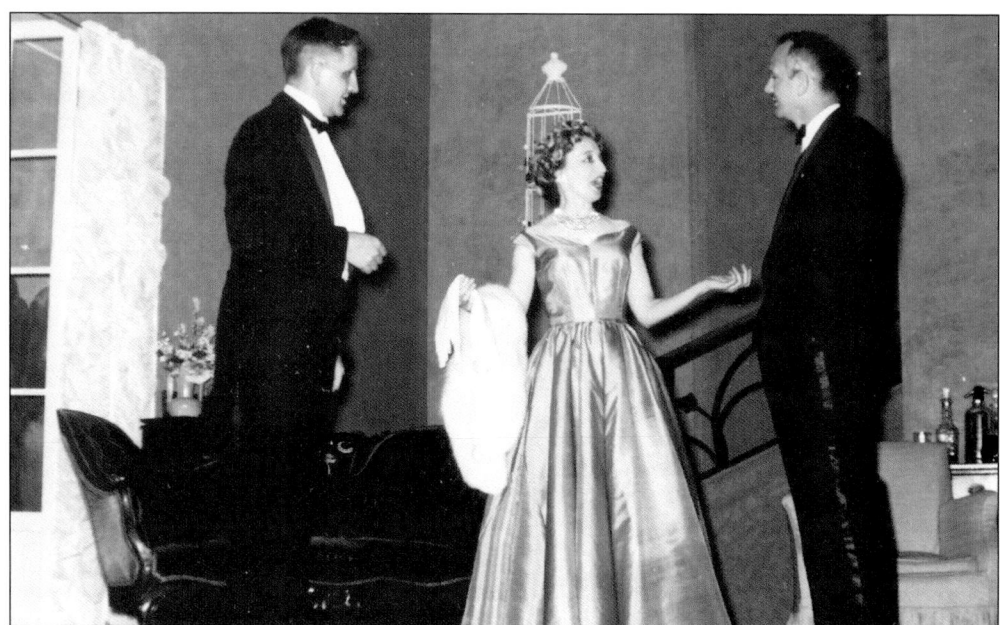

THE PLAY'S THE THING. Grant Tuttle, Arlene McCaw, and David Day, seen here from left to right, perform in a production of *Jane* put on by the Lebanon Guild of Arts and Crafts. The guild, formed in 1951 to encourage the arts and crafts in Lebanon, had more than 100 members at its peak. Many were involved in the play productions, which included 25 full-length plays. The last production was in 1966. (Courtesy Harold Geer.)

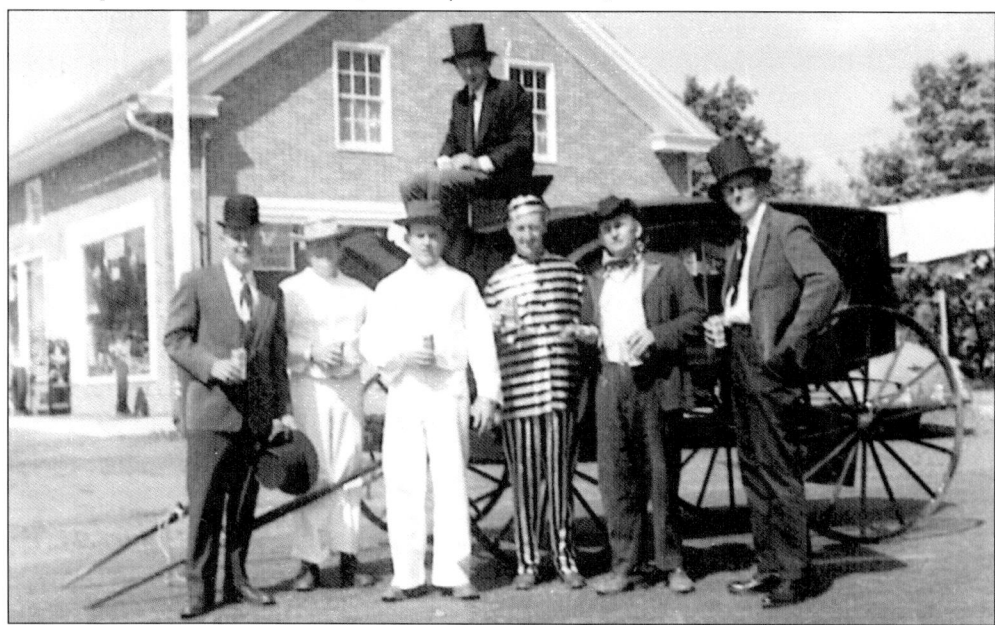

HIDDEN AWAY. In the 1950s, a group of townspeople spirited away an old hearse that the town was going to discard. They kept it hidden except for appearances at special events. In 1959, driver Harold Geer took the hearse to a parade in Willimantic. Accompanying him are, from left to right, Delton Briggs, Russ Clapp, Tom Wentworth, Tom Flannagan, Russ Tollmann, and Leslie Clarke Jr. The hearse is now owned by the Lebanon Historical Society. (Courtesy Harold Geer.)

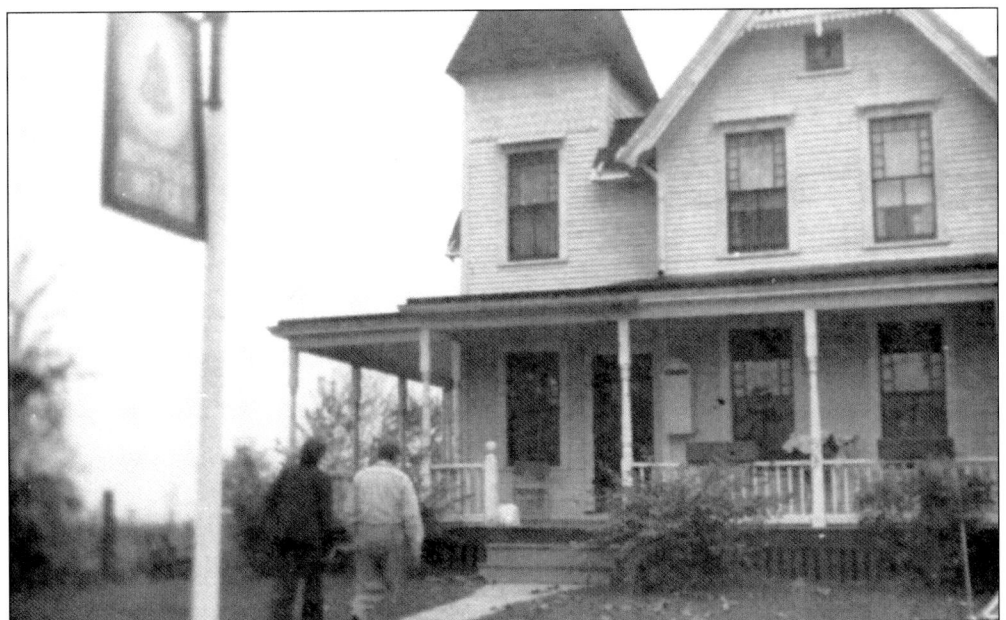

THE TELEPHONE SERVICE. This 1898 house, at 798 Trumbull Highway, was purchased by Southern New England Telephone in 1913 for the local telephone exchange. Elizabeth Troland lived here as the chief operator from 1915 to 1950. In 1950, SNET built a modern building on the lot to begin the switch to direct dialing. George Randall then bought the house and moved it to the lot next door. (Courtesy Ed Tollmann.)

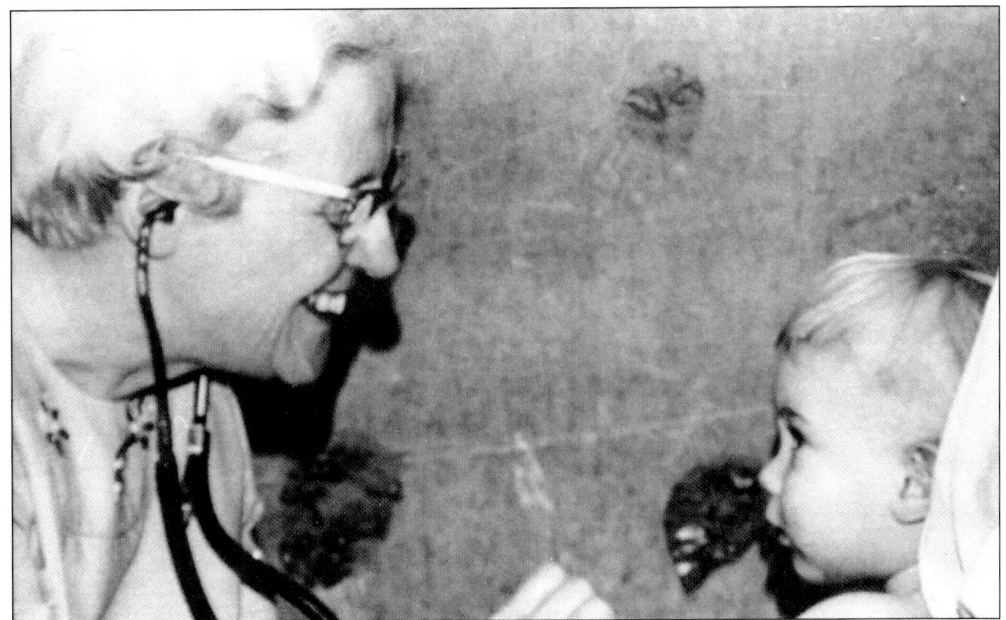

A BELOVED PHYSICIAN. Dr. Imogene Manning checks a baby at the Lebanon Well-Child Clinic in 1974. In addition to her regular practice, Dr. Manning served as the town's school medical adviser for 20 years. Although she was a pediatrician, townspeople felt they could call on her day or night for any type of medical advice. She also served as historical society president from 1975 to 1979. She died in 1982. (Courtesy LHS.)

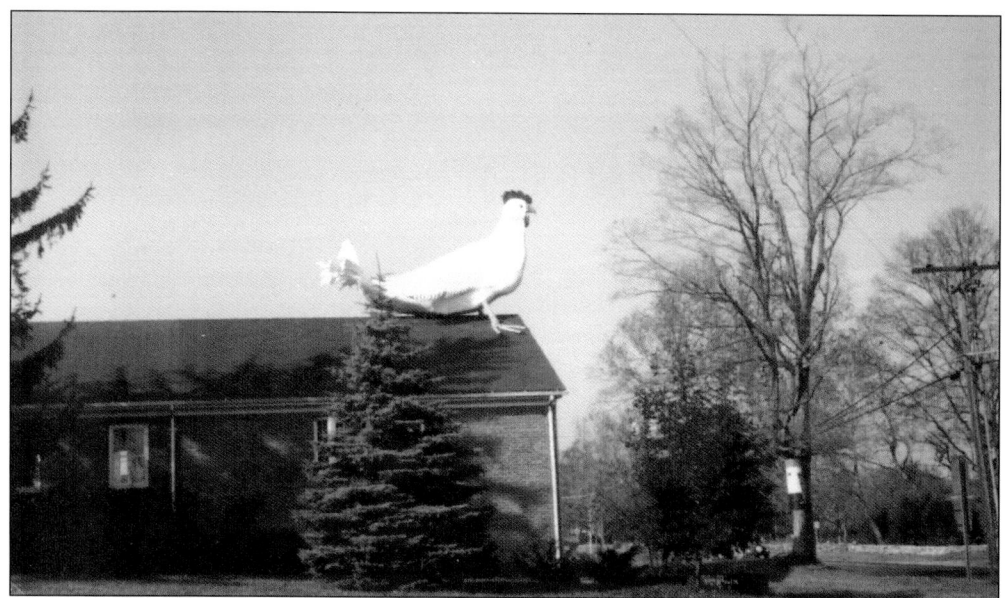

A HALLOWEEN CHICKEN. An anonymous group of residents known as the Pranksters delights in poking fun at current political and social issues in town. The morning after Halloween, residents head for the green to see what the Pranksters put up during the night. The most famous was the huge chicken that appeared on top of the library when a large egg-production facility was proposed in Lebanon. (Courtesy Barbara Wengloski.)

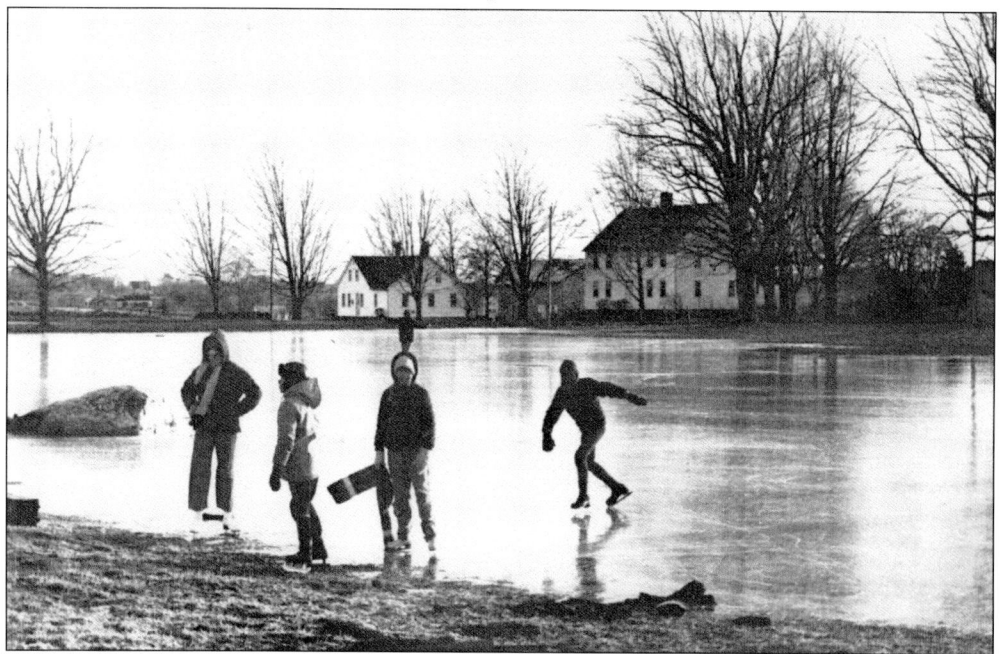

THE SKATING POND. Ice-skaters enjoy the pond created on the town green each year when water collects behind a small dam that is closed in early winter. The early 19th-century house on the left in the background was moved in 1990 to another lot on the street. The Colonial house on the right dates from c. 1740. The old barn in the center has been converted to a farm stand. (Courtesy LHS.)

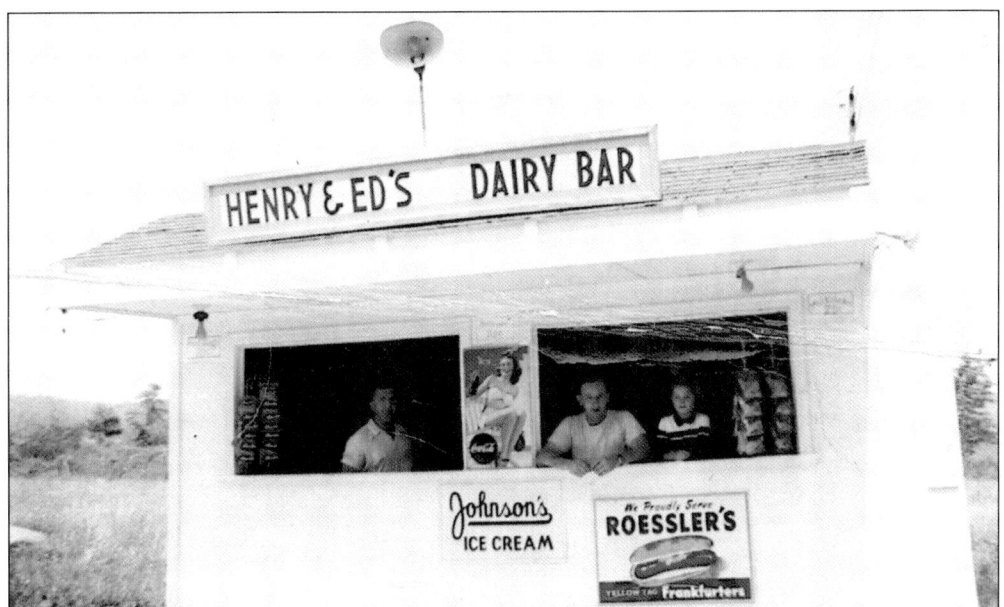

ICE CREAM, ANYONE? In the 1950s, Henry Haddad and Ed Clark opened a dairy bar on Route 87, south of the Oliver Road intersection. Ed's daughter Susan Coutu helped out. Ed Clark served 35 years as superintendent of the Lebanon Country Fair. He also opened the first horse ring in the region and was a former owner of the Lebanon Green Store. He was first selectman from 1979 to 1987. (Courtesy Ed Tollmann.)

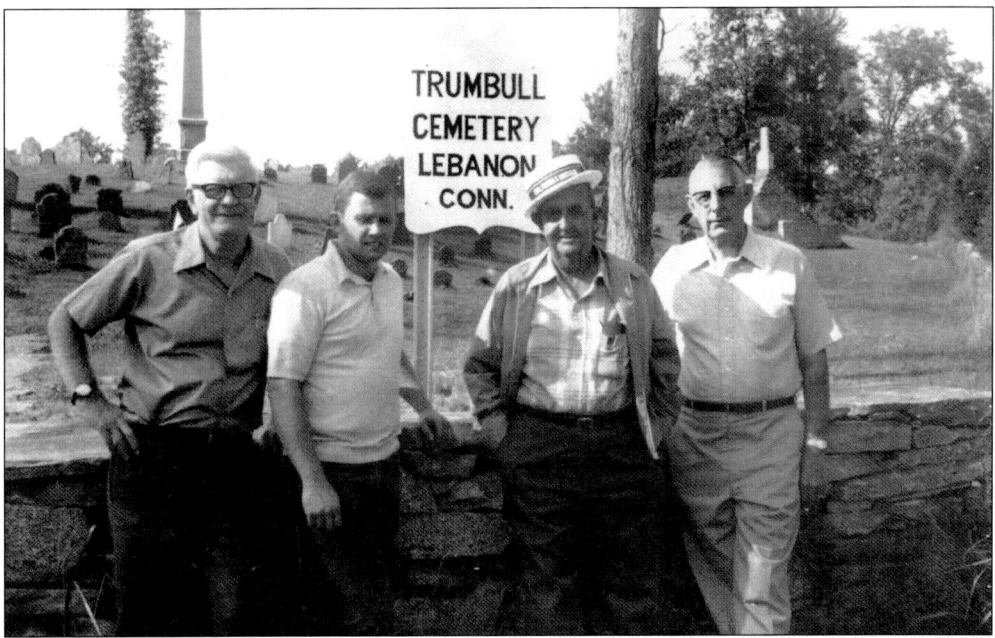

A CARING COMMISSION. The Lebanon Cemetery Commission was established in 1972 to provide better care for all town cemeteries, some of which suffered from neglect. Here, from left to right, Phillip Kohler, Ed Tollmann, Henry Aspinall, and Jared Hinckley, all members of the new commission, stand in front of their new sign at the Trumbull Cemetery. This cemetery has fine examples of early Colonial stone carving. (Courtesy Ed Tollmann.)

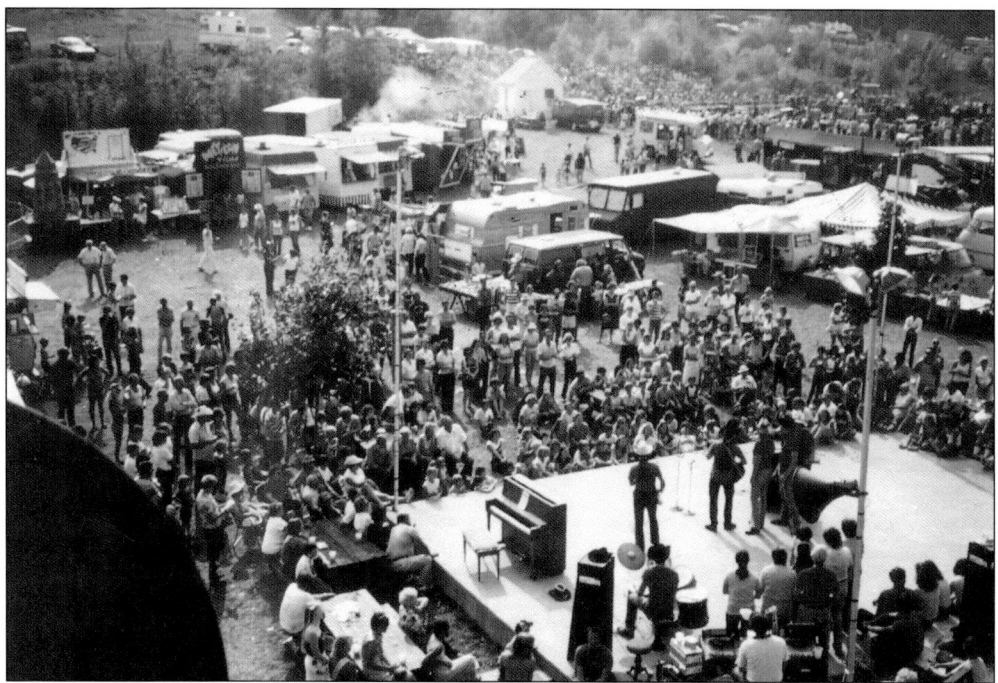

THE COUNTRY FAIR. The Lebanon Lions Club, chartered in 1952, sponsors the Lebanon Country Fair. It has grown from a small fair held on the town green to a major state fair attracting more than 30,000 visitors to the club's fairgrounds on Mack Road. The fair is a major fund-raiser for the club's charitable work. It is a showcase of agricultural exhibits, home arts, commercial exhibits, entertainment, and midway attractions. (Courtesy Ed Tollmann.)

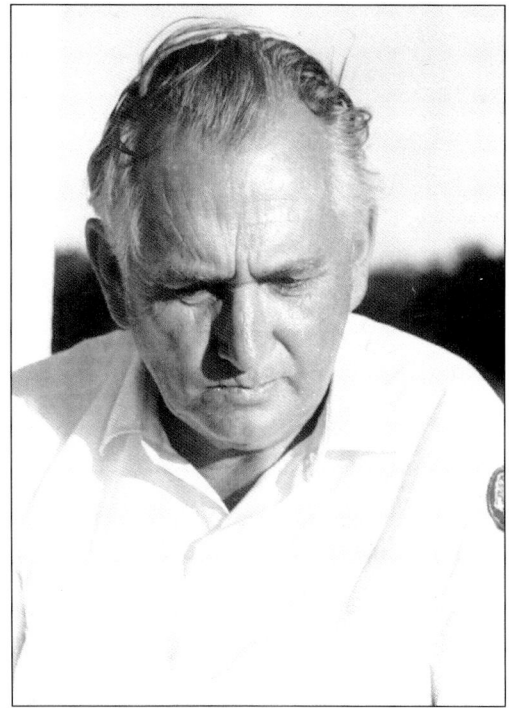

THE VOICE OF THE FAIR. Russell Tollmann, former first selectman, is shown in the tower on the Lions Club fairgrounds, where he announced events on the microphone just below. For years, he was known as the voice of the Lebanon Country Fair. From his high vantage point, he would spot people he knew and call out their names and a greeting. His friendly chatter made everyone feel welcome. (Courtesy Ed Tollmann.)

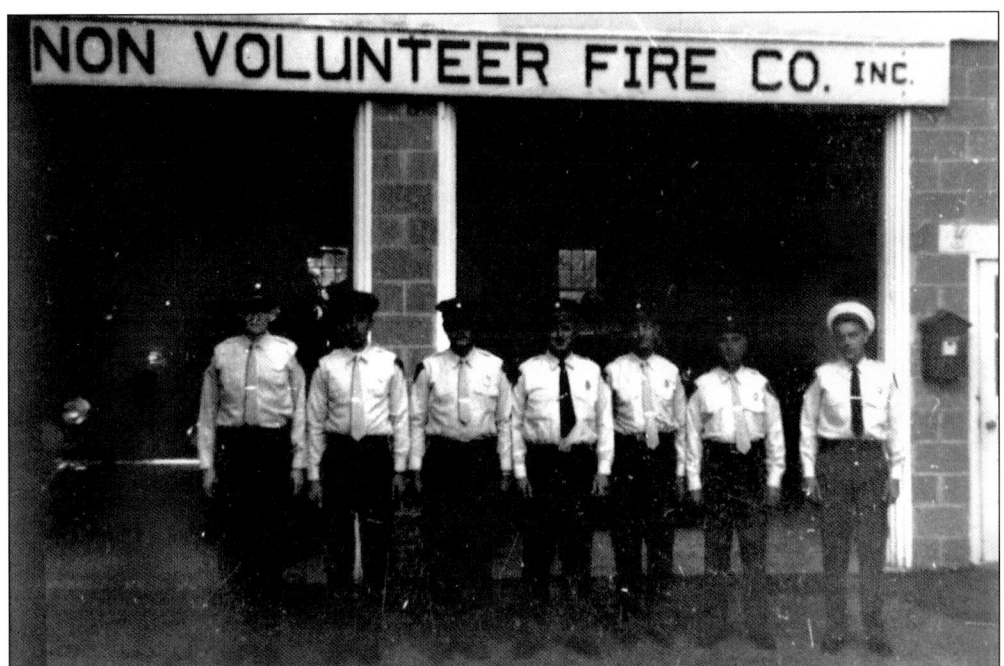

VOLUNTEER FIREFIGHTERS. The Lebanon Volunteer Fire Department was organized in 1943. The first firehouse was built across from the town hall in 1946. The volunteers did much of the construction work. Standing in front of the building in 1963 are, from left to right, members Robert Cady Sr., Jim McCaw, Doug Black, Adam Gantic, Don Jones, John Laibrandt, and Bill Brewster Sr. (Courtesy Jennie Brewster.)

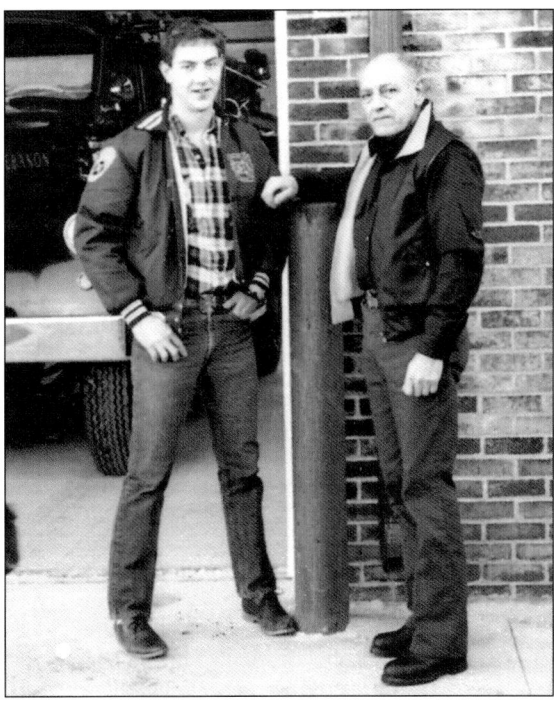

THE FIREFIGHTING TRADITION. William Brewster Sr., a charter member of the Lebanon Volunteer Fire Department, served as assistant chief for 12 years, as chief for 6 years, and as treasurer for 35 years. His son William Brewster Jr., appearing with his father at the dedication of the new fire safety complex in 1987, is also a firefighter. He designed the firefighters' memorial in front of the complex. (Courtesy Jennie Brewster.)

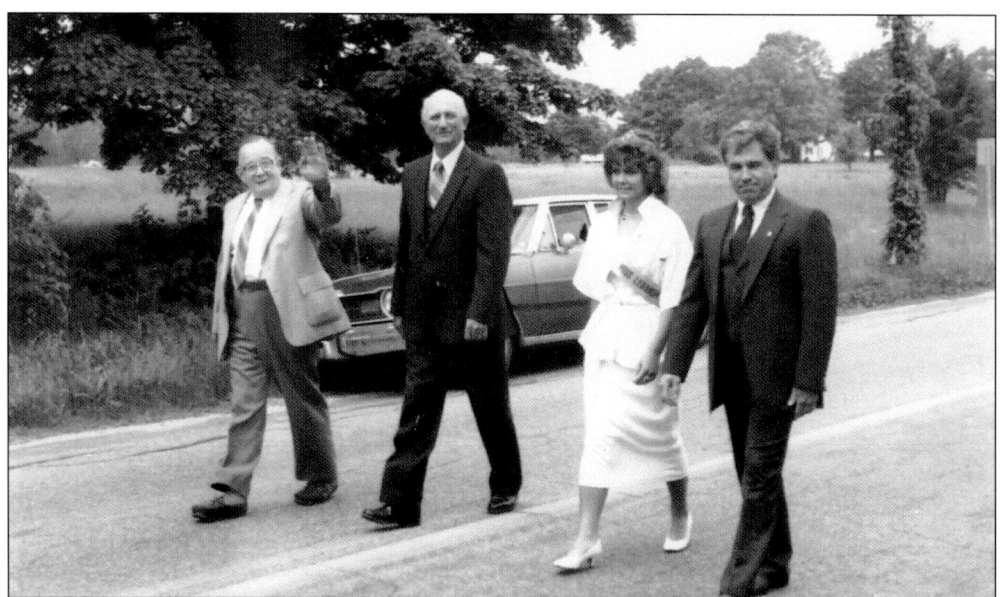

PARADE MARCHERS. Leading the annual Memorial Day parade in 1986 are, from left to right, first selectman Ed Clark, selectman Ed Bender, unidentified, and selectman Robert Leone. Now retired, Ed Bender managed the family farm on Rafferty Road for many years. A former dairy farmer, Robert Leone held the post of second selectman for 28 years, retiring from politics in 2001. He is a popular local auctioneer. (Courtesy LHS.)

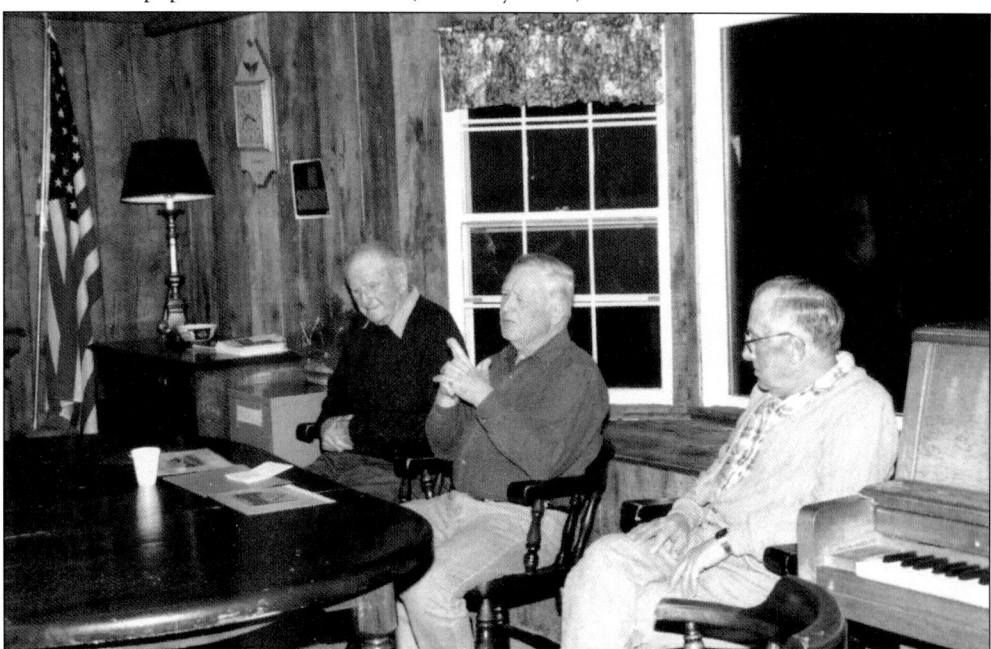

REMINISCING. At a meeting of the historical society in 1996, Frank Bartizek, Delton Briggs, and Ted Littlefield, seen here from left to right, drew on their memories of the "good old days" to entertain the audience with stories about Lester Main's General Store. The store, located where the library now stands, was the place to buy "everything," meet friends, catch the latest gossip, and lounge on the porch in summer or around the potbelly stove in winter. (Courtesy LHS.)

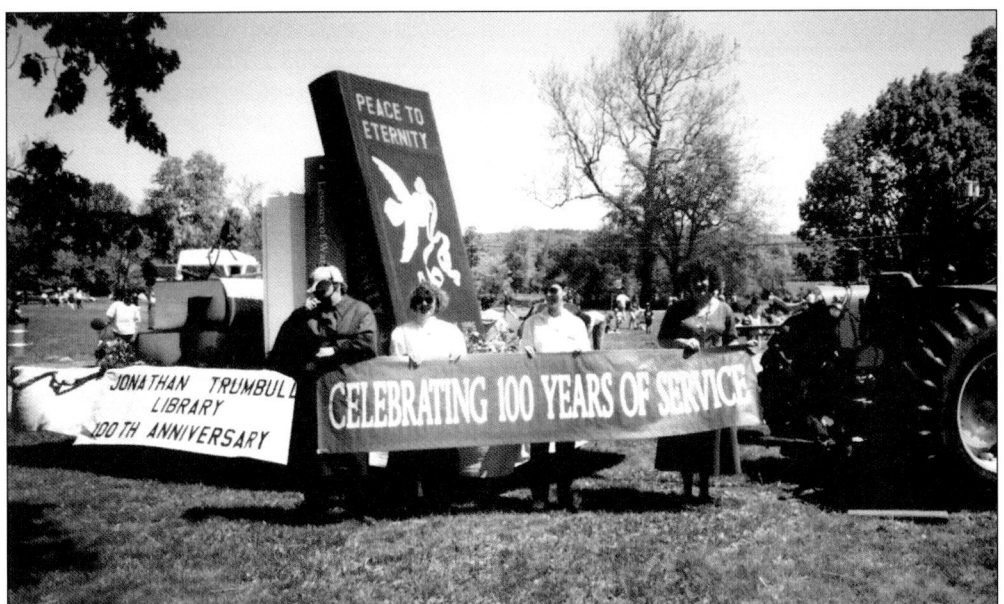

THE LIBRARY CENTENNIAL. The Jonathan Trumbull Library turned 100 years old in 1996, and many special activities took place during the year to celebrate. The library's float in the Memorial Day parade featured giant replicas of books. Marching with the banner are, from left to right, Mary Beth Yarmac, Sue Kane, Barbara Wengloski, and Linda Slate. (Courtesy Barbara Wengloski.)

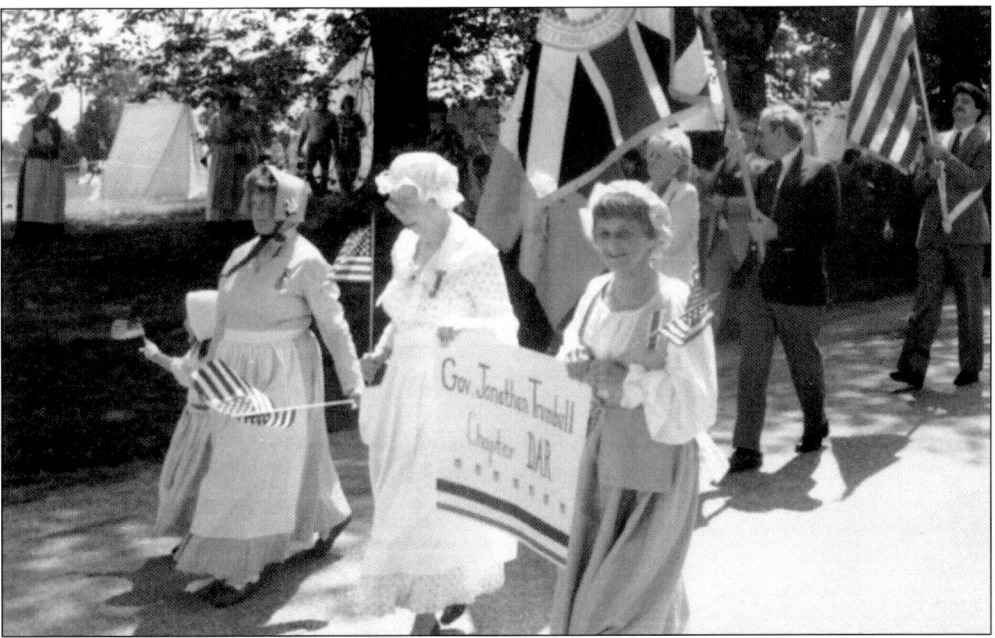

DAR MARCHERS. Every year, a contingent from the local chapter of the Connecticut Daughters of the American Revolution marches in the Memorial Day parade. In this undated parade photograph, Nancy Lyon (left) walks with her granddaughter. Jean McArthur (center) and Virginia Mullaly (right) carry the chapter banner. The chapter is named, of course, after Gov. Jonathan Trumbull of Lebanon. (Courtesy Virginia Mullaly.)

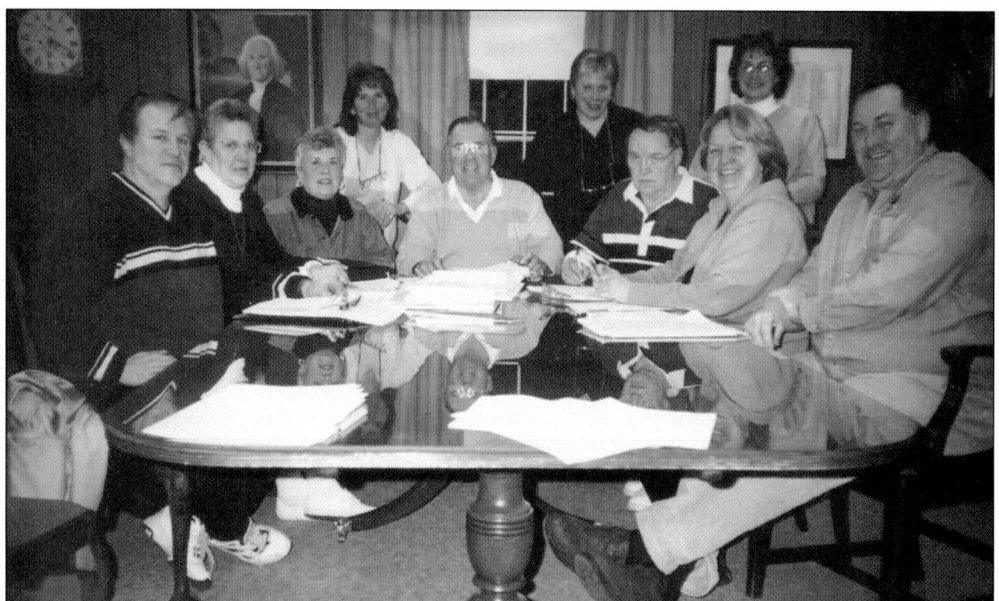

THE TERCENTENNIAL COMMITTEE. This committee was appointed by the selectmen in 1998 to organize the town's official tercentennial celebration in 2000. Members, seen here from left to right, are as follows: (sitting) Robert Leone, treasurer Jennie Brewster, Sandra Chalifoux, chairman Robert Wentworth, secretary Russell Blakeslee, Marion Russo, and Tom Hinsch; (standing) committee member Leah Tanger, parade subcommittee chairman Glenda Murphy, and fund-raising subcommittee chairman Joyce Okonuk. The subcommittees were set up by the tercentennial committee to organize various activities. (Courtesy LHS.)

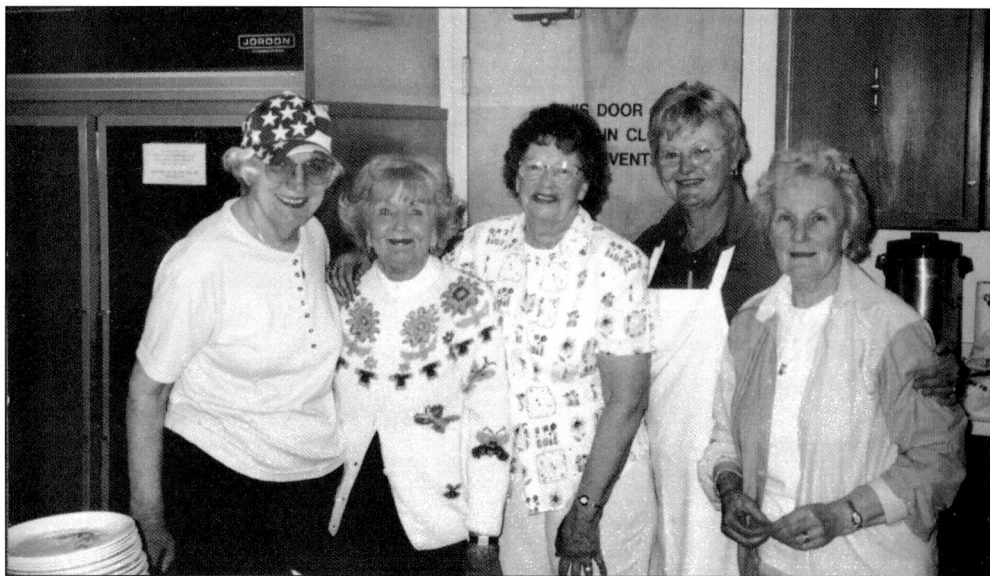

GOOD COOKS. The Commission on the Aging has been serving the needs of elderly residents since it was formed in 1976. Recently, the commission started a monthly luncheon and program for a large group of more active retirees dubbed the "Junior Seniors." Preparing one of the lunches, held at the fire safety complex, are, from left to right, Sylvia Ryan, Dee Kruppa, Priscilla Donnelly, Sandra Morin, and Evelyn Buckley. (Courtesy William Jahoda.)

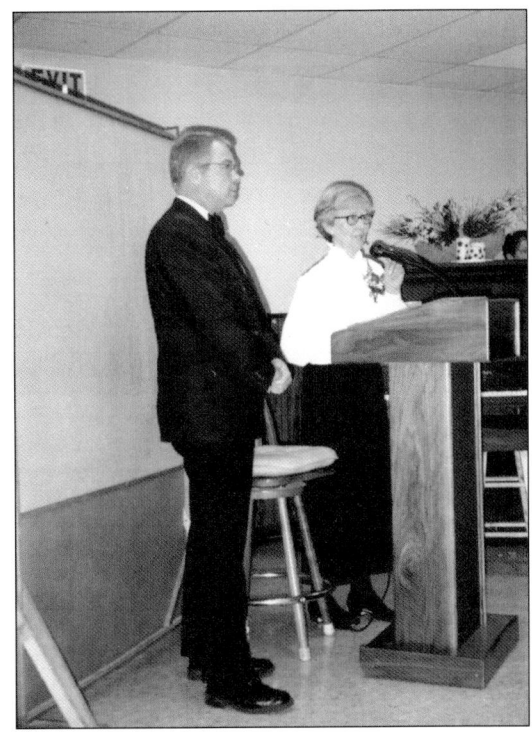

THE SOUND OF MUSIC. Alberta "Bertie" Hawkins is the founding director of the Lebanon Community Chorus, organized in 1972. A devoted volunteer, Bertie had built up the original 12-member group to one totaling more than 60 members when she retired in 1993. The chorus performs only occasionally now, when Bertie comes out of retirement to lead them for a special event. Cal Lord, program master of ceremonies, stands next to her. (Courtesy William Jahoda.)

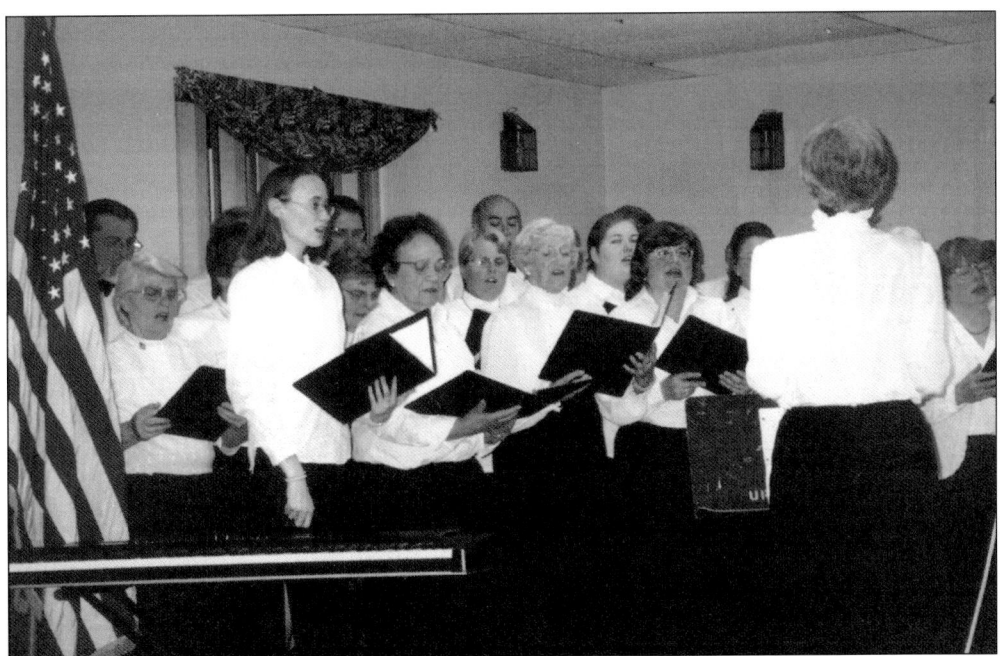

PERFORMANCE TIME. Members of the Lebanon Community Chorus reunited for a special performance at the historical society's 2003 annual meeting. Pictured in front are, from left to right, Gretchen Lathrop, Jacquie Proulx, Rose Miller, Jean Souter, Ellen Gillon, and Dot Davis (at the far right). The chorus was known for its professional performances of sacred and secular music. (Courtesy William Jahoda.)

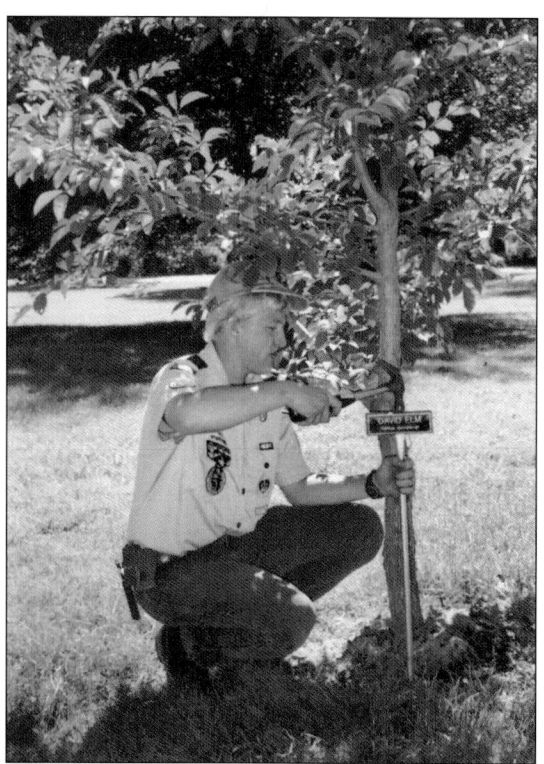

AN EAGLE SCOUT PROJECT. For his 2000 Eagle Scout project, Rob Miles worked with mentor Dr. William J. Jahoda to make identification signs for trees around the town green. The David elm, planted by Dr. Jahoda in 1999, is resistant to Dutch elm disease, which devastated the American elm. It is the first one planted in Connecticut. Dr. Jahoda is raising more seedlings for distribution around town. (Courtesy William Jahoda.)

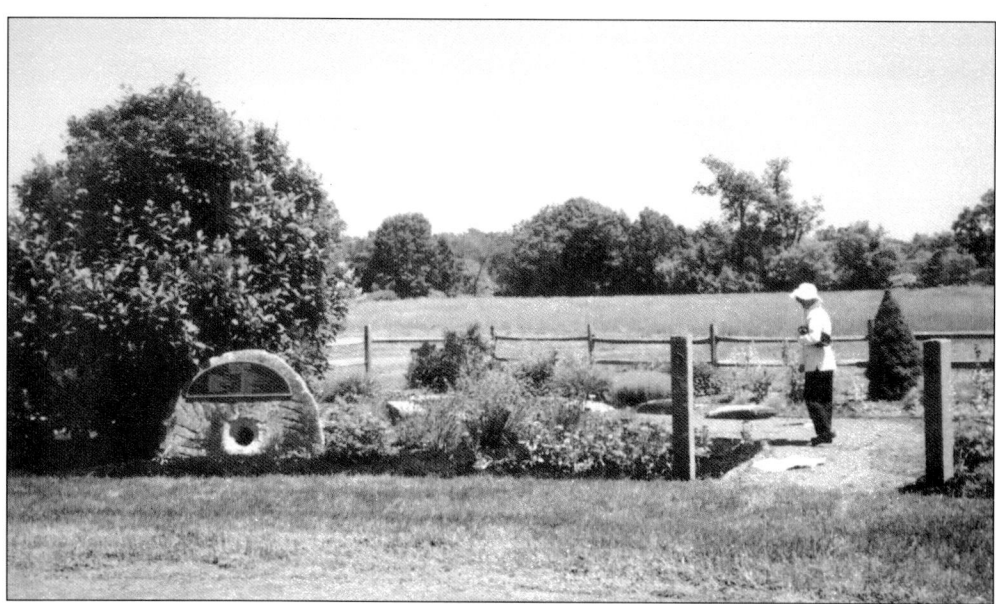

THE HERITAGE GARDEN. Marge Jahoda wanders through the Heritage Garden, created by the Lebanon Garden Club on the grounds of the Jonathan Trumbull Jr. House, the town-owned museum. Beginning in 1998, club members designed and planted a three-section garden displaying various types of plants from the Colonial, Victorian, and contemporary periods. Every spring, the club beautifies the town center with annual plants around public buildings. (Courtesy William Jahoda.)